MODERN
SPORTFISHING BOATS

MODERN SPORTFISHING BOATS

FRANK T. MOSS

INTERNATIONAL MARINE PUBLISHING COMPANY
Camden, Maine

Typeset by Journal Publications, Camden, Maine
Printed and bound by The Alpine Press, Stoughton, Massachusetts

Published by International Marine Publishing Company
21 Elm Street, Camden, Maine 04843
(207) 236-4342

Library of Congress Cataloging in Publication Data

Moss, Frank T.
    Modern sportfishing boats.

    Includes index.
    1. Fishing boats.   I. Title   II. Title:
Sportfishing boats.
SH452.9.B58M67   623.8'2314   80-84744
ISBN 0-87742-122-6   AACR2

To Mildred, who knows that a man's boat is not always his other wife

Contents

Special Tables and Formulas

List of Abbreviations

gph	gallons per hour	nmpg	nautical miles per gallon
kph	kilometers per hour	mi	mile
rpm	revolutions per minute	kn	knot
kwh	kilowatt hour	CB	citizens' band
Ah	ampere hour	SSB	single sideband
lb	pound	VHF	very high frequency
t	ton	hp	horsepower
kg	kilogram	SHP	shaft horsepower
l	liter	BHP	brake horsepower
gal	gallon (U.S.)	GBH	gross brake horsepower
Imp gal	Imperial gallon	BSFC	brake specific fuel consumption
m	meter	FWC	freshwater cooled
cm	centimeter	SS	stainless steel
cyl	cylinder	OB	outboard
dia	diameter	IB	inboard
CID	cubic inch displacement	I/O	inboard/outboard
nm	nautical mile		

Preface

The author acknowledges that the ideal way to report on sportfishing boats would be to ride and fish on every boat under consideration. Unfortunately, this was impossible, so the next best course of action was taken: to obtain as much illustrative and technical material as possible, and to include reports and comments of owners whenever these could be obtained.

Understandably, builders and owners of sportfishing boats are partial to their particular vessels. The author does not share this partiality, not owning a boat at the time of this writing. Every attempt has been made to present each boat in its relationship to known standards of excellence. Builders' and owners' statements are quoted for their usefulness in making comparisons.

Not all builders were able to supply the same kinds or volume of illustrative material or performance data. Some presentations are, therefore, less elaborate than others. This was not intended to favor the more elaborate descriptions, but to make available all the information possible in each instance. The length of a presentation is not a reflection of the author's regard for a particular boat, but rather a measure of the material available on the boat at the time of writing.

A few very good and popular boats were not included because data and/or good illustrations were not available. No boat of known or suspected inferior quality has been included, but exclusion of any boat or line of boats does not imply any judgment of inferiority. It is hoped that the result is an objective, well-documented collection of the top-quality sportfishing boats now available.

These boats are of high caliber with respect to engineering, construction, and performance. Participating builders and owners have been extremely helpful in supplying bushels of information, from which the important facts have been selected. It has been a pleasure to work with such responsive people.

MODERN SPORTFISHING BOATS

Damaris IV *was an early New England commercial fisherman converted to swordfishing and pleasure cruising. Harpooning for sport was popular in the Northeast for many years before the advent of rod-and-reel swordfishing. (Photo by Ellsworth Ford, A.F. Sozio Studio, New York, NY)*

CHAPTER 1

The Origin of Sportfishing Boats

The idea of creating a new type of boat specifically to meet the requirements of sportfishing is a modern one. For thousands of years boats were considered essential to fishing but were regarded primarily as water transportation. Most of the fishing was for the market. It is true that Shakespeare portrayed Cleopatra fishing in the Nile from her pleasure ship, calling each perch a freshly hooked Mark Anthony, but fishing for sport as we know it today had to await the development of a very modern sense of adventure and a new code of sportsmanship among noncommercial fishermen.

Awareness of a need for boats designed to meet the requirements of saltwater sportfishing did not come until the first and second decades of the present century. The earliest fishing chair was a plank across the stern with a leather cup nailed to its after edge to take the butt of the rod. Rodholders were pieces of pipe clamped to the inner surface of the gunwale. An elevated control station atop the deckhouse in the form of a flying bridge was science fiction that had not yet been dreamed up.

The early sportsman and writer John Frederick Holder vividly described the pains and frustrations of fishing for marlin and tuna out of the famous Catalina Tuna Club, using knuckle-buster rods and reels and one-lung harbor motor launches. Holder also described fishing in South Florida and the Keys for tarpon from shallow-draft rowing skiffs. Later, when outboard motors became available, the Keys skiffs were power-driven and became the progenitors of the modern Florida bonefish and tarpon open fishing boats.

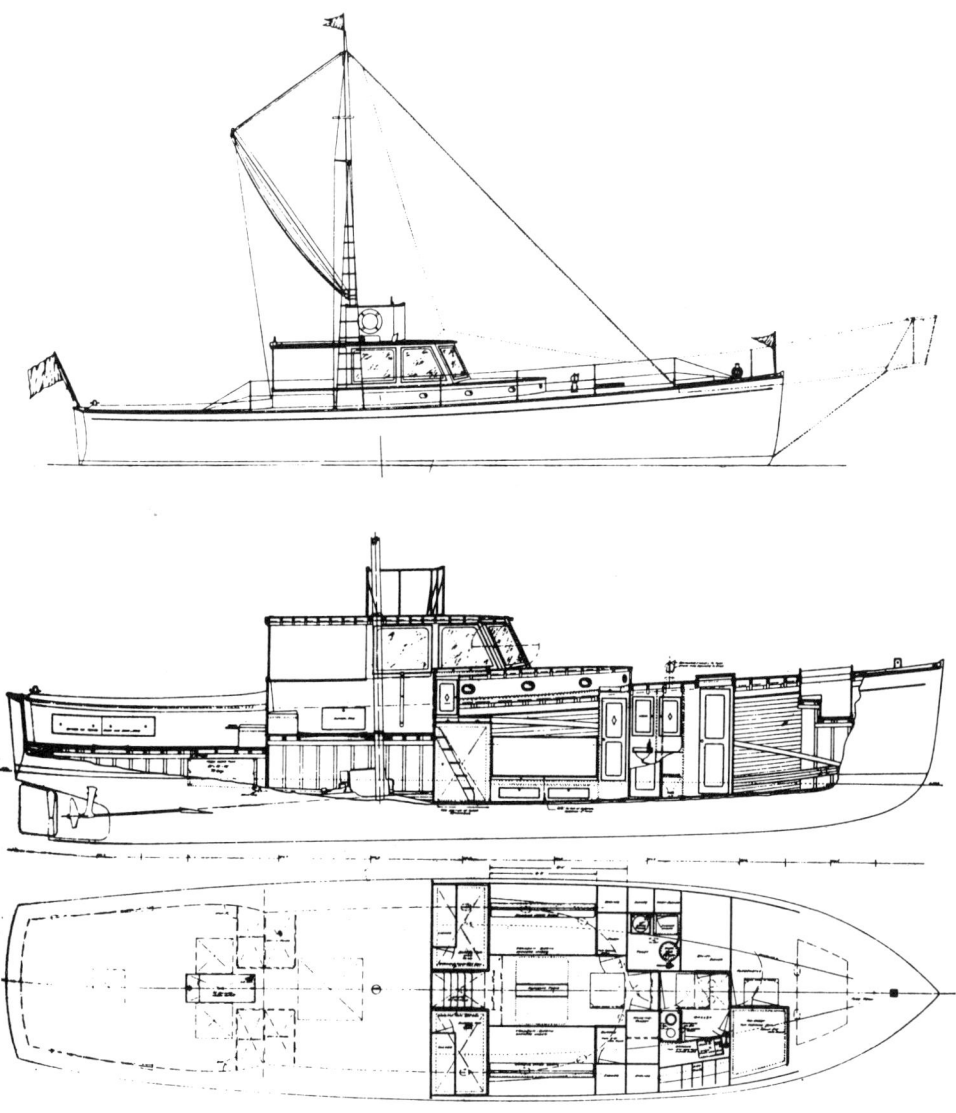

Built by Franklin G. Post & Son, Inc., of Mystic, Connecticut, to plans by Sparkman & Stephens of New York, this powerful fisherman was planned for offshore fishing between Block Island and Nantucket. Length overall, 55'4¾''; length waterline, 53'9''; beam, 12'8½''; draft, 3'10''. Power was a pair of 110-hp Chrysler Crown gasoline engines with 2.5:1 reduction gears giving a cruising speed of about 12 mph. Control stations were located at the forward end of the cockpit and the simple flying bridge. The spacious cockpit featured tackle lockers under covering boards, built-in bait and fish wells, and insulated ice lockers. Outriggers are not indicated in the plans, but probably they were added after launching. The harpooning pulpit forward and the husky boom and lifting tackle speak of the early practice of sticking swordfish rather than trying for them with rod and reel. (Plans by Sparkman & Stephens. From Yachting, *July 1936)*

An early Florida sportfisherman was Barbara Lee, *converted from a comfortable power cruiser to charter fishing by the addition of outriggers, fishing chairs, and a rudimentary flying bridge. (Photo by City of Miami News Bureau)*

With a year-round enjoyable climate and spectacular inshore and off-shore fishing, Florida quickly became one of the early centers of sport-fishing-boat development. Boats designed specifically for pleasure fishing were still rare, but hundreds of existing powerboat hulls were converted to accommodate fishing chairs, outriggers, and primitive flying bridges atop the deckhouse.

By the mid-1930s, the manufacture of boats designed for sportfishing was a well-established business. Many small boatyards in Florida, the Carolinas, the Chesapeake region, New Jersey, Long Island, and New England were turning out custom-designed craft, and manufacturers like Matthews, Consolidated, Elco, Wheeler, Chris-Craft, Huckins, and others offered powerboat models that needed only the installation of fishing chairs, outriggers, and bridge controls to be called full-fledged sportfishing boats.

At the same time began a rapid interchange of ideas about equipment and fishing techniques. Boats for sportfishing came to be recognized not as

(continued on page 15)

Early big-game fisherman W.E.S. Tuker had a rough time fighting large Chilean swordfish from an improvised chair in the stern of an open power launch. Tuker is "fishing under," with the reel mounted under the rod rather than in the more conventional position over the rod shaft. The harness directs the pull of the fish to his shoulders, much higher than modern big-game harnesses. Sportsmen like Tuker proved that very large fish could be taken with relatively simple equipment — provided teamwork was good between the angler and his crew. (Photo by Hedly Doty)

Parrot, *a Sparkman & Stephens design, was a familiar sight off Montauk, New York, in the 1940s. About 60 feet long, she was powered with a pair of big Lathrop gasoline motors for a top speed of over 16 knots. The open bridge of this double-cabin design was popular with private anglers. Trussed outriggers trolled marlin baits and the harpoon forward dealt with any swordfish foolish enough to fin up within sight. In New England, cruising power boatmen very often trolled for tuna and kept a lookout for swordfish while making the long, lazy passages from port to port. (Photo by Morris Rosenfeld. From* Yachting, *Nov. 1936)*

Captain Roy Stuart's 42-foot Wheeler fisherman Sport II *was a top Florida charter fishing boat in the 1930s. Powered with a pair of Chrysler Crowns with reduction gear, she had a top speed of 15 to 16 mph. The composite outriggers did not have the after rake that later became popular, and the bridge controls were so far removed from the cockpit that the operator almost had to use a megaphone to shout orders down to his crew. But the configuration of the modern sportfishing cruiser was taking shape in this early model. (Photo by Morris Rosenfeld. Courtesy of Wheeler Shipyard Inc., Brooklyn, NY)*

Ralph Evinrude's beautiful 38-foot Matthews fishing cruiser lacked a bridge and carried her bamboo outriggers topped up to the mast amidships back in 1938, but she was considered a well-found private fisherman of the time. Many of the famous Matthews 38s were converted to private or professional sportfishing by adding flying bridges, side-mounted outriggers, and a cockpit full of fishing chairs. Top speed was 18 to 20 mph with a pair of 140 to 180 hp gasoline motors. Hulls were mahogany planking over steam-bent oak frames. A few of these classics are still fishing today. (Photo by Morris Rosenfeld)

Modern super-fishermen were foreshadowed by Paul Townsend's fast Elco fishing cruiser, Jacpau III. *Powered with two powerful Hall-Scott gasoline motors, she cruised at 20 knots. A gallows frame atop the deckhouse supported the tall outriggers, which were stiffened to their very tips. Essentially a fast power cruiser with fishing capability, this class of Elco boats set the stage for the faster tournament specialists that were to follow. (Photo by Morris Rosenfeld. From* Yachting, *Dec. 1938)*

In 1948, Elco introduced its vastly popular 30-foot sport model, which proved ideal for light family fishing and cruising. Powered with a pair of 85-hp Chrysler Ace gasoline motors, this smart little V-hull could hold speeds of 27 to 29 mph in calm water. The Elco 30, and similar models by other builders, set the stage for the great boating boom of the 1950s in which seaworthy, inexpensive, well-designed smaller sportfishing boats became available for the first time to the great market that was hungering for them. (Photo by Elco Yacht Division, Electric Boat Company, Bayonne, NJ)

An early true fishing machine was William F. Horvath's Val-Jean III, *a 35-foot Colonial pictured off Hampton Bays, Long Island, New York. A vessel of the Little Peconic Yacht Club, she was driven by twin 155-hp Nordberg gasoline motors and boasted a top speed of 24 mph. Bridge and fishing equipment were designed by the owner and his skipper, Captain Ray Overton, especially for the demands of mid- and north-Atlantic game fishing. Horvath caught a 484½-pound swordfish by rod and reel on the boat's maiden voyage out of Shinnecock Inlet, on Long Island. By the mid-1950s, the Florida rake-back to outriggers had caught on in northern waters and had proved its greater efficiency in the baiting of difficult fish such as broadbill. (Photo by Morris Rosenfeld. From* Yachting, Nov. 1954)

A handsome, powerful fisherman was Frank L. Sample's 41-footer, Acadie. *Built on a modification of the famous Maine lobsterboat hull, the Sample fisherman was noted for easy riding in rough water. Power was usually a pair of 150 to 200 hp gasoline motors with reduction gear, giving a top speed of 16 to 20 mph. The hull was traditional wooden construction. The flying bridge was no afterthought, being offered as standard equipment. The operator's position was far enough aft to afford easy communication with the anglers down below. With the wide, short hardtop, this model proved popular with professional charter fishing skippers. Accommodations below could sleep four to six in comfort. Outriggers on this model appear to be an early version of commercially produced metal tubing units — which, in this instance, were rigged unstiffened. (Photo by Douglas Photo Studio, Bath, ME. From* Yachting, *Nov. 1954)*

Pacemaker's 30-foot family cruiser in 1961 helped that company establish a foothold in the highly competitive sportfishing boat market. While not designed specifically for fishing, the boat's large, open cockpit and comfortable hardtop shelter made it popular with small-game cruising fishermen from New York to Florida. Top speed, with a pair of 110-hp Chrysler Crown motors or the equivalent, was around 18 mph, and the boat could put in a 10-hour tuna-trolling day for fewer than 50 gallons of fuel. Pacemakers became good sportfishing boats in large part through the competition activities of the brothers Don and Jack Leek. Their arch-rival was the late, flamboyant Willis Slane of the Hatteras Yacht Corporation of High Point, North Carolina. Any tournament that saw Slane and the Leek brothers on the contestant list was sure also to see fast racing to and from the fishing grounds. (Photo by Russell T. Homan, Jr.)

The handsome Boma *was top-of-the-line for the Wheeler boatyard and made her home at Havana, Cuba, in pre-Castro days. Of wood construction, she carried her outriggers with a bit of a rake and the lookout hoops on her short mast were a hint of towers to come. Note the alternate steering station down in the cockpit for good coordination between fisherman and helmsman. Powered with a pair of 200-hp gas engines, she cruised comfortably at about 15 knots, with a top speed of 17 to 18 knots. Nearly 50 feet long,* Boma *was considered a fairly large cruising fisherman in the post-World War II era. (Photo by Morris Rosenfeld. From* Yachting)

(continued from page 5)

mere transportation on the water, but as essential tools of this new form of fishing. Formation of the International Game Fish Association helped to standardize various classes of tackle and led to the adoption of a universal code of sportfishing behavior. The special qualities that marked good sportfishing boats became widely known. These included:

- Superior performance in any fishable weather.
- Service as a comfortable living base at sea.
- Service as a mobile fishing platform.
- Ability to locate and detect game fish.
- Ability to navigate and communicate.
- Ability to attract and stimulate fish by physically interacting with them.
- Handsome, utilitarian style.

In recent years there has been a tendency to call sportfishing boats "fishing machines." This has the unfortunate effect of suggesting to the general public that ocean sportfishing has degenerated into a spectator sport. The truth of the matter is that a well-found sportfishing boat actually increases its owner's personal participation in fishing. It vastly increases his mobility on the water, making it possible for him to sample species of fish and types of fishing that otherwise would be unavailable. It increases his mastery and personal skill by requiring him to become expert not only in fishing, but also in navigation, communication, trip planning and vessel management, and the understanding of basic fish behavior. In the final analysis, it provides both challenge and fulfillment.

Non-fishing-boat owners very often regard their boats as ends in themselves. The sportfishing-boat owner perceives his boat not as an end, but as a means to an end — the location and capture of elusive game fish. Yet, the fishing-boat owner is extremely conscious of his dependence on and close kinship to his boat. The boat often develops a personality that reflects its owner's, and when the fisherman speaks of himself and his boat in the same breath, he invariably says "we."

Fishermen are by nature curious about how the other fellow catches fish, and they are great copiers of what appear to be successful innovations. By the mid-1930s the style for offshore sportfishing boats was well established. The Florida outrigger and flying bridge moved north and west. The northeastern swordfish harpooning stand moved south and west and, for a while, became a status symbol. The fishing ability of some boats was judged by the number of fishing chairs that could be crowded into the after cockpit. Some Florida charter fishing craft boasted as many as eight or ten chairs. Line tangles were taken in stride as unavoidable hazards of the fishing.

Following World War II, the manufacture of sportfishing boats underwent a revolution. Fiberglass replaced wood as the major construction material, making it possible for even small yards to produce many exact duplicates of one well- or poorly designed prototype. The great boating boom of the mid-1950s saw both standardization and specialization setting in. Popular, family cruiser-fisherman models were offered by such builders as Bertram, Hatteras, Pacemaker, Chris-Craft, and Trojan. They were easily distinguished by brand-name characteristics, but all bore the unmistakable sportfishing stamp.

At the same time, a group of smaller yards was specializing in highly refined models, fishing boats that carried the stamp of quality usually found only in the most expensive custom-built yachts. The famous Rybovich boats, for example, were masterpieces of handcrafted wooden construction that, despite their high cost and elegant finish, were dependable, tough, all-weather, tournament-class vessels. Some of the early Rybovich models are still in active service after more than 30 years of hard work, and they command top prices on the used-boat market.

Specialization developed in a number of ways. In Florida, the need for ultra-shoal, open, small boats for fishing the flats of the Keys and the nearby Bahama Islands led to the development of the distinctive bonefish and tarpon skiffs. Very early models were flat-bottomed or built with a wide, shallow V-form forward, which faded to a flat bottom aft. Outboard motors provided power for running to and from the flats, and the boats were, and still are, poled over the fishing flats by their guide-operators.

Because casting with light tackle was the method employed, the hulls had to be completely open and uncluttered. This led to grouping the steering and engine controls at a single low console on the centerline, and the center-console boat concept was born. At first, the design and manufacture of flats-fishing skiffs were largely a local South Florida enterprise. One of the early mass-producers to penetrate this market was the New England–based Boston Whaler company.

Early Boston Whalers were built in 13-foot and 17-foot sizes. The blunt-nosed hull had multiple chines that softened the ride in a head chop and gave the boat good stability in rough water. Boston Whaler very early adopted the center console and floored the forward portion of the hull with a semi-raised casting platform. While Whalers seldom replaced true Keys skiffs among the Florida Keys professional guides, they proved quite popular with boat livery people in areas where toughness, seaworthiness, and ability to absorb abuse from the general public were paramount to commercial success. They also proved popular among do-it-yourself fishermen, who found that the boat trailer gave them a type of alongshore mobility that previously had been the exclusive property of larger charter boats and fishing yachts.

In southern New England, the so-called Cuttyhunk bass boat epitomized the relatively rare development of a boat type without a direct commercial fishing background. The Cuttyhunker did incorporate the lapstrake hull skin of the earlier New Jersey Sea Bright dories, but only down to the turn of the hard chine. From chine to keel the hull was

Classic lines and flashing speed are the mark of the true tournament fisherman. This 36-foot Merritt, built in Florida, epitomizes the concept of the modern fishing machine. The tower is in proportion to the length and breadth of the hull. The very slight reverse sheer looks practically flat in this slightly elevated view. A single fighting chair occupies the cockpit and can be replaced by a "rocket launcher" multiple rodholder for fast light-tackle competitive fishing. Speeds of 40 knots are not unusual in this class of fisherman, but performance at slow trolling speeds in rough water is superb. (Photo by Frank T. Moss)

Stalking the wily bonefish over the shallow Florida Bay flats calls for a small open boat with shoal draft and considerable stability. The 17-foot Mako open-console fisherman is one of a number of similar boats easily trailed to distant productive waters and completely at home in anything deeper than a heavy dew. (Photo by Bill Munro — Mako Marine)

smooth-planked. Power was single-screw, and the wheel and rudder were protected by a very strong oak skeg.

Early Cuttyhunkers averaged from 20 to 25 feet in length and were rather heavily built. Because their operators made a good portion of their living by market-fishing for striped bass between fishing parties, the distinctive Cuttyhunk stern tiller became standard equipment at an early stage. This tiller is just high enough to rest between the operator's knees or lower thighs when running and fishing standing up, facing forward. It can be folded down out of the way when not needed. Stern-mounted throttle and clutch controls complete the singlehanded operating picture.

Cuttyhunk bass boats were, and still are, designed to operate in rock-infested, tideripped, coastal waters. As one Cuttyhunk guide once confessed, "I know where the rocks are because I've been on top of every dang one of 'em!"

From flats-casting skiff to pocket-battleship tournament contender, the Mako fleet of modern center-console fishermen spans the full range of saltwater sportfishing. These boats are fueling up in a Florida canal port for the long haul across the Gulf Stream to Walkers Cay in the Bahamas for a light-tackle big-game fishing tournament. (Photo by Bill Munro)

Modern New England bass boats retain much of the traditional design, adding improvements borrowed from other successful models. Their beam is now more generous and fiberglass is the dominant construction material. Single-screw power is still popular, although most builders do not bat an eye at the owner who wants twin-screw. Both builders and users seem to remain convinced that, in the Cuttyhunk model, hull weight is a function of stability and easy motion in rough water. The fact remains that the Cuttyhunk bass boat is a highly successful model conceived and developed for a specialized form of fishing, and proved beyond any shadow of doubt in the tough testing laboratory of New England coastal tiderips.

What biologists might call a case of convergent evolution took place simultaneously on the U.S. West Coast and, of all places, in South Africa. The Oregon Cape Kawanda dory is a wide-sterned version of the traditional Atlantic commercial fishing dory. Developed especially for launching and retrieving from beaches through the ocean surf, the Cape Kawanda dory features either a good-sized outboard motor mounted in an internal well, or a modern water-jet propulsion system. The quarry is salmon for sportsmen or the commercial market, and the fishing is rugged.

A far cry from the early Boston Whaler days, this 20-foot Outrage model is rigged for big game with a fighting chair mounted on the forward casting platform. Fighting a big tuna, marlin, or swordfish from the bow of a small boat gives angler and skipper the advantage of the hull's natural ability to handle waves and wind while moving forward rather than backing down. Whalers of different models are often seen on Stellwagen Bank, in Massachusetts Bay, fishing for 1,000-pound giant bluefin tuna. The Whaler's early forte, however, was probing the northern surf for stripers and bluefish, or the Florida and Bahama flats for bonefish and tarpon. (Photo by Boston Whaler)

Nearly identical conditions exist at Cape Vidal on the Indian Ocean shore of South Africa. Bill Wisner, former associate editor of *Sportfishing* magazine, described a Cape Vidal ski-boat operation in the August 1967 issue.

> At Cape Vidal I was introduced to ski boat fishing. Cape Vidal waters are alive with marlin, sailfish, dolphin, sharks, king mackerel, wahoo, and others, but the area lacks natural harbors. Ski boat fishing was conceived as a way to launch boats through the surf.

Sporting outriggers, Dudley Roberts' 21-foot MacKenzie-Cuttyhunk bass boat trolls for game fish in Exuma Sound off the tip of Eleuthera in the Bahamas. Powered by a single 130-hp gas engine, she tops out at over 20 mph, but she can idle down to a slow 1 to 2 mph for trolling. A fold-down top provides a modicum of shelter. Two small chairs occupy the stern. Wooden Cuttyhunkers traditionally are lapstrake planked from guardrail down to the corner of the bilge. Bottom planking is smooth. Rather heavily built for their size, the older Cuttyhunkers gain in rough water comfort and stability what they lose in speed to lighter models. (Photo by Frank T. Moss)

The boats go 18 to 22 feet, there being a limit to the size of craft you can launch through the breakers. I fished aboard *Zulu Dancer*, a 22-footer skippered by Captain Dave Borland of St. Lucia. Her power was a pair of Volvo 100-hp I/O units and the cockpit carried six compact fishing chairs.

A line from the boat's bow ran out to a block moored to a submerged rock, then back to a power winch on the shore. With all hands aboard, life jackets on, the winch hauled the boat off the sand and into the water. The line was cast off and Dave headed out toward the breakers. He waited for precisely the right moment. Suddenly it came. The Volvos roared and we headed for the crashing surf at full speed.

When we hit the first curling wall of water the boat's bow leaped skyward. Up and over the roaring crest we shot, descending on the

This 18-foot South African ski-boat, powered with two antique Johnson outboard motors, is astonishingly similar in looks and method of use to its American counterpart, the Cape Kawanda dory from Oregon. The primary difference is that the South African boat carries its outboards on the transom, while the Oregon dory houses its single big outboard in an amidships inboard well. Both launch directly through ocean surf to reach the fishing grounds. The fish shown here is a barracuda. Oregon fishermen use their dory for salmon fishing. (Courtesy of South African Tourist Corp.)

seaward side with a bone-jarring jolt. Two lesser takeoffs and landings, and we were clear for offshore. The return to the beach was as exciting, but not as jarring. The boat didn't stop until she was on the sand. Aided by a special cradle, the winch, and Zulu muscle, she was drawn high, turned around, and made ready for the next trip.

The Cape Kawanda and Cape Vidal beach-launched boats share a mutual operational ancestor in the famous Sea Bright dories of New Jersey. These small, light, lapstrake powerboats had a lively sheer, a broad transom stern, and featured a unique box keel that gave the flat bottom a double-ended shape. The box keel terminated in a deadwood that carried the propeller-shaft stern bearing and a metal skeg to take the external rudder.

Sea Bright dories — or "Jersey boats," as they were often called — were launched over wooden rollers directly into the surf. The commercial fishermen operating them fished by handlines, operated fish traps, used seines, or tended lobster pots. The return to the beach, well-laden, could be hair-raising. Each Sea Bright skiff carried a stout iron ring in the bow to which a tow chain from a pair of horses was made fast to haul the boat above the surf line. Each boat's crew fished as an independent unit, but colonies of beach dory-fishermen existed up and down the shore, sharing the work of launching, retrieving, unloading the fish, and often the living expenses.

In his book, *The Sea Bright Skiff and Other Jersey Shore Boats*, Peter J. Guthorn describes the beach-fishing communities of the New Jersey shore. These communities were first organized between 1825 and 1850 and enjoyed a large and profitable market in the nearby and rapidly growing New York metropolitan area.

The earliest beach-fishing boats were about 15 feet long with a 5-foot beam. They were propelled by oars and sail and featured a centerboard or daggerboard for windward sailing work.

Power became predominant early in the present century. When New Jersey boatyards turned to the building of large, fast powerboats to supply the smuggling trade during the era of Prohibition, many of the hulls were enlarged versions of the faster, inboard-powered Jersey skiffs. The Jersey, or Sea Bright, skiff also had a strong influence on the development of fast, seaworthy pleasure boats, of which the well-known Banfield skiffs soon came to be recognized as superior small sportfishermen.

The adaptation of commercial hulls to sportfishing is another example of convergent evolution. Just as the Jersey skiffs became the progenitors of small sportfishing boats in the New Jersey–Long Island region, so the small seaworthy lobsterboats of Maine inspired a Down-East style of sportfisherman that combined the qualities of good speed with moderate power, seakindliness, and economy of initial cost.

Sportfishing in Hawaii began to boom shortly after World War II, and island shipyards began turning out slicked-up versions of the traditional Japanese fishing sampan hull. These boats were, and still are, superlative sea boats, quite at home in the rough seas and heavy chop of the inter-island passages. Of deadrise hull form, they are heavy, slow and built to last many years.

In the last decade there has been a steady and growing influx to Hawaiian ports of lighter, faster, more modern, mainland sportfishing types. Some of these are representatives of such well-known East Coast and Florida builders as Hatteras, Pacemaker, Bertram, Merritt, Rybovich, and even Boston Whaler. West Coast builders are represented by Uniflite, Pacifica, and Tollycraft.

Tradition-minded Hawaiians cannot be blamed for looking askance at

The 36-foot Little Vigilant II, *built by Hubert S. Johnson of Bay Head, New Jersey, and owned by Ogden W. Headington, was a final mutation of the long and honorable line of Jersey sea skiffs. Powered with twin 140-hp Chrysler Royal straight-eights, she cruised at 20 knots yet was an excellent slow troller for bass and bluefish. Essentially a family cruising fisherman, she lacks a bridge but carries offshore navigating equipment in the form of a permanently installed radio direction finder. The position of the outriggers — straight up and straight out — dates this boat to pre-World War II days. Hubert Johnson and other New Jersey builders perfected their designs in the cutthroat competition of Prohibition rumrunning days. With repeal, they adapted their fast, load-carrying rumrunner hull forms to the more prosaic work of economical pleasure cruising and fishing. (Photo by Morris Rosenfeld. From* Yachting)

the flashy, fast interlopers, but with more than 600 square miles of prime marlin and tuna water protected from the northeast trade winds by the massive island of Hawaii, private and professional sportfishermen based at Kailua and other Kona Coast ports are taking to the mainland imports like bluefish after a school of sand eels.

In boats, as in other fields of constant development, extreme specialization tends to become a dead-end street. Witness the rise and demise of the plank-on-edge racing cutter yachts of Victorian days. These extreme hulls fell victim to the lighter, faster, shoal-draft, American racing hulls. But once in a while a specialization is married to a radical new development, giving birth to a hybrid of great potential. Exactly this happened in 1960, when Richard Bertram stunned the powerboat world with his sweeping victory in the rough Miami-Nassau powerboat race, crashing through towering seas in his small, deep-V-hulled *Moppie*.

The deep-V hull pioneered by C. Raymond Hunt and promoted by Richard Bertram in the form of his famous Moppie *class of 31-footers revolutionized sportfishing boat design in the early 1960s. Adequately powered, the Hunt hull gallops to windward in rough seas with hardly a pound and runs down steep following seas with nary a hand on the wheel, while the skipper casually combs his hair. More than 2,000 31-foot Bertrams exist worldwide, and the original models are virtually unchanged in nearly 20 years. Like the famous Morgan horse of Vermont, the Bertram 31 was an American original with the prepotent ability to stamp its genetic imprint on an entirely new race of superior sportfishing boats. (Photo by Bertram Yacht)*

Power racing boats were, and still are, highly specialized craft. The deep-V hull, developed by C. Raymond Hunt and demonstrated by Bertram, married the radical new hull form to the specialized racing machine and produced a hybrid that took the power-yacht and sportfishing worlds by storm. The Hunt-Bertram deep-V hull soon proved to be a tremendous fishing boat. Between 1960 and 1970, more than 1,000 31-foot Bertram sport boats were launched, the majority of them destined for fishing. The model is still in production, virtually unchanged after 20 years.

The great success of the Hunt-Bertram deep-V fisherman quickly inspired imitators. The deep-V hull solved two problems of handling small boats at speed in rough water. It vastly reduced pounding in a head sea, and it greatly increased directional stability in short, steep following seas. Because the bilges of the deep-V hull are "slack" when compared with conventional hard-chine, V-bottomed hulls, the deep-V sometimes develops a slower, deeper roll at slow speed in a beam or quartering sea. But dynamic stability builds rapidly as speed increases in rough water.

Typical of modern West Coast deep-water sportfishermen is the 51-foot Seeley fishing cruiser Miss Lynne. Western anglers seldom employ professional captains, and a 51-footer is a large boat to handle without paid help, unless one has a passel of willing friends. Miss Lynne has accommodations for six to eight, can cruise 1,000 miles on a single filling of diesel fuel, and is air conditioned against the heat of southern California and the Baja peninsula. The large, insulated fish hold can refrigerate such delicate fish as albacore and yellowtail, taken far offshore or on remote sea pinnacles such as Alijos Rocks. The bridge control station is placed rather far forward by Atlantic standards, but it conforms to the trend of contemporary Pacific design. With hospitable ports sometimes many miles apart, Pacific deep-sea sportfishermen like their boats to be big, roomy, long-range, and eminently comfortable. Miss Lynne meets all these requirements. (Photo by Don Bush, Costa Mesa, CA)

Adaptation of the deep-V hull to the new, center-console, smaller open fisherman was almost instantaneous. With the deep-V hull, center-console boats as small as 20 feet often fished far offshore along with the deep-water tournament fleet. In the last few years, a new class of pocket-battleship, semi-open, tournament fishermen has arrived on the scene. These are basically deep-V hulls in the 26- to 34-foot class, inboard-powered, with minimal cuddy cabins forward and the amidships area protected by strong plastic curtains hung from the tower legs. With speeds of upward of 40 knots in smooth water, these small, light, fast fishing boats are ideal for day or light-tackle tournament fishing, where participants do not have to live on board.

Stripped of their fishing context, the qualities that mark the modern sportfishing boat are the same that brand any quality yacht. The day is long gone when a boat for fishing was any old clunker too decrepit to serve as a yacht. The opposite is now true. A sportfishing boat, by public definition, is superior. The circle of evolution is now complete. Lessons learned and concepts proved in the crucible of competitive fishing are being applied to nonfishing boats to make them faster, more comfortable, more efficient, and more seaworthy. The characteristics of the sportfishing boat of today are becoming the criteria of excellence in racing and cruising powerboats of the future.

A blue marlin reaches for the sky off Walkers Cay in the Bahamas. Modern fishing boats and equipment have opened new avenues of adventure on the ocean, a frontier that is still relatively unspoiled by human encroachment. (Photo by Bill Munro — Mako Marine)

CHAPTER 2
The Strategies of Boat Fishing

Successful fishermen know that their success depends on a high degree of boat-handling skill, fishing skill, and an understanding of the two basic strategies of boat fishing. These strategies are:

- The strategy of fish location and detection.
- The strategy of interaction between the fish and the fisherman and his boat.

These two strategies are not identical, although very often both operate at the same time. Success with one very often depends on success with the other.

The strategy of fish location and detection is based on local and regional knowledge of fish species and fish behavior, where to go to find the fish when they are in a biting mood, and how to detect them when they are not visible to the naked eye. This strategy is widely discussed in fishing literature.

Less widely understood but equally important is the subject of direct interaction between the fish and the boat. This interaction is most apparent in trolling. Tuna trollers, for example, know that every boat has a particular trolling speed at which it obtains the most strikes. This speed varies from boat to boat, and some boats possess it more than others. A smart troller soon discovers the trolling speeds that are best for his boat under different conditions of sea and weather, and with different species of fish.

Boats moving on the water are in constant interaction with fish. A fish does not know that a boat is anything other than a fairly noisy surface-dwelling creature that swims with a spinning rather than a wagging tail. (Photo by Bill Munro — Mako Marine)

Dissatisfaction with a sportfishing boat often stems from an owner's awareness that his boat is deficient in this important fish-interaction quality. Some owners will put up with a relative dog of a boat where comfort is concerned if the boat has superior fish-attracting ability. But a comfortable boat that also attracts fish is an almost unbeatable combination. Builders know this and go to considerable lengths to build into their hulls the physical properties that appear to enhance fish-boat interaction. These qualities are sometimes hard to define, but they can be described in general terms.

- Stability and good handling qualities at trolling speeds in any fishable weather.
- Ability to maintain a steady trolling speed while running into, across, or down a rough sea.
- Ability to generate an underwater sound field that is attractive to the fish, or at least not frightening to them.

The first quality is controllable through engineering, design, and construction. The second is often a mark of the boat-handling skill of the operator. The third is not controllable except by happy accident. Some boats become better game-fish trollers after a change of propellers, but there is no way that the outcome of a change of propellers can be predicted; success depends on trial and error. A knowledgeable owner will often go to great lengths to arrive at the best possible propeller-generated sound field. Learning to get the most from a boat's fish-attracting potential is one of the great challenges of sportfishing.

THE STRATEGY OF FISH LOCATION AND DETECTION

The simplest method of fish location and detection is visual inspection of the water for signs of fish. These signs include individual fish or schools of fish breaking the surface while chasing bait; individual large fish, such as marlin, swordfish, or sharks, swimming and finning out at the surface; and fish sighted swimming under the surface in conditions of good water visibility.

Indirect signs of fish include sea birds actively feeding on bait at the surface; fresh organic oil slicks caused by large fish feeding down deep on smaller, oily bait fish; a sudden change in trolling tactics of other boats; and the presence of floating sargassum weed, planks, or other debris, under which some species of fish like to take refuge.

There are natural water conditions that often indicate areas where fish may be found. Tide and current rips are excellent examples. A tiderip is formed when an ocean or coastal current flows over a ledge or bar, creating a stationary rip condition. A current rip, on the other hand, is caused when two currents of opposite direction cause a friction rip along their mutual boundary.

Game fish love an "edge," or water discontinuity. In many coastal areas there is a distinct boundary, or "line," between discolored, greenish, inshore water and clear, blue, offshore water. The offshore water is clear because it contains less plankton and suspended particulate matter. It is also usually slightly warmer and more saline. Along the Atlantic coast from Cape Hatteras to Cape Cod, the offshore mile or two along the edge of the blue water very often is best for finding white marlin.

Developing a personal strategy for visual fish location and detection is largely a matter of self-training in how to look for fish and what to look for. Scanning the surface for fins and breaking fish, for instance, is best done with one's side vision. Side vision emphasizes black-and-white contrast and is first to pick up motion and distinctive shapes.

Searching underwater for the dark purple-brown mass of a school of deep-swimming bluefins or the bright blue of a swordfish, on the other hand, is best done with one's central vision. Central vision discriminates best between nuances of color. Learning to concentrate on side or central vision is like learning to ride a bicycle. You fall a few times at first, but soon it becomes automatic.

Eyeball location of finning or underwater fish is essential to many types of fishing. The operator on the tower of this Mako open-console fisherman has 360-degree vision both to the horizon and well underwater. The tower puts his eyes almost on the level of the flying bridge of an average larger fishing cruiser. (Photo by Bill Munro — Mako Marine)

Good visibility, of course, is a prime requisite. The flying bridge and the lookout tower were invented to maximize fish-spotting visibility, but their purposes are not the same. Fin spotting is best done from the relatively low altitude of the bridge. Here you are looking for the distinctive shape and motion of a fin against the lighter background shades of the water surface.

Towers provide the altitude needed to spot underwater fish. They were first used shortly after World War II in Florida and Bahamian waters for spotting and following swift schools of migrating bluefin tuna on the shallow Bahama Banks. It did not take long for the rod and reel sword-fishermen of Long Island and New England to discover how much a tower increased the chances of spotting broadbills cruising just under the surface. Now, of course, a tower is a hallmark of the well-equipped offshore sportfishing boat; it has also become a status symbol.

Spotting and interpreting the natural signs of fish are old skills. Modern fishermen make use of new skills that were in the class of science fiction just a few decades ago. The electronic depth sounder, for instance, has revolutionized fish detection. The sounder was invented to make it possible for ships to obtain fast, accurate soundings without having to slow down or stop to use the old-fashioned lead line. Very soon, commercial fishermen discovered that an accurate depth sounder could give them valuable information about the character of the bottom.

A sharp, irregular bottom line, or bottom-flash, was a sure sign of rocky bottom. A less distinct, broader bottom indication was probably mud. With practice, a keen operator could tell the difference between sand, rocks, mud, shells, or seaweed. All of these habitats were favored or avoided by various species of fish.

Then it became evident that sounders could display schools of small fish or large individual fish between the surface and the bottom. Instantly, fishermen of all persuasions had an "eye in the water" that vastly reduced the amount of time spent in trial-and-error fish finding. What had started as an aid to navigation was now an important fish location and identification instrument. Sportsmen as well as commercial fishermen welcomed the sounder as a boon to their activities.

Special strategies for locating and baiting game fish soon emerged. One very interesting big-game system was pioneered in Hawaii by Captain Bart Miller and others fishing along the Kona Coast for Pacific blue marlin and *ahi* (yellowfin tuna). The traditional method was to troll at high speed with large artificial trolling lures. The new method involves fishing with live *aku* (skipjack tuna) over submerged seamounts a few miles off the Kona Coast.

Live *aku* are hooked in the area of the submerged seamounts, and, when the baits have been deployed on heavy tackle behind the boat, the boat is maneuvered by sounder to remain over the peak of a known, productive seamount. These small seamounts, or submerged cinder cones, appear to attract schools of bait and larger predators. An accurate deep-water

The flasher-recorder combination sounder in this Mako open-console fisherman is an important adjunct to successful game fishing. Of all electronic aids to fish detection, the flashing or recording sounder is probably the most important. (Photo by Bill Munro — Mako Marine)

sounder is an absolute must to keep the boat positioned over a seamount peak where the chances of big game-fish action are best.

A different strategy is that of locating fish by finding water of known comfort-zone temperature. Fishermen use two different means for obtaining water temperatures. One is a direct-reading dial on the bridge, activated by a thermister, or temperature probe, placed in the main cooling water intake, which gives surface temperature.

The second method requires taking temperatures at predetermined depths. This is useful in locating a thermocline, the boundary layer between warm surface water and cold water down deep. Both bait and game fish very often use a thermocline to remain in water of the desired temperature. One way to obtain depth temperatures is to use a modern depth-temperature probe. The weighted probe is lowered and water temperature is read by a meter in the boat. Depth is usually gauged by a color code on the probe's insulated electric wire drop line.

A more sophisticated method is to use what is known as an XBT — an expendable bathythermograph. Originally perfected for the U.S. Navy, the XBT employs a small bomb-like weight that is dropped overboard and falls free toward the bottom, transmitting back to the vessel instantaneous temperature readings through an ultra-thin, three-conductor wire. The fall rate of the bomb is a known factor (in one instance, 22 feet per second), and both temperature and depth are recorded on a synchronized paper-tape recorder in the vessel. The XBT can be used at almost any vessel speed. Bomb and wire are expendable.

Saltwater Game Fish Temperature Table*

Species	Range	Optimum
Albacore	60°-66°	64°
Amberjack	60°-72°	65°
Barracuda	70°-82°	75°
Bluefish	56°-79°	68°
Bonefish	70°-82°	75°
Bonito	60°-80°	64°
Cod	40°-58°	48°
Dolphin	72°-82°	75°
Fluke	56°-70°	66°
Flounder	48°-64°	54°
Kelp bass	60°-70°	65°
Marlin, black	68°-80°	70°
Marlin, blue	70°-82°	75°
Marlin, striped	65°-80°	72°
Marlin, white	65°-80°	70°
Permit	70°-82°	75°
Pollock	40°-60°	50°
Red snapper	50°-62°	57°
Sailfish	70°-82°	79°
Salmon (basic)	48°-60°	52°
Shark (basic)	50°-80°	70° +
Skipjack *(aku)*	65°-82°	73°
Striped bass	54°-70°	60° +
Swordfish	50°-68°	58°
Tarpon	70°-82°	76°
Tuna, big-eye	62°-68°	64°
Tuna, blackfin	70°-82°	74°
Tuna, bluefin	50°-78°	68°
Tuna, yellowfin	64°-80°	72°
White sea bass	60°-70°	67°
Yellowtail	60°-70°	67°

Source: Modern Saltwater Fishing Tackle

The temperature data above provide interesting clues about the preferred habitats of various fish. Albacore, for example, are extremely temperature-sensitive and West Coast fisheries people search for 64-degree water by air, using sensitive infrared detecting equipment. Boats are called to areas of optimum surface-water temperatures. Red snappers, on the other hand, are tropical in range, yet prefer cooler water. Therefore they are bottom-dwellers seldom taken near the surface.

Species with optimum temperatures over 70 degrees are almost invariably taken on or near the surface. These include the marlins, some tunas, and sailfish. The swordfish, on the other hand, prefers deep water, except in its northern range, where it finds optimum temperatures at or near the surface. Witness the surface-baiting of swords off Block Island versus the deep-bait fishing in Florida waters.

Some critics complain that electronic aids have taken the sportsmanship out of ocean fishing. This is a question of viewpoint. Experienced offshore fishermen counterclaim that electronic aids add new dimensions to their understanding of fish and the aquatic habitat. They say that understanding fish better through electronic aids does not mean they slaughter fish senselessly. Competitive fishing under the universally accepted rules of the International Game Fish Association has helped tremendously in maintaining a high level of restraint and sportsmanship among sportfishermen around the world.

THE STRATEGY OF BOAT-FISH INTERACTION

When confronted for the first time with the argument that boat-fish interaction is a definite part of fishing, one skeptic exclaimed, "Horsefeathers! A fish is a living creature and a boat is an inanimate, man-made object. How can an inanimate object possibly have an effect on the reactions of fish?"

Not an easy question to answer, especially in the absence of essential research into boat-fish interaction. Yet, as was stated earlier, all experienced tuna trollers and many billfishermen know that some boats definitely do raise and attract fish better than others. Furthermore, the fish have no way of knowing that the boat is an inanimate object in which they are not supposed to display any interest. One does not have to fish very long before coming to the conclusion that, as far as the fish are concerned, a boat is just another specimen of those noisy, surface-dwelling creatures that signal their approach from afar by beating the water to a froth with a spinning rather than an oscillating tail.

Any boat moving over fish is in constant interaction with them. Water is an excellent sound-conducting medium and all boats are noisy. Fish do not have to see a boat to know it is there. The prominent lateral lines down the sides of their bodies are sensitive sound- and pressure-wave detectors, directly bound into their central nervous systems. Moderate boat noise does not necessarily upset resident fish. But let a fast boat go charging past at

A boat's underwater sound-making equipment is the combination of its hull form and shafts, propellers, and rudders. The deep-V underbody of the Hunt-Bertram Moppie *hull makes a deep, frothy wake at slow speed, one that has proved to be excellent for raising and holding many varieties of game fish. Each type of boat has a definite speed at which it is most effective at raising and holding particular species of fish. Finding that speed for any combination of boat and fish species is a matter of experimentation and observation. (Photo by John Crouse, Miami, FL)*

high speed, creating a sound field of great intensity, and the fish are instantly put on guard.

The awareness of fish for a boat passing overhead often stimulates them to strike at lures trolled at a critical distance behind the boat. This was demonstrated dramatically at Montauk, New York, some years ago. A local resident had just taken delivery of a new bass boat equipped with a small tower for offshore fishing. He invited a charter captain friend to accompany him and his wife on a trial spin for striped bass. The weather was what tourists call ideal, but too calm for good bass fishing. There was no surf on the beach to give the water color. Big stripers were lazing over sandy bottom, clearly visible from the boat's low tower.

The owner and his wife were fishing long yellow "Jigit" eels placed the usual 120 feet behind the boat. Looking down from the tower, the charter captain could see the fish apparently opening ranks to let the boat go through, then closing ranks again about 60 feet behind the boat. On three passes over the fish they had no strikes.

All them fish...! In clear water, fish may school together near the bottom, waiting for a change of tide or incursion of turbid water to trigger the feeding response. Very often they will open their ranks to let a boat troll through, then close ranks again behind the boat after it has passed. If you can adjust the length of your trolling lines to have the lures under the wake at the exact distance behind the boat where the fish rejoin after the boat has passed, you may be able to stimulate fish into a striking mood. (Photo by Frank T. Moss)

Acting on a hunch, the skipper had the anglers reel in about half their lines, placing the trolling lures at the exact distance behind the boat where the disturbed bass were closing ranks under the wake after the boat had passed over them. Almost immediately man and wife had a double strike. They resumed trolling, carefully gauging the length of their lines to coincide with the distance behind the boat where the stripers moved in from either side to join ranks. They took eight large fish in less than two hours, while other boats, attracted by their activity but fishing the conventional longer lines, caught nothing.

According to the skipper, who was something of an analyst, the movement of the fish away from the boat's path as it passed over them was just enough to stimulate them without inducing an urge to flee. As the fish came back together after the boat had passed, the sudden appearance of the lures triggered their competitive urge, resulting in a concerted rush at the lures and strikes from the fish that got to them first. This super-stimulated mood could have lasted only a few seconds, for when longer lines were used, the lures arrived among the fish after their peak of stimulation had passed. No strikes.

Fish are apparently able to learn from experience. This ability is probably a beneficial result of the selective evolution of behavior. Anyone who has fished a virgin Canadian lake knows how ferociously the pike, lake trout, and char react to their first sight of artificial lures. But after the lake has been open to sportfishing for a few years, the same fish show more restraint in taking trolled or cast artificial lures.

The strategy, therefore, when fishing over "experienced" fish, is to take advantage of the boat's ability to stimulate the fish during the first few passes over them, and then, when the fish have stopped striking, to go away and give them a rest until a change of tide or sun angle helps them forget the recent experience. This is not to say that fish have human reactions and emotions. It is what successful pros actually do to produce reasonable catches when all the other fishermen are catching nothing at all.

The strategies of modern boat fishing may appear complex, but they are based on just a few simple principles.

- Train yourself to be alert and to understand the many signs that reveal fish or fishable habitat.
- Equip your boat with the mechanical and electronic aids best suited to your style of fishing and to enhancing your understanding of fish and the marine environment.
- Regard your boat not as an inanimate object, but as an extension of your personal powers of observation, evaluation, and action on the water.
- Keep abreast of developments in tackle, fishing tactics, and the understanding of fish behavior.
- Look upon ocean fishing as an opportunity to explore one of the last, great natural frontiers. Enrich your sense of accomplishment and adventure, not by trying to kill every last fish in the ocean, but by meeting and overcoming the challenges that ocean fishing offers.

CHAPTER 3
What Makes Them Go

When automotive engines were first introduced into the marine-power field before World War II, the majority of boat motors were heavy, cumbersome affairs. The only engines that could develop power in the horsepower ranges that we take for granted today were surplus World War I Liberty aircraft motors, the favorites of rumrunners. A Liberty stood nearly 5 feet tall, delivered from 250 to 400 hp, depending on how hard you dared run it, and had a half-life of about 100 hours between breakdowns.

Then came the age of automobile conversions. Watercooled manifolds and marine clutches were fitted to such auto engines as Model A Ford, Oldsmobile, Pontiac, Chrysler, and Buick fours and sixes, and the beautiful, powerful Packard straight-eight. The latter could gulp 15 gallons of fuel an hour at full throttle, yet idle down to a smooth 300 rpm for slow trolling.

During this period marine diesels were the dinosaurs of boat propulsion. A 60-hp Atlas diesel, for example, had 4 cylinders the size of butter churns, stood a fathom tall, ran at a top speed of 450 rpm, and twisted a

Left: Whether a boat is powered with outboard, sterndrive, or inboard engines — gasoline or diesel — propulsive efficiency depends on a proper matching of horsepower and propeller to the hull, elimination of excess weight, a clean bottom, and a power plant in top mechanical condition. (Photo by Bill Munro — Mako Marine)

propeller 3 feet in diameter, direct drive. The hull that carried it shook like an earthquake.

The Chrysler Corporation was one of the first of the big automotive firms to set up a separate marine-engine department. Three early, popular Chrysler models were the 6-cylinder Ace, rated at about 85 hp; the rugged Crown, developing about 110 hp; and the big Royal straight-eight with a 140-hp rating. By the early and mid-1940s, V-8 engines adapted from automotive models were making headlines for real power with light weight and reduced vibration.

Marine diesels did not escape the rock-crusher image until after the introduction of the revolutionary 2-cycle, straight-six, Gray 6-71 diesel, just before the advent of World War II. Taken over by General Motors, the 6-71 won fame as the "Jimmy" diesel that powered troop- and tank-landing barges. Tough and ugly, the "Jimmy" was rated at about 165 hp at 1800 to 2000 rpm and would run in a truly remarkable state of maladjust-

Patience II *was a slow, economical displacement type of cruiser-fisherman designed by naval architect Henry Scheel immediately after World War II to fill a demand for new postwar construction. A single 60 to 80 hp diesel with 3:1 reduction gear, swinging a propeller approximately 24 inches by 20 inches, would drive her at designed hull speed of 8 mph at a fuel consumption of perhaps two gallons per hour. A 100-gallon fuel supply would give this fuel-miser a good 400-mile range.* Patience II *was built by the Stonington Boat Works, Stonington, Connecticut, in 1946. (Photo by Frank J. Raymond)*

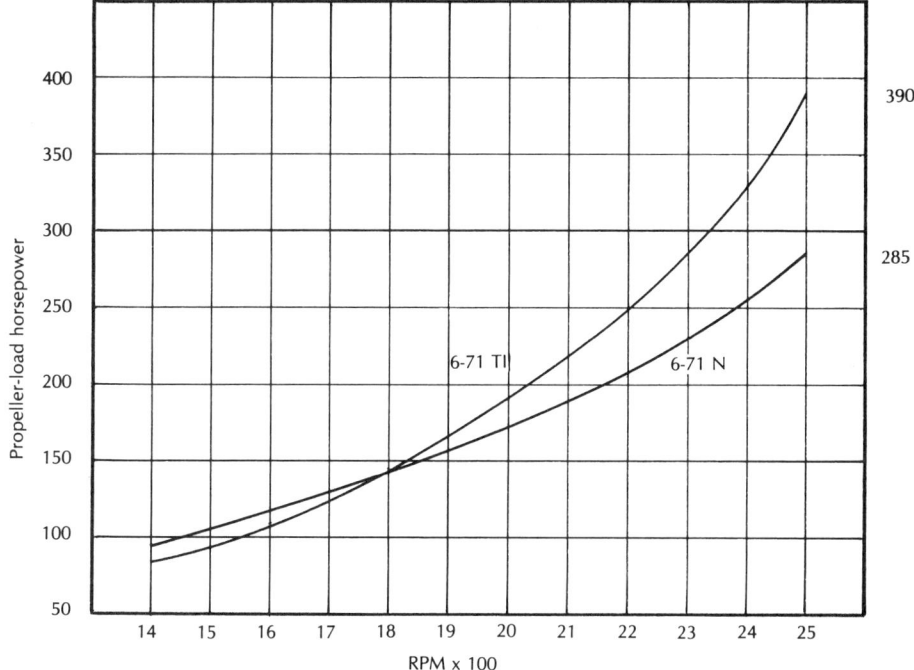

Figure 1. *This graph dramatically shows the increase of power caused by turbocharging and intercooling. The naturally aspirated 6-71 diesel peaks at 285 hp at 2500 rpm. The turbocharged, intercooled version of the same engine develops 390 hp at the same peak revolutions. Addition of TI increases power by 37 percent and, by increasing efficiency, usually decreases fuel consumption slightly for the same hull speed. (Adapted from data supplied by the Cummins Engine Co., Inc., Columbus, IN)*

ment or disrepair. The 6-71 designation meant that it had 6 cylinders, each of 71 cubic inches of displacement (CID). Today it is still a basic diesel of the smaller Detroit Diesel Allison line of marine engines.

Turbocharging has been the touchstone that has brought modern high-speed diesels into direct competition with high-output gasoline motors. Turbocharging takes advantage of latent exhaust gas energy to drive a turbine that, in turn, packs more air into the cylinders, permitting more fuel to be burned for a higher power rating at the same rpm. Intercooling of the turbo-compressed air further increases the volume of air that can be crammed into the cylinders. The letters TI in the model designation of many marine or industrial diesels mean "turbocharged, intercooled." The accompanying graph (Figure 1) clearly illustrates the power advantage of a TI diesel over an identical engine with natural aspiration.

A question frequently asked is, "Do the new engines stand up under high-speed service?" The evidence is that they do. They must be held within the speed, load, and temperature limits set by the engineers, but these limits are generally much higher than they were just a few years ago. Furthermore, their normal service life between major overhauls has been increased tremendously. Where engines of 25 years ago usually needed a ring-and-valve job every 1,000 operating hours, modern marine motors often go 3,000 to 4,000 hours before requiring the same service.

HOW MARINE ENGINES ARE POWER-RATED

In order to compare marine engines, it is necessary to know how they are power-rated. Early steam and internal-combustion engines were rated in "horsepower" to give them a rating system that meant something to people whose universal prime mover was the horse. An average healthy horse was determined to be able to lift 550 pounds in a minute of work, or 33,000 pounds in an hour of continuous work. We don't use horses as prime movers anymore, but the idea of "horsepower" as a criterion of power is so deeply ingrained in public understanding that this archaic power rating is still the dominant one in the United States and many other parts of the world.

The metric equivalent of horsepower is the kilowatt hour of work. The commonly accepted conversion factor for changing horsepower to kilowatt hours is .746. Thus, a 100-hp engine has a 74.6-kwh rating. An increasing number of U.S. manufacturers now give engine power ratings in both horsepower and kilowatt ratings. It is very easy to convert a kilowatt rating to horsepower. Simply divide the kilowatt rating by .746. For example, 150 kw divided by .746 equals 201 hp. For simplicity and clarity, this book uses the U.S. horsepower rating system.

The power rating of marine engines is complicated by the fact that engineers view ratings from several points of reference. L. Clifford Currie, manager of International Marine Marketing for the Cummins Engine Co. Inc., defines ratings for three different types of service: Pleasure Boat, Light-Duty Commercial, and Continuous Duty.

Pleasure-Boat rating. This maximum rating is intended for use in variable load applications where the average load factor does not exceed the continuous rating, and where full-throttle operation does not exceed 15 minutes in any single hour.

Light-Duty Commercial rating. This rating is intended for use in applications where the average load factor does not exceed the continuous rating and where full-throttle operation does not exceed 8 hours in any 24-hour period.

Continuous-Duty rating. This is the 24-hour continuous-duty rating and is intended for applications requiring continuous full-throttle operation.

Load Factor is the arithmetic mean of the load profile at normal-duty cycle, not including long periods at idling speeds, as in slow trolling.

In addition to the three types of duty generally recognized by engineers, there are three different classes of horsepower ratings that are applied in equal manner to each of the three duty ratings. (See Figure 2.)

Gross Brake Horsepower, or *Brake Horsepower* (GBH, or BHP), is the maximum power that an engine can deliver at maximum revolutions for each type of duty service.

Net Horsepower is the power available after deduction of such normal parasitic losses as those expended in operating the reverse-reduction gear, raw-water pump, and alternator. These parasitic losses are generally regarded as being about 6.5 percent of the Gross Brake Horsepower.

Hypothetical Propeller Power Curve is a function of the type of hull and is calculated from a formula containing an exponent representing the hull type in question. The exponent varies from 3 for a full-displacement hull to 2 for a good planing hull. Cummins uses an exponent of 2.7 for most pleasure-boat applications. The Shaft Horsepower (SHP) at any given engine speed can be calculated from the formula:

$$\text{SHP at working rpm} = \text{max SHP} \times \frac{(\text{working rpm})^{\text{Exp.}}}{\text{peak rpm}}$$

Examples

- Engine rated 421 SHP at 2600 rpm max.
- Good planing hull, exponent of 2.
- Formula: $\text{SHP} = \text{max SHP} \times \dfrac{(\text{working rpm})^2}{\text{peak rpm}}$

  a) $421 \times \dfrac{(2300 \text{ rpm})^2}{2600 \text{ rpm}} = 329.45$ SHP @ 2300 rpm

  b) $421 \times \dfrac{(2100 \text{ rpm})^2}{2600 \text{ rpm}} = 274.65$ SHP @ 2100 rpm

In the above examples the exponent of 2 gives the SHP for a good planing hull at the designated operating rpm. To show the relationship of the exponent in the equations above, let us recalculate the power curve for the same working revolutions, but using an exponent of 3 for a full-displacement hull.

  a) $421 \times \dfrac{(2300 \text{ rpm})^3}{2600 \text{ rpm}} = 291.44$ SHP @ 2300 rpm

  b) $421 \times \dfrac{(2100 \text{ rpm})^3}{2600 \text{ rpm}} = 221.83$ SHP @ 2100 rpm

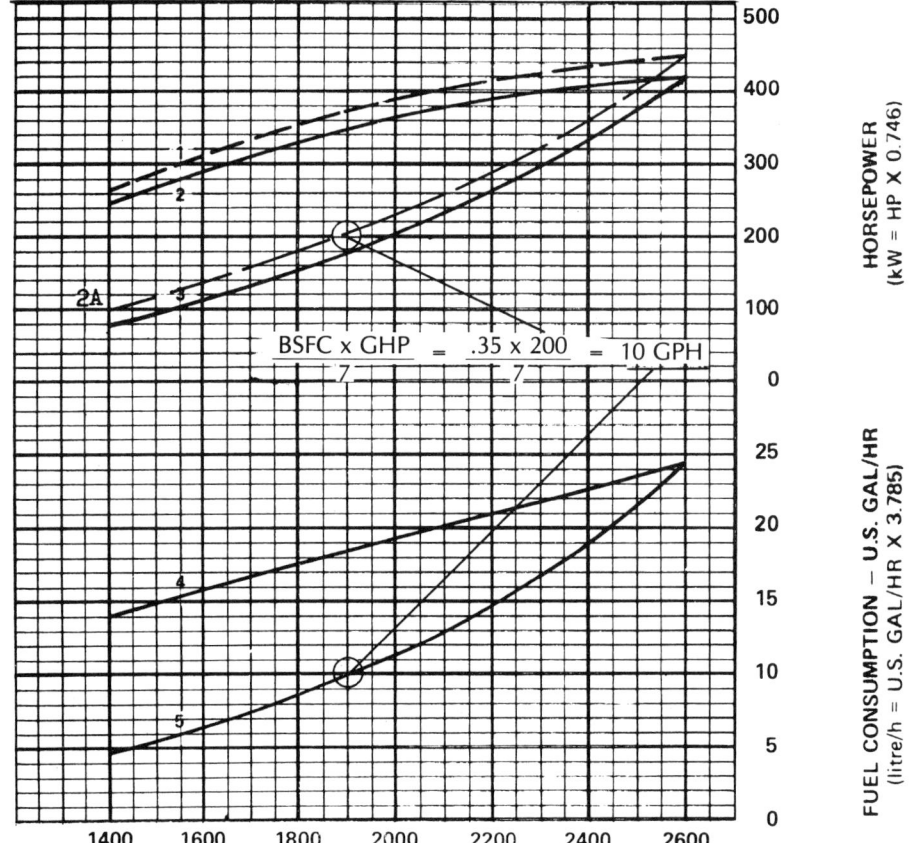

$$\frac{BSFC \times GHP}{7} = \frac{.35 \times 200}{7} = 10 \text{ GPH}$$

Figure 2. *Pleasure Boat Rating, Fuel-Power Curves, Cummins VTA-903-M Diesel*

Engine Model   *VTA-903-M*
Aspiration   *turbocharged and aftercooled*
Displacement   *903 cu in (14.8 liter)*
Bore   *5.5 in (140 mm)*
Stroke   *4.75 in (121 mm)*
Cylinders   *8*
Rating   *450 hp (336 kw) @ 2600 rpm*

Curves shown represent engine performance capabilities at SAE standard conditions. The fuel consumption curves are based on a fuel weight of 7.0 lb (3.2 kg) per U.S. gallon.

Curve 1.   Gross Brake Horsepower.
Curve 2.   Net hp with reverse-reduction gear, alternator, and raw-water pump: assumed 6.5% parasitic loss.
Curve 2A.   (See text.)

Curve 3.   Hypothetical Propeller Power Curve (2.7 exponent).
Curve 4.   Fuel Consumption for Net Shaft Horsepower.
Curve 5.   Fuel Consumption for Hypothetical Propeller.

Pleasure boat rating: *This is the maximum rating and is intended for use in variable load applications where the average load factor does not exceed the continuous rating, and where full throttle operation does not exceed 15 minutes during any one hour. (Source: Cummins Engine Co., Inc., Columbus, IN)*

From this we can see that there is no quick and easy solution to calculating the exact power and fuel requirements of a given hull, although relatively close approximations can be achieved. The accompanying graph (Figure 2) gives pleasure-boat rating curves for the Cummins VTA-903M diesel, the same engine used in the power calculations above. Currie's remarks about the curves are these:

> The attached performance curve, C-3696, is a standard pleasure-boat rating for our VTA-903M engine. Curve #1 is the Gross Brake Horsepower developed by the engine. Curve #2 shows the mechanical losses and the power available at the propeller-shaft gear coupling. Curve #2A is one I have added to show the BHP developed by the engine to overcome losses, and this is the curve we use to calculate fuel consumption shown on Curve #5.

CALCULATING FUEL CONSUMPTION

BSFC is the Brake Specific Fuel Consumption in pounds/horsepower/hours, where the average pound/gallon of diesel fuel equals 7.0.

Example (See curve: .366 is the BSFC used in test cell.)

$$\frac{.366 \times 191.25 \text{ hp}}{7} = 10 \text{ gph}$$

One can see from the curves that the fuel rate at 191 BHP, 10 gph at 1900 rpm, amounts to 19.1 hp per gph. This is generally accepted as a rule of thumb for 4-cycle diesels of various manufacturers, but it should not be assumed as applying to the engines of any particular manufacturer.

In discussing marine-power applications with the author, Currie made these observations:

> When it comes to selecting propellers, most boatbuilders specify propellers that will give a new, lightly loaded hull the highest possible speed. We much prefer to recommend propellers that will allow the engines to operate at peak revolutions and power when the hull is fully loaded with fuel, passengers, and fishing or cruising equipment, fresh water, and supplies. A 40-foot boat, for instance, may gain an extra ton of weight during its first few months, merely by the addition of equipment the owner and his family think is essential.
>
> Another problem that is seldom discussed when power is being considered is propeller cavitation. Stated simply, cavitation is the tendency of an overloaded or improperly matched propeller to entrain vapor bubbles along its fast-moving surfaces. These bubbles cause surface erosion of the metal, rapidly robbing the propeller of efficiency. We have matched thousands of propellers to hulls and have a large bank of experience from which to select propellers that will load our engines properly under most operating conditions.

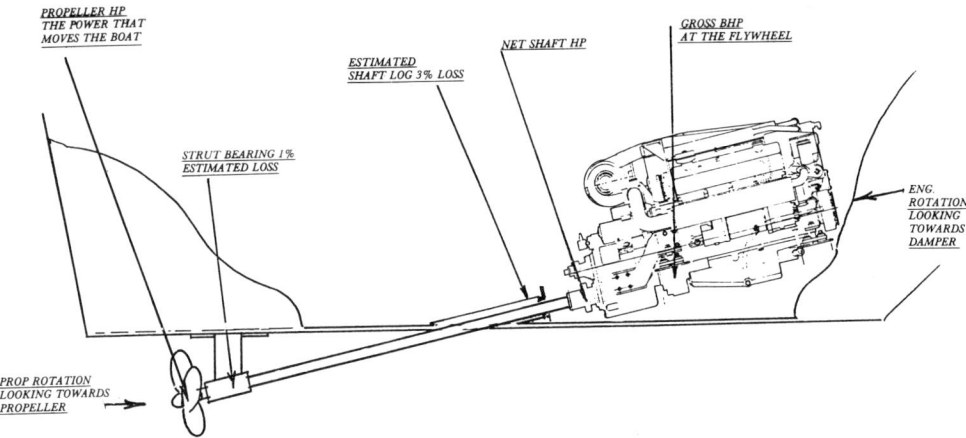

Figure 3. Engine-propeller-shaft schematic drawing showing where power losses occur between the engine and the propeller. (Source: Cummins Engine Co., Inc., Columbus, IN)

Cummins provides specially prepared Propeller Tables for all duty ratings of its engine models and reduction-gear ratios. These tables should be used together with the Cummins Horsepower and Speed Calculator when considering Cummins engines for powering a boat. The Calculator works on the circular slide-rule principle and gives estimated speeds for different types of hulls when displacement, hull type, waterline length and breadth, and hull block coefficient are worked into the Calculator.

Cummins also offers a computerized propeller recommendation service. Other engine manufacturers offer various types of propeller analysis for individual boats or for lines of boats being developed by manufacturers. Prospective owners are wise to consult the engine manufacturer as well as the boatbuilder when it comes to making a choice or compromise between top-performance or continuous-duty propeller applications.

The following tables give examples of computerized propeller recommendations worked out under the Cummins system. The engines are a pair of Cummins VTA-903M diesels with Pleasure-Boat ratings of 450 hp at 2600 rpm. Boat speed is 26 knots. Maximum propeller diameter is 30 inches. Propellers are as described in the tables. (Cummins notes that empirical equations were used in the calculations, which therefore should be considered estimates and cannot be construed as guarantees of Cummins engine performance, although they can be regarded as valuable guides.)

Engines — 2 Cummins 450-hp VTA-903M diesels

Gear ratio	1.92	2.50
Propeller	26 × 29 3-blade	28 × 30 3-blade
Make/Style	Federal Equi-Poise	Federal Equi-Poise
Pitch/dia. ratio	1.12	1.36
Blade area	294 sq in	341 sq in
Shaft speed	1354 rpm	1040 rpm

Tip speed	9,217 ft/min	7,623 ft/min
Thrust	3,957 lb	4,037 lb
Blade pressure	16.7 psi	15.8 psi
Apparent slip	19.6%	20.1%
Back cavitation	30 + %	30 + %
Gear ratio	1.92	2.50
Propeller	24 × 30 4-blade	28 × 30 4-blade
Make/Style	Federal Equi-Quad	Federal Equi-Quad
Pitch/dia. ratio	1.25	1.36
Blade area	304 sq in	413 sq in
Shaft speed	1354 rpm	1040 rpm
Tip speed	8,508 ft/min	7,623 ft/min
Thrust	3,782 lb	3,932 lb
Blade pressure	16.0 psi	12.6 psi
Apparent slip	22.3%	20.1%
Back cavitation	30 + %	30 + %

Minimum Shaft Diameter

Make/Style	*1.92 Gear Ratio*	*2.50 Gear Ratio*
Armco Aquamet 22	2.00 in (50 mm)	2.50 in (60 mm)
Monel 400	2.50 in (60 mm)	2.75 in (65 mm)
ABS Steel Grade 2	3.00 in (80 mm)	3.50 in (85 mm)

SOME PRACTICAL PROPELLER SUGGESTIONS

The wide range of propellers that will load an engine, either through direct drive or suitable reduction gears, is illustrated by the following table provided by the Lehman Power Corporation.

Engine
Lehman Ford diesel
6 cylinders, 380 CID
120 hp maximum @ 2500 rpm

Reduction Gear Ratios

MPH	*Direct*	*1.5:1*	*2:1*	*2.5:1*	*3:1*
8	17 × 10	20 × 13	26 × 15	28 × 18	30 × 22
10	17 × 11	20 × 14	25 × 17	28 × 21	30 × 24
12	16 × 12	20 × 15	24 × 19	26 × 22	30 × 26
14	16 × 13	19 × 16	24 × 20	26 × 24	30 × 28
16	16 × 14	18 × 17	24 × 21	26 × 26	30 × 30
18	15 × 15	18 × 18	24 × 22		

Following normal marine procedure, propeller sizes are in inches, with diameter always given before pitch. Thus, 19 × 16 means 19 inches in diameter by 16 inches in pitch. The table shows how one engine can power a wide variety of boat hulls. The following are examples using selections from the table.

17 × 10 This low-pitch, direct-drive propeller would be the one to use on a small converted 30-foot trawler or a converted Navy motor launch, with a single 120-hp diesel driving the boat at maximum hull speed of 8 mph.

16 × 12 With a diameter/pitch ratio of 4:3, this direct-drive propeller with the same 120-hp engine would drive a pre-war Banfield sea skiff at an easy 14 mph with full engine loading.

24 × 20 Two such propellers with 2:1 reduction gear would drive a vintage Matthews 38-foot sportfisherman at 14 mph with two 120-hp engines.

30 × 22 A small, heavy, harbor tug-workboat would hold 8 mph running free with this propeller and 3:1 reduction gear, and would retain strong towing power with the 120-hp engine at full throttle and headway of 2 to 4 mph, towing a big barge.

15 × 15 This "square" propeller with direct drive would push a center-console fisherman in the 26-foot range at 18 mph, with 120 hp at 2500 peak rpm.

These diverse examples suggest that there must be rules of thumb that govern the first stages of propeller selection.

For a slow, heavy hull, select reduction gears of 2.5:1 or 3:1 and a propeller with a diameter/pitch ratio of about 3:2, following engine manufacturer's suggestions.

For a moderate displacement, semiplaning hull with single engine power, select an engine with enough power to reach the designed top speed and equip it with 2:1 reduction gear and a propeller with 4:3 diameter/pitch ratio.

For a light, fast, planing hull, such as a modern center-console fisherman, use 1.5:1 reduction gear with low horsepower or direct drive with higher horsepower and a "square" propeller of 1:1 diameter/pitch ratio.

For a larger semiplaning hull of the so-called tournament type, select engines with 1.5:1 or 2:1 reduction-gear ratios, depending on power available, and propellers of 5:4 diameter/pitch ratio.

For a light, very fast hull, use direct drive with diameter/pitch ratio of about 4:5.

This discussion will not attempt to answer the intriguing question of why some powerboats raise game fish better than other boats. Aquatic behaviorists admit that fish are definitely influenced by external sounds. Some day we may discover that by "tuning" propellers to sing at a certain pitch, we may be able to call every fish within hearing to the stern of the boat. A few boats exhibit qualities that suggest this could be true.

But until the sonic fish-calling breakthrough is made, the best we can do is to equip our boats with engines and propellers that will push the hulls through the water with the least fuss and expenditure of energy.

WHICH POWER TO CHOOSE — GASOLINE OR DIESEL?

A basic question these days is, "Should the power of a new or repowered boat be gasoline or diesel?" The cost of fuel has many owners thinking seriously of diesel, but there is more to powering with diesel than meets the eye, so let us take an objective look at the gasoline-diesel controversy.

Exactly what are the advantages of diesel power?

- Greater range from a tankful of fuel.
- Lower cost per gallon of fuel.
- Lower cost per hour or mile traveled.
- Elimination of the gasoline explosion hazard.
- Elimination of electrical ignition systems.
- Compatibility with existing control systems.
- Rugged construction and long operating life.
- Enhanced investment value.

How much more economical is a diesel than an equivalent gasoline engine? We can start by comparing basic fuel consumption. The three major types of marine internal combustion engines burn fuel at the following rates:

Gasoline	12 hp per gph
2-cycle diesel	17 hp per gph
4-cycle diesel	20 hp per gph

These figures are averages from manufacturers' data on 1979-1980 representative engines. They indicate an increase of efficiency of at least 20 percent over similar engines of 20 years ago. They can be restated in terms of three typical engines, each developing 100 SHP.

100-hp gasoline engine	8.33 gph
100-hp 2-cycle diesel	5.88 gph
100-hp 4-cycle diesel	5.0 gph

To bring these fuel consumption figures in line with costs, let us use average 1980 fuel prices of $1.30 per gallon for standard (leaded) gasoline and $1.00 per gallon for diesel fuel. We can then convert the fuel-consumption rates into dollars for each of the three representative engines.

100-hp standard-gas engine	$10.83/hr
100-hp 2-cycle diesel	$ 5.88/hr
100-hp 4-cycle diesel	$ 5.00/hr

From this it is easy to see that the average diesel boat operates at 45 percent to 55 percent of the cost of its gasoline-powered twin. Some owners report the factor as low as 40 percent. Because diesel fuel has more work-producing ability, a gallon of diesel fuel will drive a boat farther than a gallon of gasoline. For example, suppose we have a 24-foot inboard fishing skiff that needs repowering. Before making a choice between gasoline and diesel power, we decide to cost-account the two types of power.

The old gasoline motor cruises the boat at 20 mph while burning 8.33 gallons of standard gas an hour, developing 100 hp. The boat's tanks hold 100 gallons, providing an endurance of 12 hours at 20 mph for a range of 240 miles. We are considering a 6-cylinder, 4-cycle diesel that develops 160 peak hp. At the 100-hp rating it should drive the boat at 20 mph while burning 5 gallons of fuel an hour. Now we can set up a comparative fuel-cost table.

	Gasoline	Diesel
Endurance	12 hr	20 hr
Range at 20 mph	240 mi	400 mi
Cost per tankful	$130.00	$100.00
Cost per hour	$ 10.83	$ 5.00
Cost per mile	$ 0.54	$ 0.25

How do these hypothetical figures stack up with similar figures from known, tested boats? A Florida manufacturer provided information from tests of two identical 38-foot, tournament-class boats. One was powered with twin 330-hp gasoline motors, the other with twin 270-hp, 4-cycle diesels. Fuel capacity was identical.

	Gasoline	Diesel
Top speed	27.5 mph	25.7 mph
Cruising speed	22.0 mph	23.1 mph
Cruising range	223 mi	350 mi

In another test by a New Jersey builder, three identical 40-foot, tournament-class boats were compared. One had twin 350-hp gasoline motors, one had a pair of 225-hp, 4-cycle diesels, and the third had twin turbocharged, 2-cycle diesels rating 350 hp. Here are the results:

	Gasoline	4-Cycle Diesel	2-Cycle Diesel
Top speed	26.9 mph	23.8 mph	27.5 mph
Cruising speed	20.7 mph	20.2 mph	24.6 mph
Cruising range	250 mi	425 mi	365 mi

In the case of the 4-cycle diesels, the increase of range at cruising speed was 175 miles, or 70 percent more than that of the gasoline-powered boat. The 2-cycle diesels gave a range increase of 115 miles, 46 percent greater than that of the gasoline boat, and this at a cruising speed almost 4 mph faster.

With such a rosy picture of operating economy in view, why doesn't every boat have diesel power? The primary answer is the considerably higher cost of marine diesels. Diesels of a given work capacity cost 2½ to 4 times as much as equivalent gasoline motors. If this is true, how do we find the break-even point in terms of time and dollars?

Returning to the 24-footer we considered before, we know it would cost around $3,000 for a suitable new gasoline motor. The diesel we like is pegged at $9,000. This gives a $6,000 price differential in favor of gasoline. How long would it take to make up this extra $6,000 before we could begin to realize savings from diesel operation? First we must forecast how many operating hours we will average in future fishing years.

Previous years have averaged 600 hours, and this looks reasonable for the immediate future. Average overall gas consumption has been 4 gph, or 2,400 gallons per season. Figuring that the diesel will burn about 60 per-

A 25-foot Blackfin fisherman with twin, 124-hp Volvo Penta TMD40 diesels, swinging 16-inch by 22-inch propellers through 1.91:1 reduction gears, was clocked at 33.6 knots (38.3 mph) at 3600 rpm. She cruised at 31.5 knots (35.9 mph) at 3400 rpm, burning 8 gallons of fuel per hour. This works out to a cruising range of more than 500 nautical miles at the 3400 rpm engine setting. (Photo by Blackfin Yacht Corp.)

cent of the gas engine's total, 2.4 gph and 1,440 gallons per season are reasonable estimates.

Gasoline	600 hr × 4 gph × $1.30	= $3,120
Diesel	600 hr × 2.4 gph × $1.00	= $1,440
	Difference	= $1,680

Now we can figure how soon the $6,000 will be saved.

$6,000 ÷ $1,680 = 3.57 years to break even

But suppose we lose our nice shore job, decide to take a fling at guiding bass parties with the boat, and suddenly become successful at professional fishing. Now we are operating at a rate of 1,200 hours per year. How soon will we reach break-even? (The new fuel costs will be twice what we had originally figured, or $2,880 a year.)

$6,000 ÷ $2,880 = 2.08 years to break even

To alter the situation, suppose we had been promoted to a better shore job that let us fish only 200 hours a year. How long would it take to reach break-even? Two hundred hours is one-third of 600, so the new annual fuel saving would be $1,440 ÷ 3, or $480 per year.

$6,000 ÷ $480 = 12.5 years to break even

From these exercises it is easy to see that diesel economy depends on putting in plenty of running time. In the third situation, the obvious answer would be to repower with gasoline.

Here's how a five-year, total-cost breakdown would look, figuring 200 hours of operation a year, and allowing a nominal 13 percent inflation in the cost of fuel.

	Gasoline	Diesel
Original engine cost	$3,000.00	$ 9,000.00
First year's fuel	1,040.00	480.00
Second year's fuel	1,175.20	542.40
Third year's fuel	1,327.98	612.91
Fourth year's fuel	1,500.62	692.59
Fifth year's fuel	1,695.70	782.63
Totals	$9,739.70	$12,110.53
Savings	$2,371.03	

The difference, $2,371.03, is what gasoline power would save over five years in original cost plus fuel. This shows plainly that where initial cost is important and operating hours are modest, gasoline power is probably the best buy.

Earlier we listed some of the advantages of diesel power. What are the disadvantages, other than much higher initial cost?

- Sometimes objectionable exhaust and fuel smell.
- Higher noise and vibration levels.
- Slower starting time in cold weather in some models.
- Need for very careful fuel filtration.
- Somewhat higher weight/power ratio.
- More expensive service.

How small can boats be and still profit from diesel power? The question gets us into the problem of equating engine cost with hull cost and the overall value of a complete boat. For example, a hull to duplicate our 24-footer might cost $8,000. A diesel to drive it would cost $9,000. This is 112.5 percent of the cost of the hull alone. If all we can afford is an $8,000 hull, we'll give serious thought to spending an additional $9,000 on a motor to drive it through the water.

This 28-foot Uniflite Salty Dog, with a single 270-hp Crusader gasoline engine, 1.91:1 reduction gear, swings a three-bladed, cupped 18-inch by 19-inch propeller for a top speed of 25 knots (28.5 mph) at 4200 rpm. At cruising speed of 18 knots (20.5 mph) the engine turns 3000 rpm, burning 10 gallons per hour. Tank capacity of 150 gallons allows an endurance of 15 hours at cruising speed and a range of 270 nautical miles (308 statute miles). (Photo by Uniflite Inc.)

This 46-foot Hatteras Convertible with twin 450-hp Cummins VTA-903-M diesels would top 30 mph at 2600 rpm, swinging three-bladed 26-inch by 29-inch propellers through 1.92:1 reduction gears. Cruising 27.5 mph at 2400 rpm, the engines would generate about 360 hp each, burning a total of 38 gallons per hour. With a capacity of 650 gallons, the cruising speed endurance would be 17 hours and the range 470 miles. (Photo by AMF — Hatteras Yachts)

The hull/engine cost ratio in smaller boats may be a strong factor in making decisions between diesel and gasoline power, but in larger boats it's a different story. As boats become larger, the span of cost between hull and power plant becomes greater, which means that the percentage spent on power becomes a smaller part of the total cost. For instance, consider a 42-foot tournament-class boat that has a hull and equipment worth $150,000, not counting the engines. A pair of 350-hp gasoline engines will cost at least $20,000, but this is only 13.3 percent of the cost of the hull and equipment and only 11.8 percent of the value of the complete boat.

A pair of 350 TI diesels may cost $50,000, 250 percent of the cost of the gasoline mills, but this is still only 33.3 percent of the cost of the hull and equipment and 25 percent of the cost of the fully equipped boat. In terms of percentages of invested dollars, the difference is relatively small.

If the gas engines can drive the boat 360 miles and the diesels can increase that range by 50 percent, the range with diesels should be 540 miles. For an owner contemplating frequent trips from New Orleans or Key West to Cozumel off the Yucatan coast, diesels are the logical choice. Their cost will be only 18 percent more than gasoline power.

WHAT ABOUT GAS TURBINES?

Back in the late 1960s and early 1970s, gas turbines enjoyed a brief vogue as power for boats. They had been, and still are, successful in powering hovercraft. But exhaustive tests by at least two major manufacturers showed that gas turbines, in their present form, are not suitable for pleasure powerboat use. The big problems turned out to be:

• Low fuel efficiency, especially at low speeds.
• Difficulties in dissipating waste heat.
• Very high initial cost.
• Need for exotic controls.
• Need for specially trained operating and maintenance personnel.

So the choice returns to that of gasoline power versus diesel. Each has advantages and disadvantages, but the operating differences tend to become less obvious with the passage of time. The key to a successful choice is analysis of one's personal requirements and careful shopping to find the boat-engine combination that best meets those requirements.

WHAT OWNERS THINK ABOUT BOAT PERFORMANCE

To obtain owners' opinions about the truly important performance factors of sportfishing boats, a number of owners of boats being presented in this book were contacted. The single most important quality that owners seek in a boat is reliability. The hull must be seaworthy. Engines must start up easily and quickly, run efficiently and smoothly at all speeds, and be easy to service. Owners were asked to answer questions designed to bring out their opinions concerning their boats' performance ratings. Following is the tabulated score of performance factors given in descending order of owners' scorecard ratings.

Place	Item	Score
1	Seaworthiness	118
2	Fishing efficiency	102
3	Handling ability	92
4	Fuel economy	88
5	Ease of maintenance	81
6	Investment value	80
7	Personal comfort	65
8	Cruising range	60

The three top scoring factors — seaworthiness, fishing efficiency, and handling ability — imply a demand for a high degree of reliability. The fourth, fuel economy, rated 47 percent higher than the closely related quality of cruising range. This suggests that while owners are aware of fuel costs, they appear to be satisfied with the cruising range built into most sportfishing boats.

The only class of owners that gave cruising range a consistently high score was the relatively small group of tournament-minded, long-distance cruising fishermen. Without exception, respondents stated that if fuel is available in the future, they will fish as much as or more than they have in the past.

It is interesting to note that ease of maintenance, with a score of 81, is 25 percent higher in score than personal comfort, which is next to the bottom of the list. One reader of this text suggested that this reveals the typically male attitude of desiring fishing efficiency first and comfort as an afterthought. The author does not agree. Only one returned questionnaire was from a woman, and she rated personal comfort a low fifth in score. The author is inclined to feel that the high degree of comfort built into modern sportfishing and cruising powerboats has conditioned owners to take comfort as a matter of course rather than one of personal concern.

This is a far cry from the days, not too long ago, when sportfishing boats by definition were rather spartan in comfort. In fact, a degree of discomfort was often thought to be desirable. It reminded anglers that fish are no respecters of persons, and it kept lazy guests from dozing while watching the outrigger baits for signs of a tuna or billfish.

Many responding owners had specific suggestions to make with respect to selecting power for boats. Here is a brief condensation of some of these suggestions.

Situation	*Suggestion*
1. Slow trolling, such as for stripers, kingfish, and salmon.	1. Engines that idle well and run smoothly at low rpm, yet respond instantly to sudden demands for full power. Seek local advice from professional and top amateur fishermen.
2. High-speed trolling, such as for tuna or billfish with artificial lures.	2. Engines with good variable mid-range characteristics, fast acceleration, smooth slowdown without stalling.

3. Long-distance fishing cruises.

3. Engines and fuel capacity to provide maximum range at the most efficient displacement or planing speeds. Smooth operation when trolling.

4. Tournament fishing.

4. High output for fast runs to and from distant grounds; smooth, dependable operation at all running and trolling speeds.

5. Professional chartering.

5. Maximum reliability and economy over a long working life under variable conditions. Moderate initial cost and upkeep. Ease of maintenance and self-service.

6. Rental service.

6. High reliability, foolproof operation requiring minimum of operator maintenance and skill. Quick, easy maintenance by base personnel. Good fuel economy.

In the end, the choice of what makes a fishing boat go is up to the individual owner. Fortunately, there is no dearth of accurate, reliable information about marine engines. If this discussion makes the facts governing the choice easier to understand and the choice itself less difficult, it will have achieved its goal.

Mako 25-foot inboard. (Bill Munro — Mako Marine)

SECTION ONE
Boats 15 to 29 feet

BOSTON WHALER STRIPER 15

Designer	Boston Whaler
Builder	Boston Whaler 1149 Hingham Street Rockland, MA 02370
Construction	Inner and outer fiberglass hulls filled with polyurethane foam forming a hull bond and built-in flotation.

Specifications

Length overall	15 ft 3 in	4.65 m
Beam, maximum	5 ft 8 in	1.73 m
Draft, hull	8 in	20.3 cm
Freeboard forward	NA	
Freeboard aft	NA	
Weight, normal	525 lb	239 kg
Load capacity*	1,070 lb	486 kg
Passenger capacity*	7	
Maximum power rating	70 hp	
Fuel capacity	—	
Swamped load capacity	1,650 lb	750 kg

Power options: Any (normally single) outboard motor from about 20 to the maximum of 70 hp. Normal shaft length.

Based on rated load capacity of 1,070 lb and standard human weight ratio of 13 persons per 2,000-lb ton.

Performance   (By Mercury Marine, Fond du Lac, Wisconsin)

With Mercury 402EL 40-hp motor: propeller 3-blade, 14-in pitch

Load 1,000 lb gross (1 person)	31.1 mph
Load 1,285 lb gross (3 persons)	27.4 mph

With Mercury 500EL 50-hp motor: propeller 3-blade, 17-in pitch

Load 1,015 lb gross (1 person)	36.9 mph
Load 1,325 lb gross (3 persons)	32.6 mph

With Mercury 650EL 65-hp motor: propeller 3-blade, 16-in pitch

Load 990 lb gross (1 person)	44.0 mph
Load 1,335 lb gross (3 persons)	38.4 mph

With Mercury 700EL 70-hp motor: propeller 3-blade, cupped, 10¼ in × 14 in

Load 1,040 lb gross (1 person)	43.1 mph/5500 rpm
Load 1,240 lb gross (2 persons)	39.6 mph/5300 rpm

Running fast, level, and dry, the smallest of the Boston Whaler line of fishing boats borrows the freshwater concept of pedestal fishing chairs for light-tackle saltwater game fishing. Speeds of over 40 mph are possible with single outboard motors of up to 70 hp maximum. (Photo by Boston Whaler)

Description

The name Boston Whaler is synonymous with small, fast, tough fishing boats, and the Striper 15 model is no exception. Following the general design and layout of the justly famous older Sakonnet and Montauk models, the Striper 15 incorporates a more recently developed V-bow with deep chines for speed in rough water and stability. The slightly raised forward casting platform is traditional, but the incorporation of forward and after fishing chairs follows recent trends in freshwater-bass boat arrangements.

The outer and inner fiberglass hulls are completely filled with polyurethane foam in the traditional Boston Whaler manner, providing by test 1,650 pounds of static swamped gross flotation. This is the equivalent of motor, safety equipment, fuel tank, and at least four or five adults.

The Striper 15 is the smallest boat to be given serious consideration in this book, but it is all fishing boat. For light-tackle casting alongshore or on inland waters, it is hard to beat. It's perfect for flats fishing in the Keys, and it should be a natural for beach-launching in ocean or large-lake waters. While hardly a car-topper, the Striper 15 calls for only a light trailer and tow car.

Controls at the small center console, placed well forward, put the operator amidships over the natural center of gravity for singlehanded fishing. There is plenty of room to walk around the console on either side. The unique amidships grabrails port and starboard are fine for rough-water fishing. The operator's seat can also be a 48-quart insulated ice chest and fishbox. In all, the Striper 15 is a tough, good-looking little fishing machine, eminently suited to light single-handed or couple fishing, or for use as a tender to larger fishing or cruising boats.

AQUASPORT 170 OPEN FISHERMAN

Designer	Aquasport, Inc.
Builder	Aquasport, Inc. 7925 West 2nd Court Hialeah, FL 33014
Construction	Fiberglass V-hull and superstructure.

Specifications

Length overall	20 ft 2 in	6.15 m
Beam	7 ft 10 in	2.41 m
Draft, hull	7½ in	19.00 cm
Cockpit area	60 sq ft	5.58 m²
Freeboard forward	2 ft 8 in	
Freeboard, transom	20 in	
Weight, hull (approx)	1,150 lb	523 kg
Fuel capacity	27 gal	102 l
Rated power	130 hp	

Performance

The following performance tables for the Model 170 were established with a load of two adults and 27 gallons of fuel. Tests were conducted by Aquasport and Robert Stearns.

With single 50-hp OB

RPM	MPH	GPH	MPG
3000	8.2	1.50	5.47
3500	11.1	2.29	4.85
4000	14.0	2.68	5.22
4500	19.8	3.02	6.56
5000*	24.0	3.57	6.72
5600	28.1	4.75	5.92

Best speed. Range = 181 mi @ 5000 rpm, 24 mph.

With single 85-hp OB

RPM	MPH	GPH	MPG
2500	11.1	3.44	3.23
3000	17.1	3.89	4.40
3500	23.5	4.55	5.16
4000	29.9	5.10	5.86
4500*	35.1	5.95	5.90
5000	39.0	8.06	4.84
5400	42.1	9.04	4.65

Best speed. Range = 159 mi @ 4500 rpm, 35.1 mph.

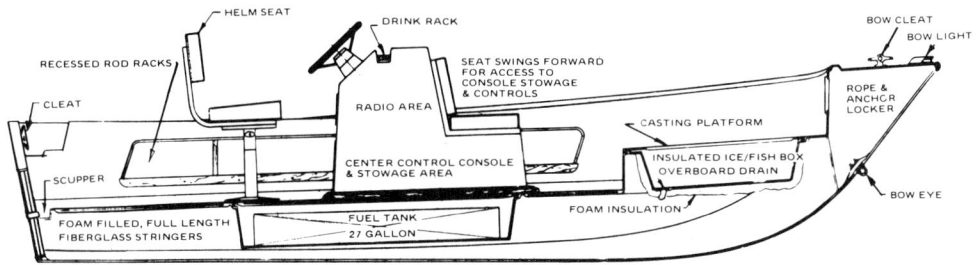

With single 115-hp OB

RPM	MPH	GPH	MPG
2000	5.7	2.36	2.42
2500	10.5	3.95	2.66
3000	18.2	4.73	3.84
3500	24.5	5.65	4.34
4000*	30.2	6.50	4.65
4500	34.2	7.66	4.64
5000	38.0	9.60	3.96
5500	43.5	11.53	3.77

*Best speed. Range = 125 mi @ 4000 rpm,
30.2 mph.*

Description

Aquasport was one of the developers of the early Florida Keys bonefish boat types, combining modern boat engineering and construction with a hull type invented specifically to meet the requirements of light-tackle, game-fish casting. The continuing popularity of the 17-foot outboard-powered model attests to its utility, versatility, and high qualities of performance and durability.

As in classic center-console construction, the steering and engine controls are grouped at the small center control station. Recessed rod racks are located under the side coamings. VHF/FM or CB radio may be installed in the console. The built-in 27-gallon fuel tank occupies the space under the console and forward part of the after fishing area. Insulated fish and ice boxes are built into the forward area seats, and added storage space is under the forward casting platform. An optional bench-type helmsman's seat is available. Twin, optional, outboard live-bait boxes can be attached to the stern. Other optional equipment includes a forward canvas spray hood and a sun top for the amidships region.

The modern boat trailer gives small fishing boats of this type unprecedented range and mobility. Boats capable of fishing well offshore with two or three skilled fishermen can be trailed to within a few miles of productive fishing areas. Boats of the Aquasport 170 class and larger usually require a paved or graded launching ramp for successful trailer launching, but such facilities are usually available near major sportfishing grounds.

A glance at the tabulated performance data uncovers some interesting information. Using the 50-hp model as an example and the standard fuel capacity of 27 gallons, we can establish that the boat could easily cruise 50 miles to and from a favored fishing spot in about 4 hours total running time, leaving a fuel reserve of

Developed from a Florida Keys bonefishing model, the modern Aquasport hull has a deep-V configuration. Spray hood (folded down) protects this model. Forward casting platform is over an insulated fish/ice box. A 115-hp motor gives speeds to 43.5 mph with 27 gallons of fuel and carrying two adults. (Photo by Aquasport Inc.)

about 10 gallons. This would be enough for 4 hours (6 gallons) of fast trolling with a 4-gallon reserve, enough for at least 25 miles of fast running at the most efficient speed of 24 mph.

A 4-gallon emergency reserve is one-sixth, or 16.7 percent, of the total fuel supply. Some operators are not satisfied with any reserve of less than 20 percent. A great deal depends on the area being fished, the presence or absence of other boats, the chances of bad weather, and of course the loading of the boat with people and fishing equipment. These small boats are especially sensitive to added weight. For example, other factors being equal, the 50-hp model indicates a range of 181 miles at its most efficient speed, an increase of 56 miles, or 45 percent, over the 125-mile range of the model with a 115-hp engine, at its most efficient speed. Part of the more powerful model's loss of range can be attributed to the combination of higher best speed (30 mph versus 24 mph), and a consequently greater demand for fuel, but part can also be assigned to the increased weight of the larger engine.

The Aquasport 170 Open Fisherman makes an excellent yacht tender for vessels large enough to carry it. There is a waterline towing pad eye set into the stem for towing on short hauls, and lifting eyes can be installed so it can be taken on board by davits or a boat boom.

Types of sportfishing in which the Aquasport 170 Open Fisherman does well include southern flats fishing (bonefish, tarpon, etc.), reef and offshore live-bait fishing (kite), northern inshore game-fish casting, light-tackle trolling, saltwater and Great Lakes deep trolling (downriggers), family bottom fishing, and light-tackle, big-game fishing.

ANGLER V-17F CC

Designer	Angler Boat Corp., Cooper Camp, and Elio Grillo
Builder	Angler Boat Corp. 4450 N.W. 128th Street Miami, FL 33054
Construction	Modified V-hull, center-console layout. Heavy-duty hand-layup fiberglass. Outboard power.

Specifications

Length overall	16 ft 8 in	5.08 m
Length, waterline	15 ft	4.58 m
Beam, maximum	7 ft 2 in	2.20 m
Draft, hull	7 in	17.80 cm
OB transom height	20 in	50.80 cm
Weight (approx)	1,075 lb	523 kg
Certified load capacity	1,150 lb	488 kg
Fuel capacity	26 gal	98 l
Maximum power	105 hp	
Power options	50 hp	
	70 hp	
	85 hp	

Performance

Normal top speed	38 mph
Normal best cruising speed	26 mph

Description

While the manufacturer was unable to supply more performance data than those given, the data suggest that the Angler V-17F CC fisherman is very close in overall performance to other boats of its size, type, weight, and power classes. The stated hull weight of slightly over 1,000 pounds (sans power) is well within the limits of easy trailing and launching, and the generous beam of 7 feet 2 inches, combined with the normal hull draft of only 7 inches, makes the boat a good one for shallow-water flats fishing. The deep forefoot promises good head-sea and rough-water handling ability.

Standard Equipment

Molded inner hull
Heavily fiberglassed stringers
26-gal aluminum fuel tank underdeck
Hollow deck cleats

SS bow and stern lifting eyes
Extra-heavy rubrail
Upholstered console seat
Console windshield and safety rail

Running lights
Insulated fishbox seat, reversible back
Rod racks
Insulated ice chest under console seat
Flush rodholders

Teak step pads
Mechanical steering and motor controls
Aluminum custom bow rail
Built-in foam flotation

Optional Equipment

Pedestal seats in lieu of fishbox seat
SS bow rail
Top and boot
Spray hood

Windshield connector
Side curtains
After curtain

While designed primarily as a fishing boat, the Angler V-17F CC is also a versatile all-purpose runabout. It can be used for daysailing, waterskiing, or as a tender for larger power or sail cruising vessels.

Simplicity and maximum useful open fishing space mark this 17-footer from Angler. The single 115-hp outboard motor illustrated can push the hull in excess of 40 mph. With passenger weight amidships, the boat runs level and dry at all planing speeds. (Photo by Angler Boat Corp.)

MAKO 18-FOOT BACK COUNTRY BOAT

Designer	Mako Marine
Builder	Mako Marine
	4355 N.W. 128th Street
	Miami, FL 33054
Construction	Hand-layup fiberglass hull and decks.

Specifications

Length overall	18 ft 2 in	5.54 m
Beam	6 ft 7 in	2.00 m
Draft, hull	6 in	15.24 cm
Transom height	20 in	50.80 cm
Hull weight	1,150 lb	523 kg
Fuel capacity	30 gal	113 l
Maximum OB power	140 hp	
Rated load	1,200 lb	545 kg
Power options	Any outboard power to maximum	

Performance

While performance data for this new model were not available at the time of writing, comparison with similar existing models suggests top speeds of over 40 mph with the maximum rated power and normal fishing load.

Description

The builder describes this unusual small fisherman as "designed for the dedicated shallow-water angler who needs a lightweight, shallow-draft, easy-to-pole, quiet boat to get him on fish." The natural habitat of a boat like this is the Florida Keys or Bahamas bonefish flats. Everything is secondary to comfort, convenience, and efficiency in light-tackle casting. The small seating well, used by the occupants while underway, can be completely decked over by means of hinged panels. The hull from bow to stern then becomes a single flush deck with almost no obstructions to snag a fly line.

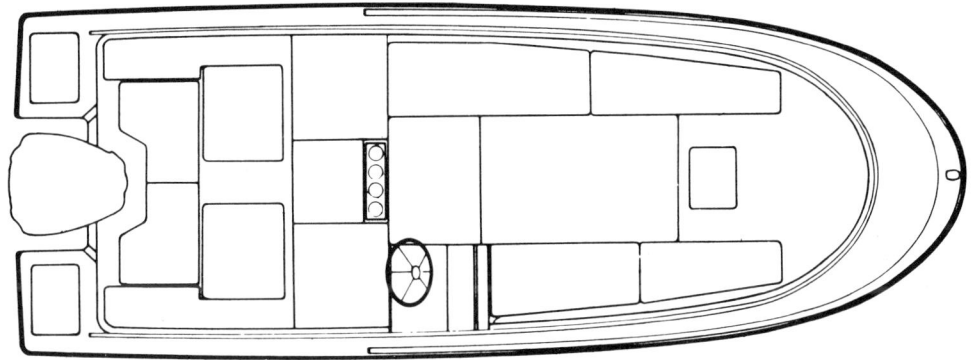

Above: Light weight, shallow draft, maximum stability, and a bow-to-stern clear casting platform are features of this 18-footer designed by Mako for fishing the back-country flats of South Florida, the Bahama Banks, and Gulf and Caribbean reefs. The *motor-control console is to starboard. Seats are in wells with backs that fold flush with the deck. Twin live-bait wells flank the single outboard power plant. Low freeboard facilitates poling, especially on a windy day.* **Right:** *"Better than being able to walk on the water,"* is what one professional bonefish guide called the new Mako 18-footer. Great stability is demonstrated in this stern-view photograph. The clear deck facilitates the use of saltwater fly-fishing tackle for bonefish, tarpon, and permit. (Photos by Mako Marine)

Left: *Fishbox, live-bait wells, tackle lockers, cooler, and gear lockers are all stowed below deck under flush hatches. The fiberglass poling pole hooks into metal holders to port. The gunwale stops some spray and protects the boat when gaffing or unhooking and releasing game fish. Power up to 140 hp gives top speeds of over 40 mph.* ***Below:*** *Running fairly level at high speed, the Mako 18-footer skirts a mangrove clump in South Florida waters. A spray hood with boot can be added forward to give some protection from wind and weather. (Photos by Mako Marine)*

Below this "aircraft carrier" deck, space is divided for various fishing uses, accessible by flush hatches. The illustration shows a pair of live-bait wells flanking the single outboard engine. There is a third live well forward. Rod storage is provided below deck for fly and casting rods up to 9½ feet long, fully rigged for fishing. The huge fishbox is a live well 5 feet wide. There is also a large cooler-locker for food and beverages.

The boat is designed for poling over the glats, therefore weight and freeboard are kept to a minimum. Poling can be done from either the bow or the stern, depending on need. Metal hangers accept the fiberglass pole inboard of one gunwale. Pedestal chair mounts are let into the centerline of the deck fore and aft for a pair of chairs, if needed. Trolling rodholders can also be let into the deck, aft.

The Mako 18-foot Back Country Boat is a highly specialized fishing machine. It is hardly what one would want for baiting large billfish or bait-fishing the bottom for table fish. But in the exciting, exacting world of light-tackle, shallow-reef, lure-and-bait casting, it appears to be at least three steps ahead of being able to walk on the water.

Standard Equipment

Heavy-duty vinyl rubrail	Electric fuel gauge on switch panel
Running and anchor lights	Trolling motor wiring conduit
Rod storage racks	Side console fuel fill
Transom-well circulating pump	Overboard vent
Bilge pump	Seat cushions (3-piece)
Electric pump, forward live well	Bow chocks (2)
Fishing rodholders (2)	Bow towing eye
Teak holder for 4 rods	Forward cleat
Mechanical steering	Stern cleats (2)

Optional Equipment

Pedestal fishing chairs (2)	Deluxe 15-in SS steering wheel
Folding top and boot	Bow lifting assembly
Morse MT, single, with cables	

AQUASPORT 200 CC PROFESSIONAL

Designer	Aquasport, Inc.
Builder	Aquasport, Inc. 7925 West 2nd Court Hialeah, FL 33014
Construction	Fiberglass deep-V hull, foam-filled multiple girder stringers, fiberglass console, teak trim.

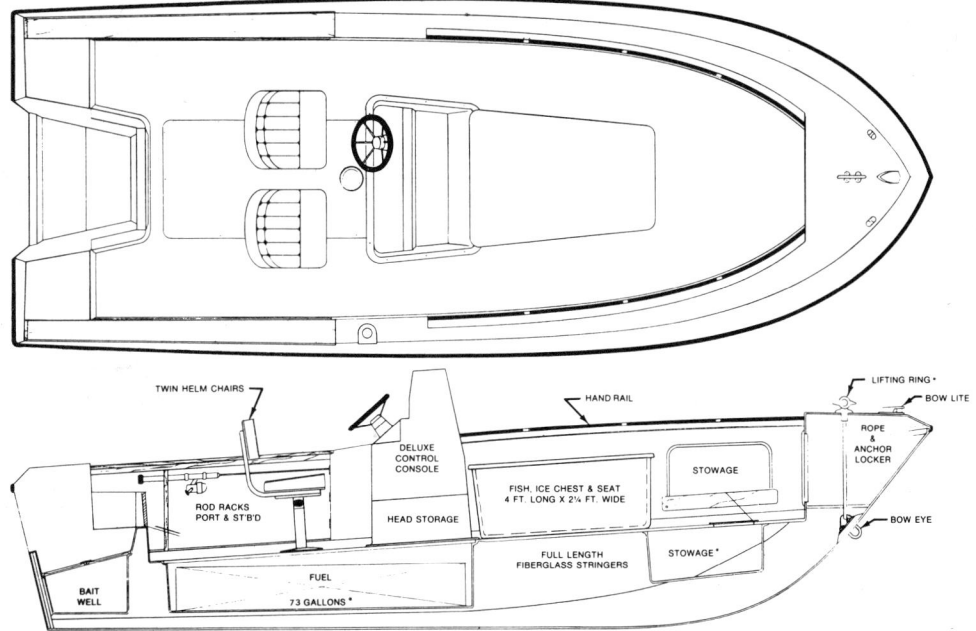

Specifications

Length overall	20 ft 2 in	6.15 m
Beam, maximum	7 ft 10 in	2.41 m
Draft, hull	12 in	30.50 cm
Freeboard forward	3 ft 6 in	1.07 m
Freeboard, transom, option	20 in/25 in	51/63.5 cm
Weight, hull (approx)	1,900 lb	864 kg
Fuel capacity*	50 gal	189 l
Rated power	200 hp	

*Optional fuel capacity of 73 gallons (276 l) is available.

Performance

The following performance table for the Aquasport 200 CC Professional model was established with a load of one adult operator, standard 73 gallons of fuel, and a single 200-hp Evinrude OB. Test by Aquasport and Robert Stearns.

RPM	MPH	GPH	MPG
1000	5.46	2.15	2.54
1500	7.14	3.18	2.23
2000	9.35	5.62	1.66
2500	16.76	7.03	2.38
3000	22.90	7.76	2.95
3500	27.17	7.83	3.47
4000*	31.58	8.91	3.54
4500	34.88	10.59	3.29
5000	39.47	12.16	3.23
5450	42.86	17.31	2.48

*Best speed. Range = 258 mi @ 4000 rpm, 31.58 mph.

The "Professional" designation in the name of this 20-foot Aquasport model is no exaggeration. The model was developed with the cooperation of professional fishing guides and reflects the guide's approach to the design of a high-performance fishing machine. Two hundred hp provides speeds of over 42 mph. (Photo by Aquasport, Inc.)

Description

The word *professional* in the name of this boat refers to the model's development from the expert suggestions of professional fishing guides who use boats of this size and type in southern and northern waters. The large insulated ice and fish box, for example, is deck-mounted forward of the console and has a large cushion top and more than 10 cubic feet of storage capacity.

The basic boat is designed for a single high-output outboard motor. The fiberglass splash well covers a built-in live-bait well. Small storage lockers flank the motor well, port and starboard. A recessed handrail protects the forward fishing area. Rods are stored in side racks, port and starboard. There is additional storage space in side lockers forward and in a storage well ahead of the fishbox. The bow cleat is also a lifting ring with tension rod down to the waterline towing bow eye. Portable head storage is under the console, which also has space for electronic gear beneath the instrument panel.

Trim of covering board back aft is teak, as are the after storage locker tops. The windshield is tinted and has a protective metal handrail. Flush-type outrigger holders complement flush rodholders. Fuel fill is to starboard, overboard-vented. Twin helm seats can be provided, while the after fishing space is large enough to take a light fighting chair with a footrest in lieu of the helm chairs.

The Aquasport 200 CC Professional is large enough and has sufficient range with the optional 75-gallon fuel supply to operate well offshore in reasonable weather. For example, in any good-weather 10-hour day, the boat has enough fuel to run 30 miles out and back at approximately 30 mph, burning about 18 gallons in cruising-speed running and an additional 25 gallons in trolling for 8 hours at 7 mph or more. This calculated expenditure of 43 gallons leaves a reserve of 30 gallons. This reserve would be good for an additional 106 miles of travel at the boat's most economical speed of 31.6 mph.

The net weight of 1,900 pounds keeps the boat well within reasonable trailing and launching weights. The Aquasport 200 CC Professional is not intended for cruising. It is what it was designed to be: an excellent fishing machine that lends itself to a wide variety of inshore and offshore angling and even specialty-market commercial fishing.

— — — — — — — — — — — — — — —

BOSTON WHALER REVENGE 21

Designer	Boston Whaler
Builder	Boston Whaler 1149 Hingham Street Rockland, MA 02370
Construction	Inner and outer fiberglass hulls filled with polyurethane foam, forming a hull bond and built-in flotation.

Specifications

Length overall	21 ft 4 in	6.51 m
Beam, maximum	7 ft 4 in	2.24 m
Draft, hull	10 in	25.4 cm
Freeboard forward	NA	
Freeboard aft	NA	
Weight, normal	1,800 lb	818 kg
Load capacity	1,286 lb	585 kg
Passenger capacity	10	
Maximum power rating	200 hp	
Fuel capacity, normal	40 gal	151 l
Extra fuel, saddles	36 gal	136 l
Swamped load capacity	3,700 lb	1,682 kg

Power options: Any (normally single) outboard motor from the recommended minimum of 65 hp to the maximum of 200 hp. Twin motors can be accommodated.

Left top: A single 200-hp motor drives the Revenge 21-foot Boston
Whaler at better than 35 mph. The small motor shown kicked up is used
for slow trolling for stripers and weakfish. *Left bottom:* The deep, flar-
ing bow is designed for fast, nonpounding running in rough water. The
hull's dynamic lift is evident in this quiet southern backwater. *Below:*
"Feather-white" is the word for this windy condition, but the Revenge
21 rides like a duck at her mooring buoy while the small fry fish for
flounder for supper. (Photos by Boston Whaler)

Performance (By Johnson Outboards and Mercury Motors)

With Johnson 200-hp motor: propeller OMC 14½ in x 19 in, test weight 2,630 lb

Passenger load	RPM	Speed	Acceleration 0-250 ft
180 lb (1 person)	5425	45.76 mph	7.60 sec
480 lb (3 persons)	5400	45.02 mph	7.99 sec
930 lb (6 persons)	5325	44.21 mph	8.72 sec

With Mercury 1150EL 115-hp motor: propeller 3-blade, 17-in pitch

Load 2,375 lb gross (1 person)	36.6 mph
Load 2,895 lb gross (4 persons)	35.9 mph

Description

The Boston Whaler Revenge 21 is a relatively new development in design for this firm in that it features a small cuddy cabin under a sculptured forward deck. A sloping, full-width windshield provides protection. The control station is located to starboard, behind the windshield. This is a style of layout that should appeal to families with children, who need more protection from wind and spray than is afforded by the more open models.

The performance of this model under load is very good. For example, from the performance tables provided by Johnson and Mercury, the boat with 200 hp loses only 1.55 mph in speed between the lightest gross loading, 2,810 pounds with one person, and the heaviest gross loading tested, 3,560 pounds with six persons. This is a loss of only 3.4 percent in speed for an increase of 750 pounds, or 26.7 percent in weight.

The area forward off the walk-through windshield doubles as a raised casting platform made safe by the addition of a stout safety rail. With a cushion set, the large, dry, forward enclosed area converts to minimal overnight accommodations for two. As an alternative, storage lockers for fishing tackle, scuba gear, and other equipment can be specified. A lockable teak door can be fitted.

The cockpit is large enough for a pair of light fishing chairs or even a light fighting chair with a footrest. Flush-mounted outrigger holders can be added amidships; rodholders can be placed at convenient points in the cockpit. As with all Boston Whaler models, a complete list of accessories and optional equipment is available from the manufacturer. The Revenge 21 ably meets the needs of owners who like to mix fishing with daysailing and other water sports.

ANGLER V-22F CC

Designer	Angler Boat Corp. and C.A. Smith, Hollywood, FL
Builder	Angler Boat Corp. 4450 N.W. 128th Street Miami, FL 33054
Construction	Modified V-hull, center-console plan. Heavy-duty hand-layup fiberglass. Outboard or I/O power.

Specifications

Length overall	22 ft	6.71 m
Length, waterline	20 ft 4 in	6.19 m
Beam, maximum	8 ft	2.44 m
Draft, hull	10 in	25.4 cm
Molded depth	4 ft 1 in	1.25 m
OB transom height	25 in	63.5 cm
Weight (approx)	1,940 lb	882 kg
Certified load capacity	3,600 lb	1,636 kg
Fuel capacity	NA	NA
Maximum power, OB or I/O	235 hp	
Power options	115 hp, OB or I/O	
	175 hp, OB or I/O	
	235 hp, OB or I/O	

Performance (235 hp)	*OB*	*I/O*
Normal top speed	54 mph	43 mph
Normal best cruising speed	32 mph	32 mph

With a single sterndrive motor and the control console placed well aft, the large forward fishing area is ideal for a family group bottom fishing or deep-jigging, or even as the location of a fighting chair for big game. A top speed of 54 mph is claimed with 235 hp. (Photo by Angler Boat Corp.)

Description

The 22-foot Angler is a larger version of their popular 17-footer. With outboard power, it is one of the fastest of the open, center-console fishing boats. Emphasis is on clean, uncluttered design. The limitation of 8 feet in beam allows the boat to be trailed on U.S. highways with no legal penalty for over-width dimensions.

Hull weight of 1,940 pounds (sans power) increases to around 2,425 pounds with average I/O or high-output OB power. This is within the capacity of medium- to heavy-duty trailing equipment. The stern is designed to take either a single large or twin medium-power outboard motors. The cockpit deck is self-bailing and flush fore and aft. This 22-footer is large enough to take a low tower. A fighting chair can be mounted either forward or aft. While fuel capacity was not given in the manufacturer's literature, it is assumed to be consistent with that of other boats of its size and class.

With a designated hull draft of only 10 inches, the V-22F CC is shoal enough to work all but the shallowest flats, yet its size, weight, and power potential fit it for serious offshore fishing when properly equipped. This Angler boat is an excellent example of the trend toward versatile, highly efficient fishing machines for tournament and light-tackle competitive fishing.

Standard Equipment

Molded inner hull and deck
Hollow cleats
SS towing eye and stern lifting eyes
Extra-heavy rubrail
Upholstered console seat
Console windshield and handrail
Flush rodholders
Teak step pads

Mechanical steering and motor controls
Aluminum custom bow rail
Baitwell
Raised forward casting platform
Running lights
Insulated icebox under console seat
Insulated fishbox seat with reversible back

Optional Equipment

Spray hood and side curtains
Aft cockpit cover
Windshield connector

Top with boot
Rod racks on console or side walls

BOSTON WHALER V-22

Designer	Boston Whaler
Builder	Boston Whaler 1149 Hingham Street Rockland, MA 02370
Construction	Inner and outer fiberglass hulls filled with polyurethane foam forming a hull bond and built-in flotation.

This new V-hull from Boston Whaler shows promise of developing into a fine offshore light-tackle fisherman. Outriggers and a low tower would make the V-22 competitive with a wide range of open fishing chariots. The hull should hold speed well in rough seas. (Photo by Boston Whaler)

Specifications

Length overall	22 ft 3 in	6.79 m
Beam, maximum	7 ft 5 in	2.27 m
Draft, hull	14 in	33.6 cm
Freeboard forward	NA	
Freeboard aft	NA	
Weight, normal	1,950 lb	886 kg
Load capacity	2,000 lb	909 kg
Passenger capacity	13	
Maximum power rating	240 hp	
Fuel capacity	70 gal	265 l
Swamped load capacity	5,000 lb	2,273 kg

Power options: Any single- or twin-outboard installation from the recommended minimum of 85 hp to the maximum of 240 hp.

Performance

Performance data were not available at the time of this writing. Readers interested in complete performance information are invited to contact the manufacturer.

Description

Largest and most powerful of the Boston Whaler fleet at the time of this report, the V-22 is a center-console model with exceptional working and fishing space. The maximum beam of 7 feet 5 inches and hull weight of under 2,000 pounds put it in the medium-weight class for highway trailing. Speeds should be consistent with those of the Revenge 21, considering the greater size and weight and higher power rating.

With a forward spray hood and low tower, the boat could be easily converted into an extremely efficient offshore, light-tackle, tournament competitor. Yet it is not too large for alongshore trolling and casting, or even for working southern bonefish flats or tarpon sloughs. The swamped load capacity of 5,000 pounds is equal, at the rate of 13 persons to the ton, to 32 normal adults and one wet Labrador retriever.

MAKO 238 WALK-AROUND CABIN

Designer	Mako Marine
Builder	Mako Marine 4355 N.W. 128th Street Miami, FL 33054
Construction	Hand-layup fiberglass hull, decks, and superstructure.

Specifications

Length overall	23 ft	7.02 m
Beam	8 ft	2.44 m
Draft, hull	14 in	35.60 cm
Cockpit area	50 sq ft	4.65 m²
Transom height (twin)	20 in	50.80 cm
Transom height (single)	25 in	63.50 cm
Weight, hull	2,500 lb	1,136 kg
Fuel capacity	121 gal	457 l
Water capacity	NA	
Maximum power	250 hp	
Rated load capacity	2,500 lb	1,136 kg
Sleeping accommodations	2	

Power options: any single- or twin-outboard combination
totaling not over 250 hp.

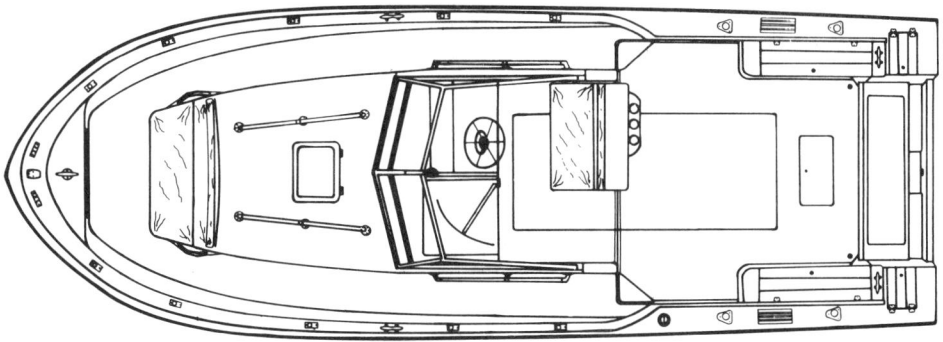

Performance

With single Johnson 235-hp, propeller 14¼-in dia. × 21-in pitch, 3-blade

RPM	Speed (mph)	Fuel (gph)	Fuel (mpg)
1000	5.29	1.90	2.78
1500	7.39	3.20	2.31
2000	8.61	5.06	1.70
2500	12.12	7.10	1.71
3000	18.05	9.60	1.88
3500	24.58	10.68	2.30
4000*	29.98	12.50	2.40
4500	34.27	15.52	2.21
5000	38.09	25.71	1.48
5200 (max)	40.12	27.07	1.48

Optimum cruising speed.

Using the optimum cruising speed as a base, the 121-gallon fuel capacity should be good for an endurance of very close to 9.7 hours and a range of 290 miles. This is impressive range for a family-style, 23-foot fisherman with outboard power. Translating to a 10-hour fishing and trolling day, the table suggests the following:

Time running (45 miles @ 30 mph)	1.5 hr =	18.75 gal
Time slow trolling (5.3 mph)	4.5 hr =	8.55 gal
Time fast trolling (8.6 mph)	4.0 hr =	20.25 gal
Total fuel		47.55 gal

This would indicate that the 121-gallon fuel capacity could be extended for two typical days, totaling about 95 gallons and leaving a reserve of 26 gallons, or 21 percent of the original. This reserve would be good for 2 hours or almost 60 miles of running at the 30-mph optimum cruising speed. These figures also indicate that the boat can be expected to operate at an average fuel rate of less than 5 gph under what are considered fairly normal operating conditions. The rate would be higher, naturally, if longer running time were required to reach more distant fishing grounds.

Based on the popular Mako 23-foot hull, the new 238 cabin model features a walk-around deck forward and an elevated, protected control center amidships. The result is a small, fast, very fishable, family boat with overnight sleeping accommodations for a small family and excellent protection for daysailing and fishing. (Photo by Mako Marine)

The boat is described by the builders as being quick but not radical in maneuverability, quite dry at speed in choppy water, and under excellent control at slow fishing speeds.

Description

Mako Marine describes the 238 Walk-Around Cabin model as "the perfect extension to the Mako center-console line . . . for fishing, diving, waterskiing, and cruising for the family."

The cabin is large, light, and airy, with rod stowage, cabinets, a hanging locker, 5-foot headroom, and 6-foot 8-inch V-berths. While not intended for lengthy cruises, the cabin does provide overnight sleeping for a family and excellent protection for dawn-to-dusk daysailing and fishing. The control station is amidships with a raised pilot seat, windshield, and spray top and boot as standard equipment. Every inch of space is used to good advantage. The wide, walk-around decks extend from the cockpit to the bow, greatly facilitating the handling of ground tackle and docklines.

The cockpit is not as large as in some other 23-footers, but it is adequate for most game-fishing purposes and can easily take a centerline fishing chair or tournament-style rodholder, or "rocket launcher." Side seats double as fish and gear lockers. Baitwells are built into the stern corners flanking the motor well. The large fuel tank is located underdeck.

In these days of rapidly increasing fuel costs, the Mako 238 Walk-Around Cabin model answers a growing demand for small, high-performance cruiser-fishermen with comfort and safety for family anglers.

Standard Equipment

Walk-around cabin
Live-bait well
Radio or glove box
Lockable storage area
International Rule running and anchor
  lights
V-bunk cushions (3-piece set)
Custom instrument panel, external fuses
Springline cleats, 6½-in
Bow storage with teak door
Battery compartment
Marinium and SS hardware
Bow rail
Sliding side cabin windows
Helm bench seat with 2 tackle drawers,
  storage area and rod rack for 3 rods
Knife and rigging rack
Two-drawer storage cabinet
Cabin step storage box
Electric windshield wiper

Folding top and boot
Automatic bilge pump
Mechanical steering
SS towing eye
SS lifting eyes (2 aft)
Deck lifting eye
Stern cleats (2)
Bow chocks (2)
Cockpit lights
Insulated fish and bait boxes
Heavy-duty vinyl rubrail
Grabrails
Skylight cabin hatch
Louvered teak cabin door
Three-drawer storage cabinet
Cabin light (1)
Rod storage in cabin
Cabin headliner carpet
Head compartment suitable for most
  portable heads

Optional Equipment

Pompanette fishing chair
Custom rodholders (4)
15-ft Lee's outriggers (side mount)
18-ft Lee's outriggers (side mount)
Aft fishbox cushions (set)
Side curtains
Rear drop curtain
Bench seat cover
Deluxe 15-in SS steering wheel

Chain deck pipe
Compass, 4-in High Speed
Univ. Conn. kit, SS single
Custom twin steering connector
Twin drag-link steering connector
Morse MT, single with cables
Morse MT, dual with cables
Bunk filler and cushions

SEACRAFT SF 23 (OB, I/O, IB)

Designer	SeaCraft
Builder	SeaCraft 24400 S.W. 137th Avenue Princeton, FL 33032
Construction	Fiberglass hull, interliner, and deck structures. Variable deadrise hull (Carl Moesly, U.S. Patent No. 3,237,581).

Twin-outboard model has baitwells built into corners of the stern and has good working room around the motor well for fishing. Speeds to 46 mph are claimed with 115-hp motors. (Photo by SeaCraft)

Specifications

Length overall	23 ft 2 in	7.08 m
Length, waterline	NA	
Beam	8 ft	2.44 m
Draft		
OB hull, engine up	16 in	40.04 cm
I/O hull, drive up	17 in	43.18 cm
Inboard	28 in	71.12 cm
Deadrise at transom	20°	
Minimum cockpit depth	25 in	63.50 cm
Height, keel to		
windshield top	6 ft 4 in	1.93 m
Weight, bare hull	2,650 lb	1,205 kg
OB rated load	3,185 lb	1,448 kg
I/O rated load	2,278 lb	1,035 kg
Inboard rated load	2,278 lb	1,035 kg
Fuel capacity	100 gal	378 l

Power options

OB — single or twin motors to 500 maximum total hp

I/O — offered as 1979 standard equipment
One 255-hp Volvo gasoline, jackshafted
One 290-hp Volvo gasoline, jackshafted
One 130-hp Volvo diesel, jackshafted, FWC*

Continued

Specifications *continued*
> Inboard — offered as 1979 standard equipment
> > One 225-hp MerCruiser or 260-hp OMC (350 CID)
> > One 330-hp MerCruiser or 330-hp OMC (454 CID)
> > One 124-hp Volvo diesel with FWC*

*FWC = freshwater cooling standard equipment

Performance

Three different sets of test data are available for the SeaCraft 23-foot hull. The first is from the Mercury Marine testing center, Fond du Lac, Wisconsin, used with permission. The second and third are from *Boating* magazine, New York, New York, used with permission, and were conducted on a slightly different 23-foot boat configuration, the 23-foot Tsunami model, which has the same basic 23-foot SeaCraft hull. The Tsunami models are rated for a safe load capacity of 1,600 lb (727 kg).

SF 23 (Data from Mercury Marine testing center)

Power	Two 150-hp Merc Model 1150EL OB motors
Net hull weight	2,550 lb
Transom height	20½ in at 25¼-in centers
Tilt pin hole	Trimmed to #3 hole
Propellers	C-48-32746A3, aluminum, 21-in pitch, 3-blade

Load	Measured speed
Load A (3,555 lb gross, 1 person)	43.4 mph
Load B (4,055 lb gross, 4 persons)	42.1 mph

Tsunami 23-footer (Data from *Boating* magazine)

Power	Two 150-hp Merc Model 1150EL OB motors
Net load	60 gal of fuel, plus 2 persons
Propellers	13-in dia. × 21-in pitch, 3-blade

RPM	MPH*	GPH**	MPG	Trim
1500	7.63	3.80	2.00	2°
2000	8.92	6.00	1.48	4°
2500	12.41	8.20	1.51	4°
3000	22.37	10.60	2.20	3°
3500	27.37	13.20	2.07	3°
4000	34.63	16.40	2.11	3°
4500	38.22	20.20	1.89	3°
5000	42.76	25.20	1.70	3°
5300	46.08	30.00	1.54	3°

*Speeds based on times clocked with Rolex Cosmograph.
**Fuel consumption figures supplied by engine manufacturer.

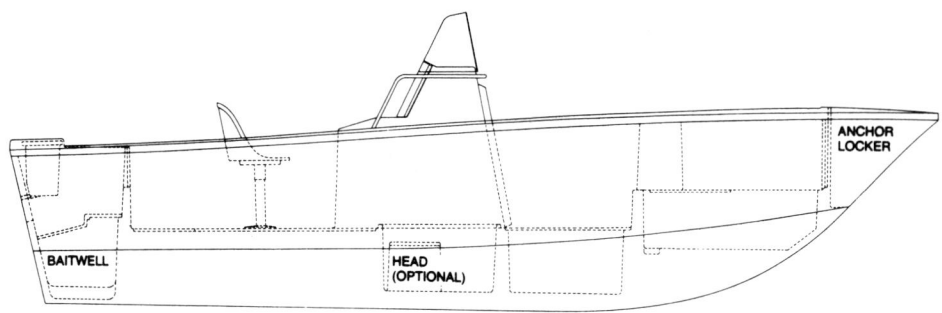

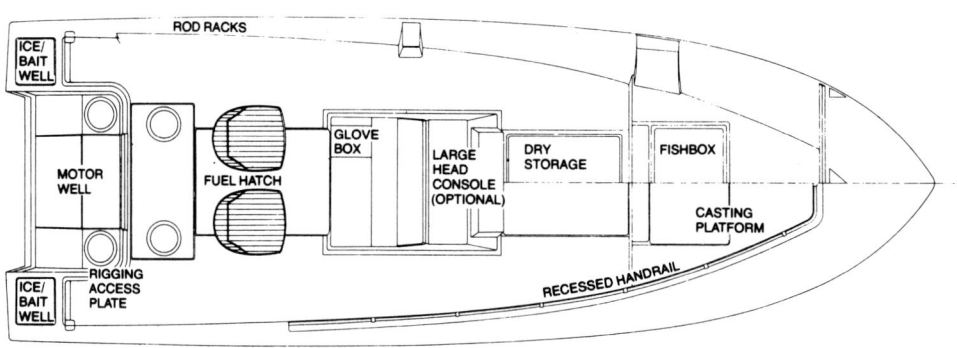

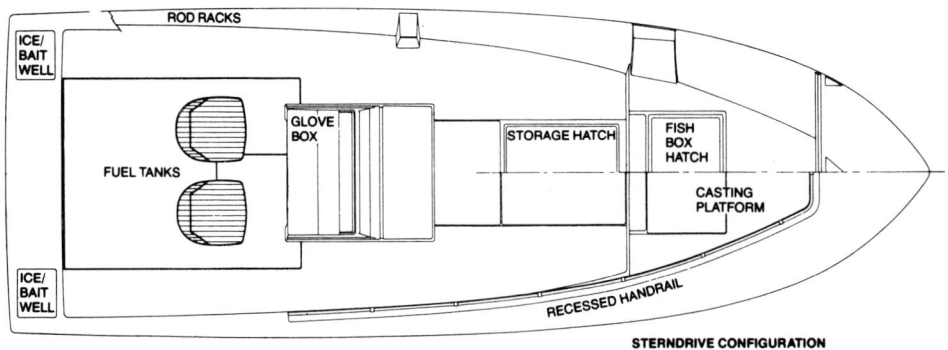

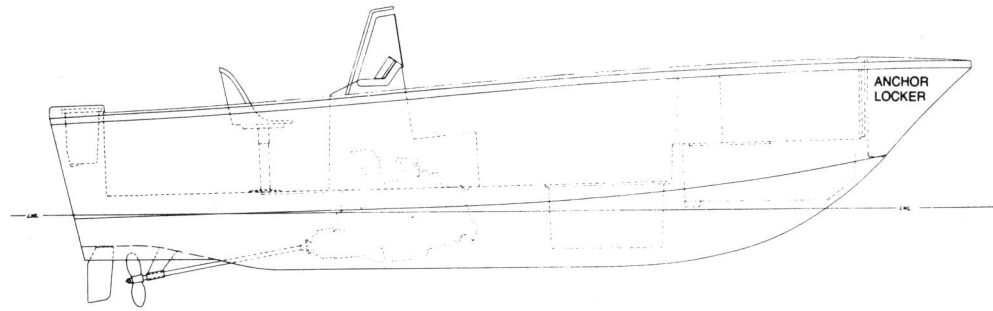

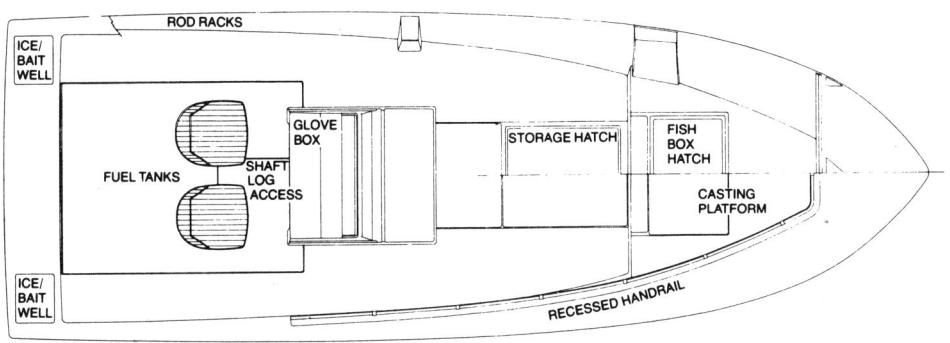

Left: *Excellent planning of interior space is evident in sketches of the outboard and sterndrive SeaCraft models. Engines aft allow a head to be located in the control console.* **Above:** *Inboard model carries the motor under the control console, opening the stern for better fishing or possible placement of a fighting chair. The propeller turns in a semi-tunnel. (Courtesy of SeaCraft)*

Tsunami 23-footer (Data from *Boating* magazine)

Power	Two 165-hp MerCruiser sterndrive units
Net load	60 gal of fuel, plus 2 persons
Propellers	15¼-in dia. × 21-in pitch, 3-blade

RPM	MPH*	GPH**	MPG	Trim
1500	8.58	4.50	1.90	2°
2000	13.95	8.00	1.74	4°
2500	22.73	10.50	2.16	2°
3000	28.90	12.50	2.31	2°
3500	34.85	17.50	1.99	2°
4000	40.46	25.00	1.61	2°
4300	43.82	29.00	1.58	2°

Speeds based on times clocked with Rolex Cosmograph.
**Fuel consumption measured with Brooks Instrument flowmeter.*

Performance data on SF single-engine I/O and inboard (IB) models were not available from the manufacturer, the data used here being from independent testing agencies. However, the top speeds, loads, etc., of the SF 23 twin-OB and Tsunami twin-OB models are practically identical. By comparing the two, we can arrive at the following generalized performance table for the twin 150-hp Merc-powered SF 23, allowing for the center-console model's larger fuel capacity of 100 gallons.

Top RPM	5300 rpm
Top speed	43.4 mph
Top fuel rate	30.0 gph/1.45 mpg
Top endurance	3.33 hr
Top speed range	144.5 mi
Cruising RPM*	3000 rpm
Cruising speed	22.37 mph
Cruising fuel rate	10.6 gph/2.2 mpg
Cruising endurance	9.43 hr
Cruising range	211 mi

Arbitrarily selected as the best fuel rate in mpg indicated by test reports.

Description

The SeaCraft 23-foot hull is unique in that it is designed for outboard, I/O (sterndrive), or inboard power with no significant sacrifice of performance with any of the three types of power. The hull design incorporates variable deadrise developed and patented by Carl Moesly and perfected in a number of years of early ocean powerboat racing. Of the hull form, SeaCraft has this to say:

> The patented SeaCraft Variable Deadrise hull [gives a] softer ride due to its V-like shape; minimum of water deflection, air pockets created by [longitudinal] steps and the natural stiffness that the steps provide. The SeaCraft hull . . . is one of the softest riding boats in rough water. It is notably softer riding than many boats with deeper vees.

The low deadrise [flatter] outer panels of the SeaCraft hull and the reduction of the V-shaped displacement created by the steps into the V-shape of the hull give it far more lateral roll resistance than comparable pure V-hulls. Outstanding efficiency in terms of speed for a given amount of installed horsepower, notably flatter-running [i.e., does not have high bow-rise].

The outboard and I/O models are relatively similar, having the propulsion power at the stern. In each, a large head console is optional, with the head tucked away under the control station and windshield. An insulated fishbox with hatch is built into the forward casting platform. Rod racks are installed under the after cockpit coamings. Dry storage is under the forward portion of the cockpit sole, ahead of the console. Fuel tanks are located under the after cockpit deck.

The inboard model differs in having the console placed slightly farther aft to act as an engine box over the single inboard engine. The hull bottom in way of the inboard propeller is depressed upward into a shallow semi-tunnel to raise the position and lower the shaft angle of the propeller. A dagger-type rudder trails the propeller and does not extend beyond the transom. Ice and bait wells are built into the inboard's stern. Remaining fishing installations are essentially the same as in the OB and I/O models.

The SF 23 models are essentially small-to-medium-game, light-trolling, and casting-fishing machines. Hull draft with outboard motors or sterndrives tilted up is shallow enough for all but the shallowest flats, yet the boats have enough size and stability to fish well offshore in almost any normally fishable weather.

Standard Equipment

Design and Construction

Antiskid-finished decks, coverboards
Gelcoated white hull, deck, and interliner
Flotation, polyurethane foam
Keel stringer, box-type, full-length, fiberglass
Lamination method, hand-layup, fiberglass-reinforced polyester
Longitudinal stringers, fiberglass box-type with molded-in ducts for cables and hoses
Self-bailing cockpit
Full-width, marine-plywood transom, molded-in

Systems and Steering

Battery boxes (2 for OB, 1 for I/O and inboard)
Bilge pumps (1 for OB and I/O, 2 for inboard)
Fuel tanks (OB 100-gal, I/O 105-gal, inboard 2 52-gal), welded aluminum
All required instrumentation, per power type
Steering, mechanical

Hardware and Lights

Bow and stern towing eyes, heavy-duty ½-in SS
Cleats, 4 SS (OB and I/O), 6 SS (inboard), stern cleats under side deck with hawse-pipes
International Rule navigation lights

Hull and Deck

Anchor/rope locker, teak-grained door and bulkhead
Bow handrail, low profile, recessed into coamings
Coaming trim, teak-grained vinyl
Fuel-tank sending-unit inspection plate (OB and I/O)
Helm and companion seats, swivel, adjustable, cushions
Iceboxes, 16-qt, with drains overboard (2)
OB motor well, full-depth, teak access door
Rubrail, heavy-duty black vinyl
Storage compartment, 240-qt, molded into deck
Ventilation, bilge

Console

Console (OB and I/O), center-mounted, fiberglass
Console (inboard), center-mounted, hinged for engine access
Console seat, side-hinged with removable cushions
Glove box, carpet-lined
Instrument and switch panels with external fuses
Steering wheel, deluxe SS
Storage shelf, teak-trimmed, in console
Windshield, Plexiglas, SS handrail

Fishing Gear

Baitwell, 120-qt in OB motor well, 80-qt in I/O model, molded into liner below deck
Baitwells, molded into stern in inboard model
Fishbox, 390-qt, under forward casting platform, insulated, with overboard drain
Rodholders, flush-mounted (2)
Rod racks, teak, 6-rod capacity, recessed under gunwales

Sterndrive (I/O) model also includes

Battery switch, vaporproof
Bilge blower, electric
Console teak doors with latch
Full engine instrumentation and power trim
Engine mounted under console, jackshaft to sterndrive unit
Fire extinguisher, 2½-lb, dry chemical
Fuel filter water separator

Inboard model also includes

Battery switch, vaporproof
Bilge blower, electric
Engine instrumentation, including hour meter
Fire extinguisher, 2½-lb, dry chemical
Fuel filter water separator
All underwater and internal parts bonded
High-speed, bronze, cooling-water pickup
Muffler, high-capacity fiberglass
Propeller, 3-blade bronze, 16-in dia. × 17-in pitch
Rudder, SS
Shaft, 1¼-in SS
Strut, SS, with Cutless bearing, zincs on shaft and hull
Transmission, Borg-Warner hydraulic, 1.5:1 reduction gear

AMF ROBALO R236 OUTBOARD AND I/O

Designer	AMF Slickcraft
Builder	AMF Slickcraft 500 East 32nd Street Holland, MI 49423
Construction	Hand-layup fiberglass hull, deck, interliner, and superstructure. Teak trim.

Specifications

Length overall	23 ft	7.02 m
Length, waterline	NA	
Beam, maximum	8 ft	2.44 m
Draft	NA	
Cockpit area (approx)	70 sq ft	6.51 m²
Freeboard forward	36 in	91.44 cm
Freeboard aft	24 in	61.00 cm
Height	NA	
Weight, normal	3,820 lb	1,736 kg
Fuel capacity	82 gal	310 l
Water capacity	NA	
Sleeping accommodations	2	

Power options

Outboard: Any single or twin combination to 250 hp

I/O: MerCruiser 228-hp, 260-hp, 198-hp
OMC 230-hp, 200-hp, 260-hp
Volvo 260-hp, 200-hp

Performance   (From AMF Powerboat performance data sheets)

Model R236 Outboard (twin 115-hp Evinrude)

Fuel	40 gal (half load)
Persons	2
Propeller(s)	2 — 13-in dia. × 19-in pitch

RPM	MPH	GPH	Trim Angle
1000	5.0	—	2.0°
1500	6.5	—	2.0°
2000	8.0	—	3.7°
2500	9.5	—	6.0°
3000	15.0	—	4.0°
3500	27.5	—	2.8°
4000	36.0	—	2.0°
4500	40.0	—	1.0°
5000	46.0	—	—

Model R236 I/O (single MerCruiser 188-hp)

Fuel	80 gal (full load)
Reduction gear ratio	1.5:1
Persons	2
Propeller	(Merc) 15.75-in dia. × 17-in pitch, Blade C

RPM	MPH	GPH	Trim Angle
1000	8.5	1.9	3.7°
1500	11.9	2.7	5.0°
2000	15.8	3.7	5.7°
2500	20.4	5.0	5.6°
3000	26.3	6.0	3.5°
3500	33.8	9.5	2.2°
4000	38.5	14.5	2.0°

Above: *With a single 235-hp outboard motor, tower, and outriggers, the 23-foot Robalo cuddy-cabin model is fully equipped for offshore fishing. Speed with two 115-hp outboards was clocked at 46 mph.* **Opposite:** *Sterndrive version of the same hull does 40 mph with 250 hp. Four deep-trolling downriggers, plus outriggers, demonstrate the versatility of this interesting all-purpose fisherman. (Photos by AMF Robalo)*

Model R236 I/O (single MerCruiser 250-hp)

Fuel	84 gal (full load)
Reduction gear ratio	1.32:1
Persons	2
Propeller	(Merc) 14-in dia. × 19-in pitch, Blade C

RPM	MPH	GPH	Trim Angle
1000	4.5	2.5	4.8°
1500	9.0	3.7	6.0°
2000	15.3	4.8	6.4°
2500	24.0	6.3	5.0°
3000	30.3	7.4	3.4°
3500	35.0	10.5	2.2°
4000	39.0	14.2	1.3°
4300	40.0	16.3	1.0°

From these figures, estimates of endurance and cruising range can be made for the two I/O models cited. While fuel data were not supplied for the outboard model, the author feels that the endurance and range of outboard models of similar total horsepower will be within 80 to 90 percent of the figures estimated for the I/O models. It is important to remember that these endurance and range figures are author's estimates, not builder's statements.

	Merc 188 (80-gal)	*Merc 250 (84-gal)*
Top speed	38.5 mph @ 4000 rpm	40.0 mph @ 4300 rpm
Top fuel rate	14.5 gph	16.3 gph
Top endurance	5.5 hr	5.15 hr
Top range	212 mi	206 mi
Cruising speed	33.8 mph @ 3500 rpm	35.0 mph @ 3500 rpm
Cruising fuel rate	9.5 gph	10.5 gph
Cruising endurance	8.4 hr	8.0 hr
Cruising range	284 mi	280 mi

The calculated endurance and range figures suggest that the preferred power in I/O for this particular hull would be the 188- rather than the 250-hp engine. The data indicate that the extra weight of the larger engine, placed in the stern of this small hull, increases trim angle at low speeds, resulting in a slightly larger fuel consumption at trolling speeds. At trolling speed of 5 mph, for example, the trim angle with the 250-hp engine is 5 degrees at about 1070 rpm and a fuel rate of 1.6 gph. By comparison, the 188-hp motor holds 5 mph with a 2.5-degree trim angle at about 600 rpm, for a fuel rate of 1.3 gph.

Description

The AMF Robalo is a very modern, stylish, high-performance, semi-open fisherman in the popular 20- to 25-foot range. A number of Robalo models are of center-console layout, but the R236 has a small cuddy cabin forward with V-berths and a full-width windshield. With canvas top and Plexiglas curtains, the boat offers more weather protection than most center-console models.

Two almost identical versions are illustrated. The I/O, or sterndrive, version is rigged with both surface outriggers and a set of four downriggers for deep trolling. This version depicts four rods being deep-trolled simultaneously with modern downrigger equipment.

The outboard-powered version, sporting a single 235-hp Johnson motor, is rigged primarily for offshore surface game fishing, with outriggers mounted on a low tower that gives the operator excellent 360-degree surface and depth vision. The tower framework and deck surface can be used as curtain supports to enclose the forward end of the cockpit. The small cuddy cabin can sleep a friendly couple overnight, but it is by no means intended for serious cruising. The boat is a small, fast, economical fishing machine, a very basic fishing platform.

Robalo construction features hand layup of the major fiberglass components. Underdeck and gunwale-side spaces are filled with a foamed-in-place flotation material that also helps to stiffen the hull and deadens sound and vibration. The fuel cell is located under the forward portion of the cockpit space.

The control station is forward to starboard behind the full-width windshield. There is a helmsman's seat behind the wheel and a matching companion seat to port. An insulated fish and ice compartment is built into the outboard space in the inner bulkhead and the space under the forward seats.

Standard Equipment

SS bow eye and cleats
Aluminum fuel tank
Teak rod racks under coaming
Transom eyes
Rodholders (2)
Fishbox aft (OB only)
Storage under bunks, in cockpit sides
Slide panel compartments (2 each side)
Shelves on cabin hull sides
Anchor rope locker with door
Fiberglass cockpit liner
Carpeted cabin with headliner
Portlights
Lockable teak cabin door
Carpeted cabin sides
Sliding-base pedestal seats (2)
V-berth cushions
Electric fuel gauge
Individually fused switches
Instrument switch protection
Battery door, teak (OB only)
Vinyl convertible top with boot
SS top frame

Nonskid deck
Welded aluminum windshield, prewired,
    tempered glass
International navigation lights
Automatic electric bilge pump
Electric horn
Welded SS bow rail
Rope rubrail
Teak trim, door, companionway
SS steering wheel
Forward hatch
Compass, 3½-in
Complete bilge access
Instrumentation
    Oil-pressure gauge
    Water-temperature gauge
    Tachometer
    Voltmeter
    Trim gauge
    Speedometer
Single-lever shift/throttle control
Fire/sound retardant in engine box (I/O)
Large Robalo identification

Optional Equipment

Antifouling paint
After curtain
Chair covers
Drop curtain
Side curtains
Camper top
Special hull color
Forward lifting ring
Outriggers, 15-ft, aluminum (2, gunwale)
Rodholders (2 extra)
Springline cleats (2)
Storage cradle
Shipping wrap
Battery master disconnect switch

Chartlight/cigarette lighter
Hour meter (engine)
Trim tabs, electric
Anchor, chocks, chain, line, deck pipe
Docking lights
Spotlight, ½-mi, remote control
Wiper, additional
Jump seats (single-engine)
Pedestal seat, additional (Pompanette)
Quick-release pedestal with 2 plates
Quick-release pedestal with 1 plate
V-berth filler cushion
Swim ladder with extension
Portable head

WELLCRAFT 24-FOOT AIRSLOT SPORT FISHERMAN

Designer	Richard Cole
Builder	Wellcraft Marine Corp.
	8151 Bradenton Road
	Sarasota, FL 33580
Construction	Cathedral main center hull with narrow sponsons port and starboard. Hand-layup fiberglass hull, deck, and interliner.

Specifications

Length overall	24 ft 5 in	7.44 m
Length, waterline	21 ft 6 in	6.56 m
Beam, maximum	8 ft	2.44 m
Draft	2 ft 4 in	0.71 m
Cockpit area	66 sq ft	6.14 m²
Weight, normal	5,000 lb	2,273 kg
Height above waterline	5 ft 8 in	1.73 m
Fuel capacity	122 gal	461 l
Water capacity	—	
Sleeping accommodations	2	

Continued

*Below: Single-outboard version of this Wellcraft 24-foot Airslot Fisherman is level-running at full speed. Bait tank/fishwell is built into the motor-well bulkhead, a real convenience when the fishing is fast. **Opposite:** Single sterndrive unit drives the same hull at well over 30 mph. The cockpit occupies nearly half of the hull, providing lots of useful fishing space. (Photos by Wellcraft)*

Specifications *continued*

Power options

Single 188-hp MerCruiser I/O gasoline
Single 233-hp MerCruiser I/O gasoline
Single 225-hp OMC I/O gasoline
Twin 140-hp MerCruiser gasoline
Single or twin outboard to 300 hp

Performance

With twin 140-hp MerCruiser I/O gasoline engines, 181 CID each
Full fuel tank and two persons; propellers 15¼-inch diameter by 21-inch pitch,
3-blade; 115 usable gallons of fuel. Test on measured course timed by Longines
stopwatch, made by *Boating* magazine, used with permission.

RPM	MPH	GPH	MPG	Endurance	Range	Angle
1500	7.89	3.0	2.63	38.3 hr	302 mi	2.5°
2000	10.08	4.5	2.24	25.6 hr	257 mi	4.5°
2500	17.99	7.5	2.40	15.3 hr	276 mi	5.0°
3000*	25.38	9.5	2.67	12.1 hr	307 mi	3.5°
3500	30.90	19.0	1.63	6.0 hr	187 mi	2.0°
4000	36.79	23.0	1.60	5.0 hr	184 mi	1.0°

Recommended most efficient cruising speed.

This boat's performance is remarkable in that the range at the most efficient
cruising speed, 307 miles at 3000 rpm with these engines, 25.38 mph, is calculated
to be actually slightly greater than the range at the slow displacement speed of
7.89 mph. Both range and endurance compare favorably with some much larger
boats. Owner Milt Rosko, whose evaluation appears later, claims a maximum
range of 325 miles at 25 mph.

Milt Rosko's 24-foot Wellcraft Airslot with twin sterndrives is trailed to distant fishing areas, fishes for everything from bay flounder to blue marlin 50 miles from shore. (Photo by Milton Rosko, Jr.)

Description

Wellcraft's 24-foot Airslot Sport Fisherman is unusual in more ways than one. Its cathedral hull features a rather blunt bow with a fairly deep main-hull forefoot and two integral side sponsons that extend well forward to form the twin air slots for which the hull is named. Despite its unconventional design, it is called "the driest 24-footer I've ever fished from" by well-known fisherman-writer-owner Milt Rosko.

Another unusual feature is the well-deck effect of the forward side and bow decks beside the small cuddy cabin. This, coupled with a stout metal safety rail forward, makes handling ground tackle in heavy weather a cinch. The third unusual feature is the rather remarkable range in a boat with 8-foot beam, not too large or heavy for trailing overland behind a suitable towing vehicle.

A softtop cover with side curtains that fastens to the windshield affords weather protection for up to four persons without using the cuddy cabin. Two

Softtop and spray curtain provide protection. Sunken step-deck around the bow is a feature greatly appreciated when handling ground tackle or coming into a busy pier. (Photo by Milton Rosko, Jr.)

bunks and a small head in the cuddy provide weekend cruising accommodations of a sort for a couple, or a family with small children. The cuddy cabin can also serve as overnight sleeping quarters while on the highway between fishing ports.

Milt Rosko rigged his boat with outriggers, two fishing chairs in addition to the regular helmsman's and companion seats, and installed VHF/FM and CB radios, two depth sounders of different types, and a radio direction finder. He trails the boat out of his Watchung, New Jersey, home on assignments for major boating and fishing publishers. He claims an average of 250 water-hours of use a year, saying, "We fish approximately 50 days per year, cruising for 30 percent of the time and trolling for 70 percent."

His personal evaluation score is:

Fuel economy	Super
Handling qualities	Super
Seaworthiness	Super
Overall design	Good
("Needs 2 inches more freeboard.")	
Cruising comfort	Good
Fishing efficiency	Super
Ease of maintenance	Super
Investment value	Good

He calls this boat his ultimate fishing machine, exactly suited to his need for a trailable, high-performance boat that can be handled by him, his wife, and two children at modest operating expense. Comparing the Wellcraft Airslot with other boats he has owned, he says, "The Airslot 24 has a remarkably soft ride in heavy weather. The boat is very stable when anchored for bottom fishing or chumming. The head in the cabin is a great convenience for the family. We've caught everything from flounders in the bays to marlin 50 miles offshore."

The outboard version pictured here was added to the Wellcraft line in 1979. Effective fishing room aft is increased, and there is a storage compartment that doubles as a fishbox built into the motor-well bulkhead. Locker space in both OB and I/O versions is generous. While the boat is a bit small to support a tower, it handles outriggers or downriggers for deep trolling very well. The hull is unconventional to many saltwater eyes, seeming to be a carryover from freshwater building practice. But extensive ocean tests under fishing conditions from New England to the Gulf of Mexico have proved it to be unique in comfort and weatherliness.

And it seems to catch fish like a demon. This, in the final analysis, is the true mark of a good fishing boat.

COBIA C24CC CARIBBEAN

Designer	Cobia Boat Co.
Builder	Cobia Boat Co. Sanford, FL 32771
Construction	Hand-layup fiberglass hull, decks, and superstructure.

Specifications

Length overall	23 ft 7 in	7.19 m
Length, waterline	NA	
Beam, maximum	8 ft	2.44 m
Draft	NA	
Cockpit area (estimated)	75 sq ft	6.98 m²
Freeboard forward	NA	
Freeboard aft	NA	
Height	NA	
Weight	4,200 lb	1,454 kg
Fuel capacity	140 gal	529 l
Water capacity	NA	
Sleeping accommodations	2	
Power options		

Twin 140-hp Volvo I/O gasoline engines
MerCruiser, OMC, and other engines by selection

The low tower on this sterndrive Cobia 24-footer substantially increases the helmsman's ability to spot fish or obstacles in the water. Speeds have been recorded to 38 mph with sterndrive power. (Photo by Cobia Boat Co.)

Performance

The builder reports that a Cobia C24CC model equipped with tower and offshore fishing equipment was tested out of Fort Houston Marine, Houston, Texas. The boat was powered with twin 140-hp Volvo sterndrive gasoline units and had a hull weight of approximately 4,200 pounds, with 140 gallons of fuel.

Top speed	38 mph (rpm not available)
Cruising speed	28 mph @ 3000 rpm
Cruising fuel	7 gph total @ 28 mph
Endurance	20 hr @ 3000 rpm, 28 mph
Cruising range	560 mi @ 3000 rpm, 28 mph

Deep-V hull with outboard power is very dry and level-running. Accommodations are provided for two for weekend cruising. Fishing space is excellent for trolling or bottom fishing. (Photo by Cobia Boat Co.)

Description

The Cobia C24CC is described as having a deep-V fiberglass hull and may be powered with twin sterndrive or outboard motors. The sterndrive option is illustrated here. Transparent curtains can be rigged to the forward support members of the low tower to enclose the forward portion of the cockpit for weather protection.

A self-draining fishbox is built into the stern of the sterndrive model. Rod stowage racks are located port and starboard under the coaming covering boards. The full-length ribbed teakwood step pads on either side of the coaming are good safety features. Down below, a simple V-berth and covered head complete the simple cruising arrangement.

Standard rodholder arrangement calls for two flush-mounted holders on either side, one pair for the outrigger rods, the other pair for stern flatlines. Another arrangement could be a multiple "rocket launcher" holder mounted on the centerline just forward of or on top of the sterndrive engine box. Some boats of this general type have mounted a light fighting chair on the stern engine box, but the boat as a type seems better suited to light-tackle, stand-up fishing with rod gimbal belts and light rod harnesses worn by the anglers.

The wide transom platform is a feature not frequently seen on eastern sportfishing boats and should be handy for billing or gaffing active game fish. A tilt-down ladder is helpful for swimmers or skindivers boarding the boat. Overall, the design is an appealing one for dayfishing, and the cruising range is adequate for extensive offshore trips in normally fishable weather.

Standard Equipment

Convertible top with boot
Molded fiberglass interliner
SS bow rail
Interior courtesy lights
Deluxe instrument panel
  (standard I/O only)
Swivel pedestal seats (2)
Swim boarding ladder (I/O only)
Heavy-duty vinyl gunwale molding
Flush-mounted rodholders

Teak rod storage holders
Helmsman seat, fore-aft adjustable
70-gal aluminum fuel tank
Bilge pump and blower (I/O only)
Cabin bunk cushions
Deluxe cabin headliner and sideliner
Full bulkhead with door
Portable chemical toilet
Fishbox or storage compartment in cockpit
  sole

Optional Equipment

Side curtains
After curtain
Pillowback reclining lounge seats
Jump seats (I/O only)
Deluxe outdoor carpet
Super Style interior deluxe pack
Deluxe instrument panel (OB only)
Upholstered box with 25-qt cooler
Electric windshield wipers
Teak swimming (transom) platform
  (I/O only)

Two-tone hull
BIA-certified basic foam flotation
Rear seat platform
Extra 70-gal aluminum fuel tank
Bilge pump and blower (optional, OB)
Sanitary chemical head with dockside
  discharge
Galley with icebox or electric refrigerator
Camper canvas
Mooring cover

AQUASPORT 246 FAMILY FISHERMAN

Designer Aquasport Inc.

Builder Aquasport Inc.
7925 West 2nd Court
Hialeah, FL 33014

Construction Fiberglass deep-V hull with foam-filled multiple girder stringers.
Fiberglass superstructure, teak trim.

Huge cockpit of the Aquasport 24-foot Family Fisherman is ideal for introducing children to light-tackle trolling, deep-jigging, and bottom fishing. Twin 115-hp outboards give speeds to over 44 mph. Fold-down softtop with curtains provides weather protection. (Photo by Aquasport Inc.)

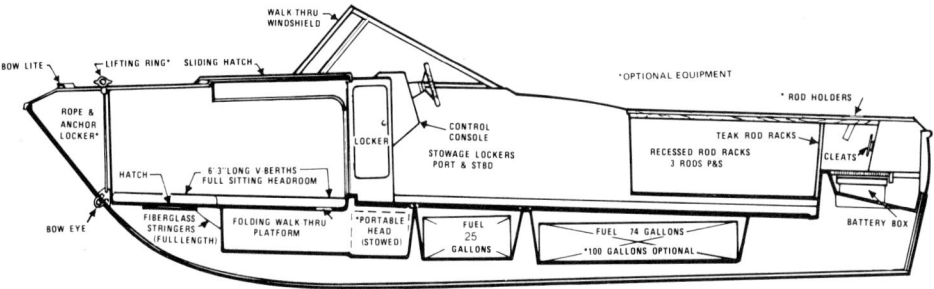

Above: *Nautical test expert Bob Stearns adjusts speed/fuel test equipment on another Aquasport model. Accurate testing under working conditions is essential for determining the endurance and cruising range of powerboats. (Photo by Aquasport Inc.)*

Specifications

Length overall	24 ft 6 in	7.47 m
Beam, maximum	8 ft	2.44 m
Draft, hull	12 in	30.50 cm
Cockpit area	70 sq ft	6.51 m²
Freeboard forward	4 ft	1.22 m
Freeboard, transom	20 in	51.00 cm
Weight, hull (approx)	2,650 lb	1,204 kg
Fuel capacity, standard	74 gal	280 l
Fuel capacity, option 1	100 gal	378 l
Fuel capacity, option 2	125 gal	473 l
Maximum power	280 hp	
Sleeping accommodations	2 V-berths	

Performance

The following performance table was developed from the Aquasport 246 CC Professional model, which is essentially the same hull and power configuration used in the Aquasport 246 Family Fisherman. Load was one adult operator, 120 gallons of fuel, and two 140-hp Evinrude OBs, for a total of 280 hp. The test was conducted by Aquasport and Robert Stearns.

RPM	MPH	GPH	MPG
1000	5.83	3.54	1.65
1500	7.52	4.21	1.79
2000	8.80	5.63	1.56
2500	15.38	6.92	2.22
3000	20.76	7.76	2.68
3500	25.86	10.23	2.53
4000*	30.46	10.71	2.84
4500	35.71	13.64	2.62
5000	39.58	17.30	2.29
5600	44.38	25.00	1.78

Best speed. Range = 340.8 mi @ 4000 rpm, 30.46 mph.

Description

The performance and fuel economy of this class of small, family fishing boats are truly amazing. Consider how a two-day fishing trip would work out in terms of fuel. Allow for running 30 miles out and 30 back each day at the best speed of 30 mph (10.7 gph). This, in two days, accounts for about 44 gallons. Then allow 8 hours of trolling each day at 5 to 6 mph, 3.5 gph. This totals 56 gallons. The grand total for the two-day trip is 100 gallons, leaving an emergency reserve of 20 gallons (20 percent of that consumed). This, in a pinch, could run the boat for almost 2 hours, or better than 50 miles, at the vessel's most efficient speed.

The Aquasport 246 Family Fisherman features a flush-decked bow containing V-berths 6 feet 3 inches long with full sitting headroom. A portable head stows under the forward end of the cockpit deck, accessible from the cabin via the walk-through well platform. Standard fuel capacity consists of two tanks, one of 74 gallons and another of 25 gallons. An optional 100-gallon tank can be installed in lieu of the 74-gallon tank.

The wide, stern splash well will take either a single high-output outboard motor or a pair of medium-to-high twins. The large, uncluttered cockpit can take a variety of chair and deck locker arrangements. There are side racks for six rods. A 28-gallon freshwater tank is available as an option in lieu of the 25-gallon fuel tank shown in the sketches. Freshwater equipment includes pump, hose, and nozzle. Live-bait wells can be transom-mounted.

The Aquasport 246 Family Fisherman offers limited cruising accommodations for two persons, and daysailing and fishing comfort for up to six. Protective canvas spray curtains and sun top are available as options, as are a small galley unit, bunk cushions, and a wide variety of similar accessories. The boat is large enough to support a light tower. Enclosure of the lower tower area, abaft the windshield, with transparent plastic curtains cut to fit provides a large shelter from bad weather that gives most of the comfort of a conventional cruiser's deckhouse.

The boat is an attractive alternative for the family with growing children who are old enough to enjoy fishing, yet hardly big or rugged enough to take the sometimes rigorous conditions found at sea in open and center-console boats.

BLACKFIN 25 INBOARD OFFSHORE FISHERMAN

Designer	Blackfin Yacht Corporation
Builder	Blackfin Yacht Corp. P.O. Box 22982 Fort Lauderdale, FL 33335
Construction	Nearly 50 percent glass content in alternating matt and woven glass roving. Deep-V hull, teak trim.

Specifications

Length overall	25 ft 2 in	7.68 m
Length, waterline	21 ft 7 in	6.60 m
Beam, maximum	8 ft	2.44 m
Deadrise	24°	
Draft		
Single gasoline	31 in	0.82 m
Twin gasoline/diesel	23 in	0.34 m
Single diesel	32 in	0.85 m
Cockpit area	50 sq ft	4.65 m²
Freeboard forward	3 ft 5 in	1.04 m
Freeboard aft	2 ft 4 in	0.71 m
Height, waterline to tower top	10 ft	3.05 m

Continued

Running at speed, the 25-foot Blackfin Inboard Offshore Fisherman is dry and nonpounding. The deep-V hull exhibits excellent directional stability both into and down the seas. Speeds to 42 mph are possible with twin gasoline engines. (Photo by Blackfin Yacht Corp.)

Specifications *continued*

Weight		
Single gasoline	5,100 lb	2,313 kg
Twin gasoline	6,100 lb	2,767 kg
Diesel	6,200 lb	2,812 kg
Fuel capacity	135 gal	510 l
Water capacity	(variable)	
Sleeping accommodations	(custom, 2-3)	
Power options		
Single gasoline	OMC	260 hp
	Pleasurecraft	250 hp
	MerCruiser	255 hp
	Crusader	270 hp
	Crusader	350 hp
Single diesel	Caterpillar	3208
	Detroit	6V53
	Cummins	V555
	Caterpillar	636T
Twin gasoline	OMC	190 hp
	Pleasurecraft	185 hp
	Pleasurecraft	215 hp
	OMC	225 hp
Twin diesel	Volvo	TMD40

Performance

The Blackfin 25 is a true high-performance hull more in the style of open-water racing machines than fishing boats of the traditional stripe. Manufacturer's performance data are designed to show comparative ranges of speed, fuel consumption, and range rather than exact performance of each option of power.

Power	Approx. Top Speed	Fuel Rate	Endurance
Single gasoline	40 mph / 64 kph	9 gph	15 hr
Twin gasoline	42 mph / 68 kph	14 gph	9.6 hr
Diesel	30 mph / 48 kph	6½ gph	20 hr

The published fuel data do not indicate whether the fuel rates quoted are maximum- or optimum-speed, but even so, the speed-endurance product is impressive. Relatively small, high-speed boats of this type, however, feel added weight quite rapidly, and the weight of a tower, fighting chair, and normal fishing tackle, bait, and supplies for four anglers for a day's fishing may easily add up to three-fourths of a ton.

The cockpit on the 25-footer is large enough for a full-sized fighting chair, twin fishing chairs, or "rocket launcher" for standup fishing. Power is located under the center control console. (Photo by Blackfin Yacht Corp.)

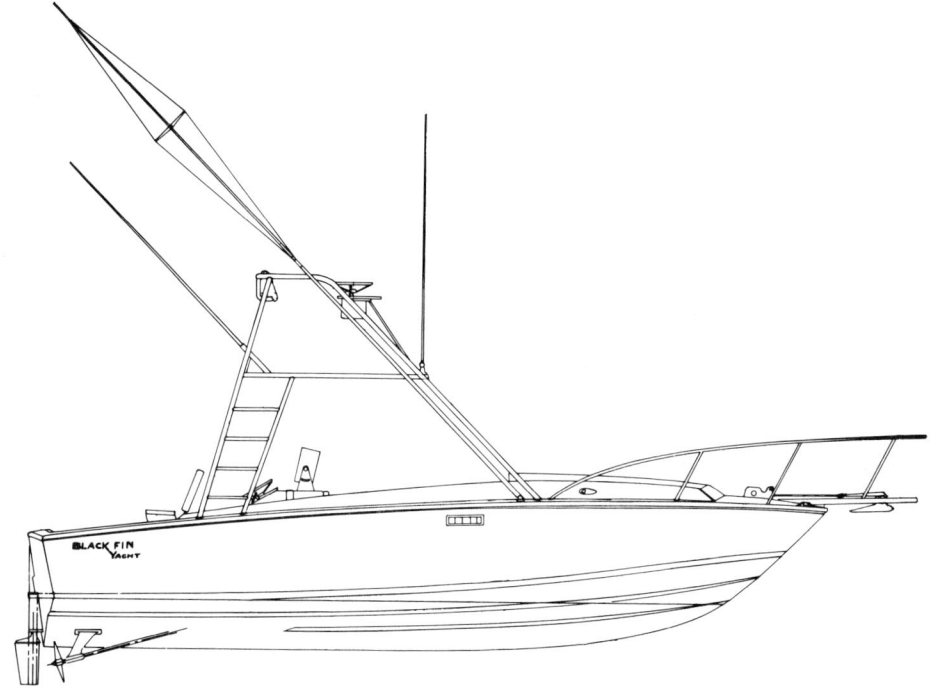

Description

The manufacturer describes the hull design this way:

> The Blackfin design was the first to utilize direct-drive inboard power in mid-size, deep-V hulls. It is not an adaptation of any other existing stern-powered hull. The 24-degree deadrise hull was designed and engineered to carry the engine mass amidships at the point of perfect balance. The result: superior ride and handling offshore.

Single-engine models feature a combined engine box and center-control console on the centerline. Twin-screw models feature a separate engine box over each engine with a flush-deck walkway between. The control console is part of the starboard engine-box structure. Down below, twin 7-foot V-berths provide adequate sleeping for two persons or for two friendly couples. Admittedly, cruising accommodations are minimal, but they are sufficient for day-to-day fishing or for short weekend trips.

The model featured has a low tower. Enclosure of the tower structure beneath the tower deck, using transparent plastic curtains, makes the forward portion of the cockpit into an effective weather shelter with adequate visibility for the helmsman. Holding the beam to 8 feet complies with U.S.-highway trailer-width restrictions. The gross boat weight of a little over 3 U.S. tons calls for a heavy-duty trailer and tow vehicle, but this is no greater than the weight of a good many larger highway house trailers. The boat itself can serve as living quarters for a couple on a cruise overland to distant fishing areas.

That practical fishermen had a hand in designing the Blackfin 25 is obvious.

Tackle stowage is provided below and there is a 50-gallon insulated well below the deck that can be used for bait, fish, ice, dry storage, or even extra fuel or fresh water. Engines are fully exposed for inspection and servicing by lifting the box covers. With the inboard engines located amidships, there is nothing to hamper active work while fighting or gaffing the biggest game fish.

Directional stability in rough water is said to be phenomenal. The 24-degree deadrise, deep-V hull tracks straight and true down following seas with either single or twin power. The combined matt-roving fiberglass layup results in a hull that is very strong for its weight, with high impact strength, yet a desirable degree of flexibility.

The builder points out that while the design is standardized for quality control in manufacture, a high degree of customizing is possible in finishing the boat. In fact, the builder encourages close participation of clients in planning and executing the fishing layout so as to produce a fishing machine of truly outstanding efficiency, exactly reflecting individual owners' tastes and requirements.

Standard Equipment

Full 7-ft cuddy cabin
Under-bunk stowage
Three-piece Herculon bunk cushions
Console or motor-box seat cushions
Helm chair with fore-and-aft slide
Companion chair with 360° swivel
Marine aluminum fuel tank, 135-gal,
    with shutoff
Automatic bilge pump
Bilge blower
Underdeck 50-gal fish or storage tank
Pump and blower monitor lights
Fiberglass muffler system
Fuel filter/water separator
Cabin light, 12 v. DC
Marine battery and box, heavy-duty
Rodholders (2)
Electric fuel gauge
Complete instrumentation
Weather-protected gauges and switches
Complete circuit-breaker switch panel
Navigation lights, international
Tinted windshield with handrails
Rack-and-pinion steering system
SS steering wheel
Three-blade bronze propeller(s)

Heavy-duty bronze rudder(s)
1¼-in SS shaft(s)
Heavy-duty bronze strut(s)
Zinc shaft collars
Heavy-duty seawater intake strainers
Underwater through-hull seacocks
Flush fuel fill with overboard vent
Sliding fiberglass cabin deck hatch
Teak louvered cabin door
Rope locker with louvered door
Handcrafted solid teak trim
Heavy-duty SS bow and stern eyes
Single-lever control
Heavy-duty vinyl rubrail with nylon
    rope insert
Waterline boottop
Forward deck access hatch
Access hatches to all mechanical
    components
Complete and immediate engine access
Self-bailing, nonskid cockpit deck
Hand-laid fiberglass construction
Integral hull, deck, and liner bonding
Underwater fittings electrically bonded
Nonskid forward deck walkways

SURF HUNTER 25

Designer	C. Raymond Hunt Associates
	63 Long Wharf
	Boston, MA 02110
Builder	Surf Hunter Corp.
	50 Fort Street
	P.O. Box D-4
	Fairhaven, MA 02719
Construction	Hand-layup fiberglass hull, deck, and superstructure.

Specifications

Length overall	25 ft	7.63 m
Length, waterline	21 ft 6 in	6.56 m
Beam, maximum	9 ft	2.75 m
Draft, hull only	1 ft 6 in	0.46 m
Cockpit area	90 sq ft	8.37 m²
Freeboard forward	3 ft 10 in	1.19 m
Freeboard aft	2 ft 5 in	0.73 m
Height, waterline to windshield top	7 ft	2.14 m
Fuel capacity	100 gal	378 l
Weight, normal		
Fisherman model	6,000 lb	2,728 kg
Weekender model	6,500 lb	2,956 kg
Sleeping accommodations	2	

Power options (by arrangement)

Fisherman	Twin 140-hp Volvo I/O engines (gasoline)
Weekender	Single 225-hp Chrysler inboard (gasoline)
Fisherman	Single 140-hp Volvo AQD diesel

Performance

While no formal test data were available from the builder, a letter gives the following information.

> The open boat [Fisherman] with cuddy cabin is powered with a pair of Volvo 140-hp I/Os, and the Weekender with an inboard Chrysler 225-hp gas engine. Fisherman displaces 6,000 pounds, and Weekender 6,500 pounds, both with 100 gallons of fuel in two aluminum tanks.
>
> The 4-cylinder Volvos deliver about 25 mph at 4000 rpm with total fuel consumption of 8 gph. Top speed is close to 32 mph at 16 to 18 gph (top rpm not stated). The heavier Weekender with Chrysler 225-hp does 22 mph at 3300 cruising rpm, and top speed of 27. Fuel consumption at cruising is 8 to 9 gph and 16 at top speed.

This information suggests that the Fisherman, with twin 140-hp Volvo I/O units, carrying 100 gallons of fuel, has an endurance of about 12½ hours at 25 mph cruising speed, and a cruising-speed range of about 312 miles. The Weekender, with single 225-hp Chrysler inboard engine, has an endurance of 11 to 12½ hours at 22 mph and a suggested cruising range of 240 to 275 miles at that speed.

The builder goes on to say: "We have a hull in process for the Volvo 140-hp AQD diesel, with which we expect our Fisherman (kept on the light side) will do 18 mph with a fuel consumption of about 3 gph."

This indicates a single-diesel fuel rate of 6 mpg for a cruising-speed range of around 600 miles, truly outstanding range performance for a 25-foot boat.

The builder concludes: "The *Wild Goose*, a Fisherman with 230-hp I/O, burns an average of 5 gph in an all-day fishing jaunt, and while cruising at 21 mph, burns 8 gph."

This suggests an all-purpose endurance of about 20 hours at various running and trolling speeds, a fuel rate of 2.63 mpg at 21 mph, and a cruising-speed range of more than 260 miles with this power. With the exception of the projected performance of the light, single-Volvo-diesel boat, performance is comparable with that of boats of similar size and general type. The single-diesel projected performance is within reason if the weight of the vessel is kept down, and 18 mph proves to be the hull's most efficient speed in terms of miles per gallon.

Translated into actual bulk of fuel, the economy of boats of this type is quite evident. Reasonable speed in decent weather is a must for modern ocean game fishing. At the same time, availability of fuel in the future will probably be a strongly determining factor in putting and keeping active fishermen on the water. The Surf Hunter 25 is apparently a boat that will accommodate well the fuel situation of the future.

Left: The Surf Hunter 25-foot Fisherman is a neat, nautical-looking boat with Down East conservatism applied to modern construction. (Photo by Norman Fortier)

The large cockpit of the Fisherman model is ideal for surface or deep trolling, or for casting along reefs and into the surf.

The deep-V hull form is nonpounding and dry-running. Dynamic lift is evident at speeds in excess of 30 mph. (Photos by Norman Fortier)

Above: The Weekender model with inboard power is a handsome little ship with comfortable accommodations for two. Below: The Weekender's cuddy cabin interior is neat and uncluttered and makes maximum use of space without the common sin of overcrowding. (Photos by Norman Fortier)

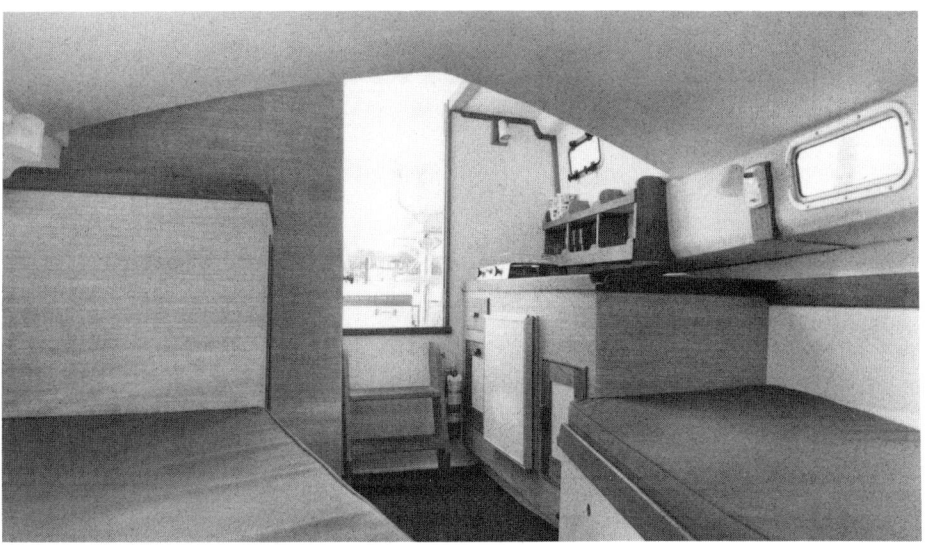

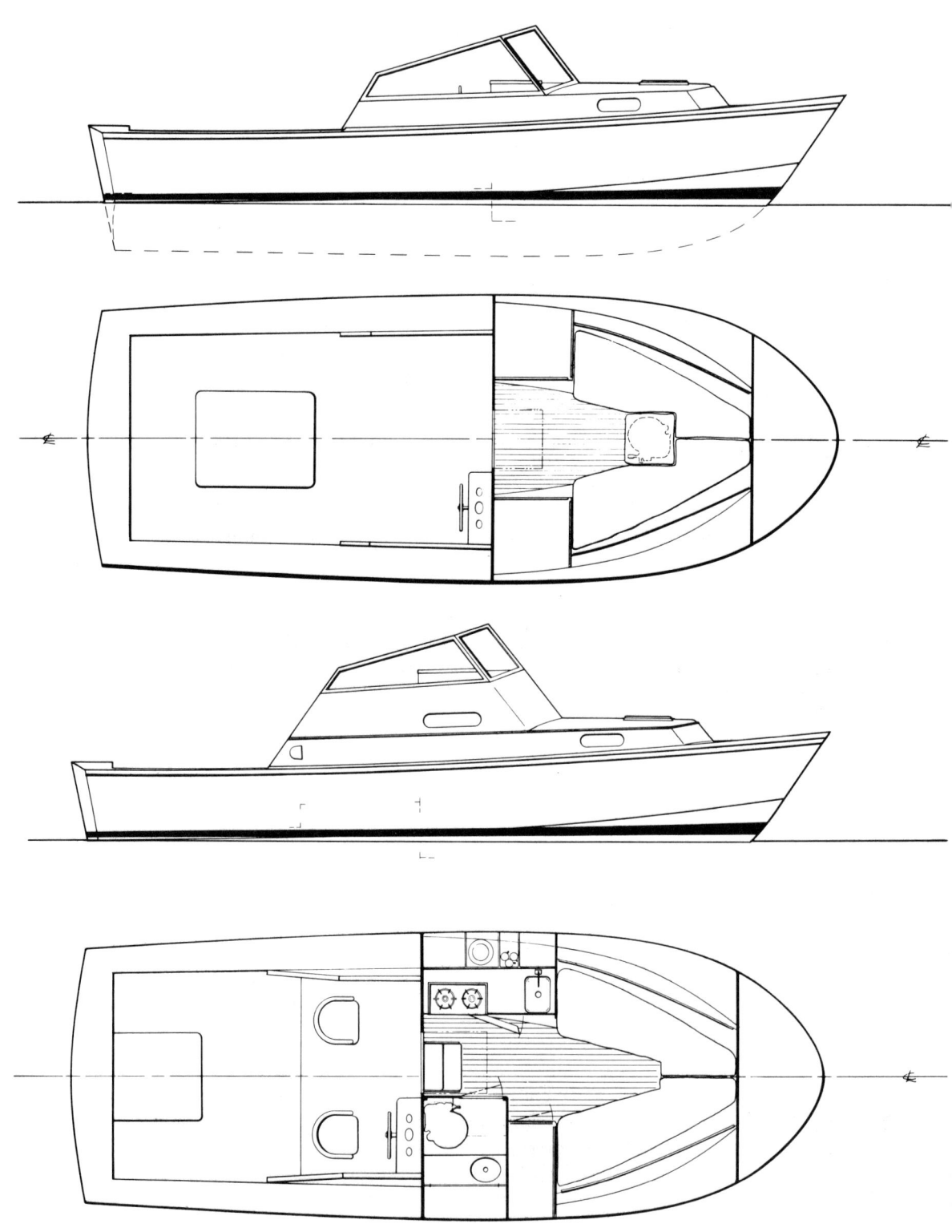

Description

Designed by C. Raymond Hunt Associates Inc., developers of the famous deep-V speed hulls, the Surf Hunter 25 is a modern version of the time-tested New England bass boat. The Fisherman version, with low profile and small cuddy cabin forward, provides maximum uncluttered space for casting and inshore trolling. It is highly adaptable to light-tackle, big-game trolling or chumming. While not intended for cruising, it does offer adequate overnight shelter for two anglers. Economy of operation and maintenance is very high.

The Weekender version, with a slightly higher superstructure profile, features an enclosed head below and a small but efficient galley in addition to the two-person V-berth forward. There is a short bridge-deck amidships, presumably to take an inboard motor without needing an engine box. Effective cockpit fishing space is still large for a boat of this size.

The lines of both versions are very clean, uncluttered, and nautical. These boats look like boats, not amphibious house trailers. With a fairly small annual production, the builder is able to give considerable personal attention to each boat.

Performance in rough water is said to be outstanding. The deep-V hull is good in both head and following seas and has considerable inherent directional stability. The roll is slower than in boats with conventional V-bottoms, but this is not a sign of lack of stability. A slow roll is often a blessing when quartering a boiling tiderip or running home before a smoking summer sou'wester.

Owner's Evaluation

Captain Dave MacEachern, charter fishing operator out of Yarmouthport, Massachusetts, gives this report on his 1979 Surf Hunter 25, the *Wild Goose.*

Fuel economy	Good
Handling qualities	Super
Seaworthiness	Super
Overall design	Super
Cruising comfort	Super
Fishing efficiency	Super
Ease of maintenance	Good
Investment value	Super

Captain MacEachern fishes charter parties in Massachusetts Bay and around Martha's Vineyard. He averages 800 hours of use per year, with 40 percent of the time spent in running and 60 percent in trolling. His normal top speed is 40 mph and he cruises at 28 to 30 mph with a 230-hp OMC I/O gasoline unit. He estimates his ultimate cruising range at 500 miles at 25 mph. This is at variance with the author's estimates taken from data provided by the builder, however.

Commenting on the boat, Captain MacEachern had this to say:

> For me, this is my ultimate fishing machine. I'd like an after tiller station, bass-boat style, but this would be costly with I/O power. The Surf Hunter design seems to be the best compromise of economy, speed, handling, and comfort I've found. It's truly a great fishing boat.

It's not so big as to put me in the poorhouse trying to operate it, and not so small that I have to worry about rough weather. I can fish comfortably with a party of three and still have storage for gear. My overall fuel consumption is 5 gph, which isn't bad.

As a professional fisherman, Captain MacEachern gives top priority to the qualities of seaworthiness, fuel economy, fishing efficiency, and handling ability. The next most important categories for him are ease of maintenance and investment value. Lowest on his list of priorities are personal comfort and cruising range. This reflects the attitude of many guides — "If they get too damned comfortable, they'll fall asleep and not catch me any fish!"

Captain MacEachern finds his primary satisfaction from fishing to be "bringing all the variables and unknowns together to find big stripers and watch a novice catch his first fish."

Standard Equipment

From literature provided, the builder's policy appears to be to furnish a complete boat with engines to order, 100 gallons fuel capacity, interior arrangements as agreed, and all engines with freshwater cooling. Inboard engines have 1.5:1 reduction gear and V-drives. Other engine options can be negotiated, including outboard power. A standard equipment list is not provided as such, but the builder does provide a list of optional equipment at extra cost.

Standard Options (builder's title)

Marine nonpolluting sanitary system, Type 1 - IWSS
Electric windshield wipers
Helmsman seat(s)
Teak cockpit rod racks (4)
Made-up docklines (4), fenders (2)
Anchor and chocks, rode and chain
Bow rail, SS
Navy top
Engine box cushion
Transom lettering and bow numbers
Water tank, 20-gal, polyethylene
SS galley sink and hand pump
Ice chest

Fishbox, baitwell
Shipping cradle
115 v. AC shore-power connection with isolation transformer
Radio, sounder, other electronics
Combination bilge and washdown pump
Compass, 4-in, Danforth Constellation
5-lb CO_2 fire extinguisher with mounting bracket
Portable air horn
Tuna tower
Outriggers
Auxiliary tiller and after control station

GRADY-WHITE 254 KINGFISH

Designer	Grady-White Boats Inc.
Builder	Grady-White Boats Inc. P.O. Box 1527 Greenville, NC 27834
Construction	Hand-layup fiberglass with glassed-in stringers, polyurethane foam flotation. Molded decks and superstructure.

Specifications

Length overall	25 ft 4 in	7.72 m
Length, waterline	21 ft 2 in	6.46 m
Beam, maximum	9 ft 6 in	2.90 m
Draft, hull	19 in	48.26 cm
Cockpit area	62 sq ft	5.8 m²
Freeboard forward	4 ft 4 in	1.31 m
Freeboard aft	3 ft	0.92 m
Height above waterline	7 ft	2.16 m
Weight (single V-8)	5,100 lb	2,318 kg
Fuel capacity	125 gal	473 l
Water capacity	25 gal	95 l
Sleeping accommodations	4	

Power options (maximum, 330-hp single-screw, 340-hp twin-screw)

Single 260-hp OMC sterndrive
Single 260-hp Merc sterndrive
Single 260-hp Volvo sterndrive
Single 330-hp Merc sterndrive

Twin 140-hp OMC sterndrive
Twin 140-hp Merc sterndrive
Twin 165-hp Merc sterndrive
Twin 170-hp Merc sterndrive

Performance

The builder was unable to provide tabulated performance data but was able to supply this information:

The best power package for the boat is the twin 140-hp MerCruiser sterndrives. At 4200 rpm we're attaining speeds of 38 to 40 mph. At between 3200 and 3500 rpm we're running approximately 28 to 30 mph. At 3500 rpm we noticed one situation where we used 9½ gph for the two engines. We do offer some single-engine options for the boat; however, we would much prefer to stick with the twin installation as this is by far the most popular power for the Kingfish.

Outriggers and a light fighting chair equip this 25-foot Grady-White Kingfish for offshore game fishing. Speeds to 40 mph and range to 380 miles at 28 to 30 mph are indicated for this efficient small family fisherman. A wide selection of single or twin engines is offered. (Photo by Grady-White Boats Inc.)

From the statement above, the following table of performance has been prepared for the power recommended, 125 gallons of fuel.

Top speed @ 4200 rpm	38-40 mph
Cruising speed @ 3500 rpm	28-30 mph
Cruising fuel rates	9½ gph, or 2.95-3.16 mpg
Cruising endurance	13.16 hr
Cruising range	380 mi (averaged)

The table is an empirical one, prepared only to show comparative fuel, endurance, and range data. It should not be regarded as the result of any controlled test.

Description

The Grady-White 254 Kingfish is an example of that popular class of small fishing boat, the high-performance family fisherman. Initial investment is moderate, but within the restrictions of size and weather, its endurance, speed, and range are the equal of larger vessels. The rather low, stern engine box provides seating for daycruising, and there is room for a pair of portable fishing chairs or even one light fighting chair on a pedestal mount.

Rod racks are built into the cockpit sidewalls and the stern deck has bait, fish, and ice lockers built in. The control station is to starboard behind the low windshield, and matching helmsman's and companion seats flank the centerline entrance to the cabin. Cockpit coaming height is adequate for comfort and safety. Especially good is the slightly sunken side-deck arrangement beside the low cabin trunk. This greatly increases confidence and safety when handling ground tackle in rough weather or when coming alongside the pier.

The compact cabin can sleep four in a pair of V-berths in the bow and two single berths amidships. The amidships berths extend aft under the raised control-bridge deck, the bunk space flanking a centerline, insulated storage or fish well. A marine head can be installed between the V-berths, and a tiny galley and sink are placed port and starboard between the bunk ends. For a family of four the cabin is adequate for overnight or weekend fishing expeditions.

Owner's Evaluation

Jeff Click of East Lansing, Michigan, gives us the following owner's evaluation. Qualifying comments are noted.

Fuel economy	Good
Handling qualities	Super
Seaworthiness	Super
Overall design	Super
Cruising comfort	Good*
Fishing efficiency	Super
Ease of maintenance	Good**
Investment value	Super***

    *"Good—only because of lack of cabin space."

    **"Good—Mercury suggests boat be pulled out of the water every 100 hours of operation to grease fittings in the outdrive."

    ****"Super—I would guess the investment value to be as good as or better than any other quality boat."

Click fishes the eastern shore of Lake Michigan for coho and chinook salmon, lake trout, etc. He lists his top speed as 49 mph with a single 330-hp MerCruiser power plant, and he cruises at 30 mph. He operates an average of 200 hours a season, doing 5 percent cruising and 95 percent trolling. He estimates his maximum range at 260 miles at 30 mph.

Regarding the boat's performance, he says, "In its size range I have never seen a boat that has more fishing capability. It has the capability of a good many 30-footers. When we change boats we will trade up. By that time, I hope, Grady-White will have a larger model available. If fuel is available, I will continue to fish at the present rate, if not more."

Standard Equipment

Full fiberglass hull liner
Ventilating windshield with tempered glass
Sliding cabin windows with screens
Fixed forward cabin windows (2)
Fabric-covered foam bunk cushions
Under-bunk storage compartments (5)
Cabin liner side shelves
Deluxe nylon cabin headliner
Bow compartment rope locker
Forward cabin hatch with cushion seat
Galley storage compartment
SS sink
Alcohol stove
Built-in icebox
Fold-up table
Cabin lamp
Full-size berths (4)
Cabin-step storage box
25-gal water tank
Teak lockable cabin door, with sliding access hatch
Bow lifting ring
Heavy-duty aluminum gunwale molding
Marinium deck hardware

Recessed nonskid walkway around cabin
Side cabin handrails
SS steering wheel
Full instrument panel
Pedestal chairs, swivel and sliding
Horn
Large insulated storage or fish well with overboard drain
Helm and companion sea drinkholders
Lockable cockpit side storage compartments with fishing rodholder racks
Self-bailing cockpit with nonskid fiberglass floor
Cockpit lights
125-gal aluminum fuel tank
Rod racks
Side storage shelves
Removable after storage wells (2)
Center insulated after storage well with drain
Insulated engine box with built-in drinkholders
Bilge pumps (1 automatic, 1 manual)
BIA-approved lighting and ventilation

Factory Options

Folding top and side curtains with boot
Drop curtain
Helm station cover
Motor box cushion (single and dual)
Windshield wiper(s)
Marine head
Rodholders, flush-mounted, Marinium (4)
Outrigger kit, 15-ft
Transom teak swim platform with ladder

Pedestal chair cover(s)
Chair gimbals for fishing
Chain pipe deck fitting
Dockside power
Shipping cradle
Single-engine options to 330 hp
Twin- and single-engine options as listed
Hydraulic trim tabs

MAKO DEEP VEE 25-FOOTER

Designer	Mako Marine
Builder	Mako Marine 4355 N.W. 128th Street Miami, FL 33054
Construction	Hand-layup fiberglass hull, decks, and console.

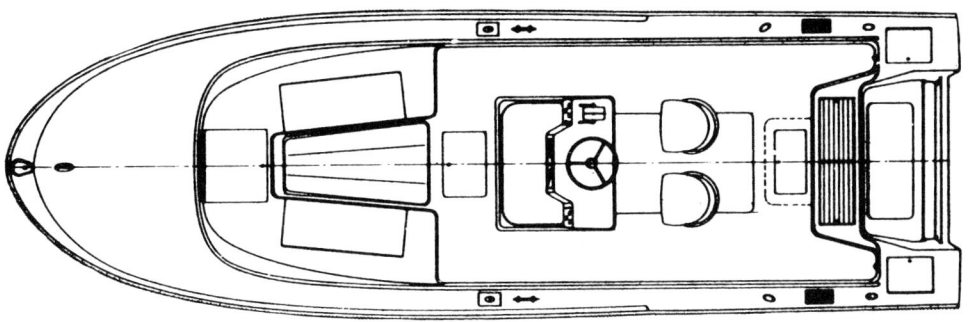

Viewed from overhead, the Mako Deep Vee 25-footer gives the impression of uncluttered, open fishing space. Hull runs fast and dry in a chop. (Photo by Mako Marine)

A low tower and outriggers make this Mako 25-footer an efficient light-tackle fishing machine. A small trolling motor saves wear and tear on the main engine and provides an extra margin of safety. (Photo by Mako Marine)

Specifications

Length overall	25 ft 6 in	7.78 m
Beam, maximum	8 ft	2.44 m
Draft, hull	14 in	35.56 cm
Cockpit area	90 sq ft	8.37 m²
Transom height (twin)	20 in	50.80 cm
Transom height (single)	25 in	63.50 cm
Fuel capacity, standard	86 gal	321 l
Fuel capacity, additional option	38 gal	142 l
Fuel capacity, total	124 gal	463 l
Maximum power	300 hp	
Rated load	2,500 lb	1,136 kg

Performance

From Mercury Marine: Twin Merc 140ELPT, 140-hp motors; propellers, 13¼-in dia. × 17-in pitch, 3-blade aluminum; 3,375 lb net hull weight.

Gross load	4,525 lb
Measured speed	44.4 mph @ 5700 rpm

Assuming the reasonable full-speed fuel rate of 8.7 hp/gph, the twin Mercs would burn about 32 gph at 44.4 mph for a mileage rate of 1.39 mpg. Running at 50 percent power (16 gph), the best cruising speed should be about 33 mph for a fuel mileage rate of slightly better than 2 mpg. Endurance at this speed would be about 7¾ hours and range, a little over 250 miles.

Downriggers on the stern adapt this Mako 25-footer to deep trolling. A dolphin-fish leaps on spinning tackle. (Photo by Mako Marine)

Low freeboard and wide side deck add a measure of safety to tagging and releasing a hammer-head shark. (Photo by Mako Marine)

Description

The Mako Deep Vee 25-footer is one of the larger open, center-console models from this builder. It is a widely proven type, adaptable to many forms of game fishing. Equipped with outriggers and a low tower, it does well in offshore competitive work. As a small charter vessel it can easily fish parties of up to four persons. The ride is fast and dry in choppy water, and stability and maneuverability at slow trolling speeds are excellent.

Viewed from above, the impression is of ample open space for fishing operations. There is room enough for a light fighting chair or two fishing chairs between the console and the built-in stern fishbox, although some skippers prefer to mount this heavy artillery up forward in the bow. Light outriggers are mounted in side-deck holders where a tower is not carried. Large seat lockers forward provide plenty of stowage space for gear or fish. Twin live-bait wells double as coolers back aft, flanking the motor well. A modicum of shelter for passengers can be provided by a neat folding canvas spray hood forward of the console.

Rigged with a low tower and topside controls, the Mako Deep Vee 25-footer becomes an impressive fishing machine. The hull is stable enough to support two men aloft in moderately rough weather, and enclosing the tower legs with plastic curtains creates a large sheltered area that still retains the open boat's full-horizon visibility.

Lockable side lockers hold fishing tackle and equipment. There is space enough for an array of electronic fishing gear behind the console sprayshield. The beam of 8 feet makes the boat legally trailable on most state and all U.S. highways without the need for a special over-width permit. A huge fishbox is built underdeck. Tackle and small equipment drawers are built into the console.

As an open fisherman, the Mako 25-footer can be drifted over all but the shallowest flats, but it still gives an excellent account of itself offshore. With the addition of specialized equipment it can handle any fishing job from deep-trolling for Great Lakes salmon to baiting billfish and giant tuna.

Standard Equipment

Recessed rod lockers with lockable doors
Live-bait well
Modular radio or glove box with lockable door
Lockable storage area
Tinted windshield
Nonskid sole and deck
Console, dry storage
Custom chairs or fishbox seat (2)
Custom instrument panel, lights, external fuses
Mechanical steering
Running and anchor lights
SS towing eye
SS lifting eyes (2 aft)
Deck eye cleat

Stern cleats (2)
Bow chocks (2)
Springline cleats
Teak side step pads
Bow storage, teak door
Antenna wire conduit
Insulated fish and bait box
Battery shelf or pad
Custom bow rail
Teak hatches for all boxes
Heavy-duty vinyl rubrail
Marinium or SS hardware
Bow lifting assembly
Foamed-in fuel tank
Fuel fill, side deck, and overboard vent

Optional Equipment

Custom rodholders (4)
Outrigger kit, Lee's, 15-ft
Outrigger kit, Lee's, 18-ft
Chair gimbal (each)
Knife and rigging rack
Cushion for seat filler
Aft fishbox cushion
Casting-deck cushions (5 pieces)
Folding top and boot
Casting platform spray hood and boot
Drop curtain
Connector, top to spray hood
Console cover
Chair covers (each)
Fishbox seat covers (each)
Recessed console box with sliding door
Console holder for 5 rods
Console rodholder (3 per side)

Windshield handrail
Fiberglass and teak filler section
Deluxe 15-in SS steering wheel
Deluxe 17-in SS steering wheel
Recessed tackle box
Additional fuel tank, 38-gal
Bilge pump, electric
Bilge pump, automatic
Chain deck pipe
Compass, 4-in, high-speed
Univ. Conn. kit, SS, single
Custom twin steering connectors
Morse MT, single with cables
Morse MT, dual with cables
Leaning post in lieu of custom chairs
Leaning post, separately
Rocket launcher in addition to leaning post (for 5 rods)

DUSKY 26-FOOT SPORT FISHERMAN

Designer	Dusky Marine Inc.
Builder	Dusky Marine Inc. 110 N. Bryan Rd. Dania, FL 33004
Construction	Fiberglass hull, interliner, and decks.

Specifications

Length overall	26 ft	7.93 m
Length, waterline	NA	
Beam	11 ft 3 in	3.43 m
Draft	29 in	73.66 cm
Cockpit area (approx)	180 sq ft	16.74 m²
Freeboard forward	NA	
Freeboard aft	3 ft 1 in	0.95 m
Height	NA	
Weight, average	7,500 lb	3,409 kg
Fuel capacity		
Normal	104 gal	393 l
Optional extra	60 gal	227 l
Water capacity	NA	

Power options
  Gasoline
    Twin 225-hp Commander (8-cyl, 302 CID Ford block)
    Twin 255-hp Commander (8-cyl, 351 CID Ford block)
    Twin 220-hp Crusader (8-cyl, 305 CID GM block)
    Twin 270-hp Crusader (8-cyl, 350 CID GM block)
    Twin 350-hp Crusader (8-cyl, 454 CID GM block)
  Diesel
    Twin 130-hp Renault diesels BWG
    Twin 145-hp Renault diesels BWG
    Twin 210-hp Renault diesels (Twin Disc)*
    Twin 240-hp Renault diesels (Twin Disc)
    Twin 200-hp Chrysler diesels (Twin Disc)
    Twin 250-hp Caterpillar #636T diesels (Twin Disc)
    Twin 124-hp Volvo #TMD40 diesels
    Twin 220-hp Volvo #TAMD60B diesels (Twin Disc)
  Twin Disc refers to trade name of clutch-reverse gear.

Performance

Detailed performance data on the Dusky 26-footer were not available, but the builder reported that top speed with two 225-hp gasoline motors is approximately 40 mph. Cruising endurance at 3000 rpm on both engines, with 90 gallons of fuel,

The unusual arrangement of the Dusky 26-footer provides seating for 4 or 5 persons without cramping the essential fishing space. Engines are under the wide central seat. The cuddy cabin has V-berths and a small head. A portable fishbox is in the stern. (Photo by Dusky Marine Inc.)

is given at about 8 hours. Assuming a cruising speed of about 30 mph, this suggests a maximum cruising range of about 240 miles with this fuel capacity.

An owner claims a maximum range of 300 miles at 30 mph with two 250-hp Fiat diesels and a fuel capacity of 140 gallons. His top speed was given as 38 mph.

Description

Purely a fishing machine is the way to describe the Dusky 26-footer. The huge cockpit occupies two-thirds of the boat and measures more than 180 square feet. The cockpit deck is broken only by the short, wide engine box, which is also a tackle locker and comfortable cruising seat for three or four persons, and by the convenient center console placed well forward in the hull. There is room aft for a full-sized fighting chair with footrest, plus two flanking fixed or portable fishing chairs.

Clear plastic curtains around the forward portion of the tower convert the forward part of the cockpit into a commodious shelter from wet or windy weather without detracting from the boat's 360-degree open visibility at deck level. The tiny cuddy under the flush forward deck can hide a marine head, a small V-berth, and extra fishing tackle. Basically a daycruiser, this boat is designed for hard, fast fishing, and cruising comfort is not given even an afterthought.

The Dusky 26-footer takes advantage of the inherent space-saving quality of inboard engine installations. The stern is uncluttered by engines or boxes and is of full height for safety and convenience in handling big fish. No outdrive projects

The tower on this Dusky places the operator's eyes a good 15 feet above the water. Outriggers are tower-mounted for greater elevation. (Photo by Dusky Marine Inc.)

Tower console contains VHF/FM radio, sounder, binoculars. Loran is located in overhead box beneath the cockpit sun shelter. (Photo by Dusky Marine Inc.)

beyond the transom. The engines' weight is concentrated amidships, leaving the stern as well as the bow buoyant to respond to irregular seas. The engines are accessible for service, and the engine box serves the triple purposes of covering the engines adequately, providing needed seating, and housing the important tackle and small-tool lockers.

Photos show a level-running hull with remarkably little spray or bow-wave formation. The wide beam affords a length/beam ratio of 2.3:1 and stability to support a tower of better than minimal height. Operator's eye level standing in the tower is about equal to that of an operator on the flying bridge of a 45- to 50-foot conventional fishing cruiser. The boat works best as a fishing machine for anglers who sleep ashore between trips or operate from a larger cruising vessel. It is small enough for minimal initial and operational costs, yet large enough to fish anywhere at sea during daylight.

Owner's Evaluation

Jack A. Gowan of Birmingham, Alabama, rates the performance of his Dusky 26-foot Sport Fisherman as follows:

Fuel economy	Super to good
Handling qualities (below)	Good
Handling qualities (tower)	Super
Seaworthiness	Good
Overall design	Super
Cruising comfort	Super
Fishing efficiency	Super
Ease of maintenance	Good
Investment value	Good

Gowan operates in the Gulf of Mexico out of the northwest Florida port of Destin, running 400 hours a year. His boat's mechanical performance was given

The cockpit is large enough for a full-sized fighting chair. Spare rods are stored in a special holder behind the engine compartment. (Photo by Dusky Marine Inc.)

earlier in this section. (He also owns a 46-foot Bertram cruiser.) He splits his operating time equally between cruising and trolling and does not define what he means by cruising. He calls the Dusky "very close" to being his ultimate fishing machine.

"This is a super well-made boat. I think it is an excellent buy. With good maintenance it should prove a very good investment. It has lots of guts and speed. I feel safe in this boat."

Standard Equipment

Hydraulic steering
Deck and hull laminated together
Self-bailing cockpit
104-gal aluminum fuel tank
Chrome-on-brass tank fill and vent
Electric fuel gauge
Flush fuel fill with overboard vent
Heavy-duty fiberglass exhaust system
    and mufflers
Bronze propellers, rudders, and struts
SS shafts, 1¼-in dia.
Underwater fittings electrically bonded
Custom steering wheel
Windshield and handrail on console
Full instrumentation and switches
Custom engine box with cushions for
    4 adults

Access hatches to all mechanical
    components
SS bow rail
Twin fishing chairs with gimbals
Chrome-on-brass cleats fore and aft
Bow chocks
Navigation lights
Marine batteries (2)
Perko chrome-on-brass rodholders (2)
Full 7-ft cuddy cabin
Underbunk storage
Bunk cushions and cabin light
Rope locker with hatch
Teak cabin door
Teak cockpit step pads
SS screws
Waterline boottop

Installed Optional Equipment

Tower with hydraulic steering
    and Morse controls
Teak radio compartment mounted
    to tower
Tower cushioned seats
Tower sun top
Half-tower
Auxiliary 60-gal fuel tanks (2)
Twin baitwells, aft
Large baitwell, forward
Pompanette 60-in insulated fishbox
Pompanette 48-in insulated fishbox
Cigarette lighter
Electric air horn
Chain deck pipe
Springline cleats
Teak dive-swim platform
Teak bow pulpit with SS handrail
Teak deckplate, aft
Perko rodholders
Pompanette SS rodholders
Spotlight
Cockpit gunwale lights

Automatic pilot
Motor box options
    Fire extinguisher and teak-trimmed
        cabinet
    Insulated bait box with teak cover
    Tackle drawers with teak doors
    Storage locker with teak doors
    Teak 6-rod rod rack
    Teak beverage holders
    Teak knife holder
SS sink with freshwater tank

Docking lights
Compass: Danforth, Maximum, or Richie

Outrigger options
    Tower center outrigger
    Tower lifting eye
    Perko heavy-duty 18-ft poles mounted
        to deck
    Perko Marlin, mounted on tower
    Perko Gamefisher mounted on deck,
        tower brace

Perko outrigger spreaders (per pair)
Pompanette Junior, SS, mounted on tower
Pompanette outrigger spreaders

Gas-vapor detector system
Engine hour meters
Dytech SeaTemp gauge
Dytech digital tachometer in lieu of standard
Perko sea strainers
Oil drain hose
Oil filter relocator
Heavy-duty Fram water separator fuel filters
Automatic bilge pump, aft
Boat levelers
Propellers, extra pair
Spare prop shaft compartment with shaft

Saltwater washdown, pump and hose
115 v. AC inlet with outlet
Bottom paint
Deluxe transom lettering
Twin battery system
Triple battery system
Quad battery system
Pompanette Y2RC fighting chair, gimbal, rodholders
Coaming cushion, aft
Custom striping
Canvas
  Console cover
  Motor box cover
  Chair cover
  Full sprayshield with side curtains
  After cover mounted to tower
  Tower sun top

UNIFLITE 28-FOOT SALTY DOG

Designer	Uniflite, Inc.
Builder	Uniflite, Inc. P.O. Box 1095 Bellingham, WA 98225 P.O. Box 68 Swansboro, NC 28584
Construction	Fiberglass hull, decks, and super-structure. Fire-resistant resin used throughout.

Specifications

Length overall	28 ft 2 in	8.60 m
Length, waterline	24 ft 5 in	7.46 m
Beam, maximum	10 ft 10 in	3.32 m
Draft	34 in	0.86 m
Cockpit area	100 sq ft	9.3 m²
Freeboard forward	4 ft 2 in	1.28 m
Freeboard aft	3 ft	0.92 m

Continued

Rigged for serious offshore fishing, the 28-foot Uniflite Salty Dog shows excellent dynamic lift and very little thrown water while running at 25 knots. This is one of the few boats of its type offered with optional twin- or single-engine inboard power installation. (Photo by Uniflite Inc.)

Specifications *continued*

Height, waterline to windshield	8 ft	2.44 m
Headroom, cabin	6 ft 3 in	1.91 m
Weight, normal	9,000 lb	4,091 kg
Fuel capacity	150 gal	1,191 l
Water capacity	30 gal	113 l
Sleeping accommodations	2	

Power options
   Twin Crusader 220-hp gasoline
   Single Crusader 270-hp gasoline
   Other options by arrangement

Performance

With single 270-hp Crusader gasoline engine, 3-blade propeller, cupped, 18-in dia. × 19-in pitch, 1.91:1 reduction gear.

Top speed	25 kn (28.5 mph) @ 4200 rpm
Top fuel rate	22 gph

At trolling speed the deep-V hull makes a wide, deep, frothy wake of the kind usually attractive to ocean game fish. The cockpit can accommodate two fishing chairs or a full-size fighting chair. A small radar antenna could be placed between the sun dodger and the tower station deck. (Photo by Uniflite Inc.)

Top fuel economy	1.14 nmpg (1.30 mpg)
Top fuel endurance	6.8 hr
Top-speed range	170 nm (194 mi)
Cruising speed	18 kn (20.5 mph) @ 3200 rpm
Cruising fuel rate	10 gph
Cruising fuel economy	1.70 nmpg (1.94 mpg)
Cruising endurance	15 hr
Cruising-speed range	270 nm (308 mi)

With twin 220-hp Crusader gasoline engines, 3-blade propellers, cupped, 16-in dia. × 14-in pitch, 1.52:1 reduction gear.

Top speed	31 kn (35.3 mph) @ 4200 rpm
Top fuel rate	38 gph
Top fuel economy	0.82 nmpg (0.93 mpg)
Top fuel endurance	4.0 hr
Top-speed range	124 nm (141 mi)

Cruising speed	22 kn (25.1 mph) @ 3000 rpm
Cruising fuel rate	26 gph
Cruising fuel economy	0.85 nmpg (0.96 mpg)
Cruising endurance	5¾ hr
Cruising-speed range	127 nm (145 mi)

The tables above are from Uniflite performance reports with direct interpolation to provide endurance and range. They suggest that this boat, with comparable diesel power, could probably sustain cruising speeds of 18 to 20 knots with a maximum cruising range of well over 400 miles.

Description

Uniflite's 28-foot Salty Dog model began life a number of years ago as a modification of a hull developed for the U.S. government as a small, fast utility boat. Its usefulness as a competitive sport or commercial fisherman soon become apparent. The hull is a modified deep-V, with accent on ruggedness rather than style. But equipped with outriggers, chairs, and a light tower, the little vessel quickly takes on the look of a fisherman's boat. It is interesting to note the apparently greater mechanical efficiency of the single-screw model over the twin-screw model, suggested by the performance tables. Additional engine weight may be the determining factor here.

The large, open cockpit area is broken by a raised deck over the engine compartment. This greatly increases the effective open deck area. A large fish-well hatch is located in the center of the after cockpit space. This might have to be bridged by a sturdy truss member if a fighting chair with footrest were to be installed. Otherwise, two permanent or portable fishing chairs and a pair of forward jump seats would provide adequate trolling seating for up to four anglers. The cockpit deck is nonskid and self-bailing.

Down below, a commodious V-berth occupies the forward end of the cabin, with an enclosed head and locker to port and a small galley to starboard. No attempt is made to cram more into the living quarters than will serve a nautical couple in comfort. The interior decor and finish are color-keyed in hand-rubbed wood grain, wood paneling, and accent fabrics. A removable triangular table can be set up in the space between the feet of the V-berths.

The Salty Dog is essentially a softtop boat with the helmsman's station elevated for better visibility. Controls and instruments are grouped for easy use and instant reading. Either single or twin engines in gasoline or diesel can be accommodated. The most economical power, in terms of fuel, would probably be a single diesel in the 160- to 220-hp range, with about 2:1 reduction gear. A cruising fuel economy of 2 to 2½ mpg at 15 knots or more should be possible, and if the speed were held down to 8 or 9 knots, fast trolling speed, the fuel economy should exceed 3 mpg, or nearly 500 miles for the fuel capacity of 150 gallons.

With a very generous beam of 10 feet on its 28-foot length, the boat has excellent stability and can easily carry a tower. The cockpit layout lends itself to stand-up, light-tackle fishing, tournament style, with four rods worked out of a "rocket launcher" type of multiple rodholder set in the center of the cockpit. The deep forefoot gives a soft ride in head seas and the generous deadrise provides excellent directional stability in beam and following seas. However it is used, the Salty Dog is one boat that thoroughly lives up to the reputation of its name.

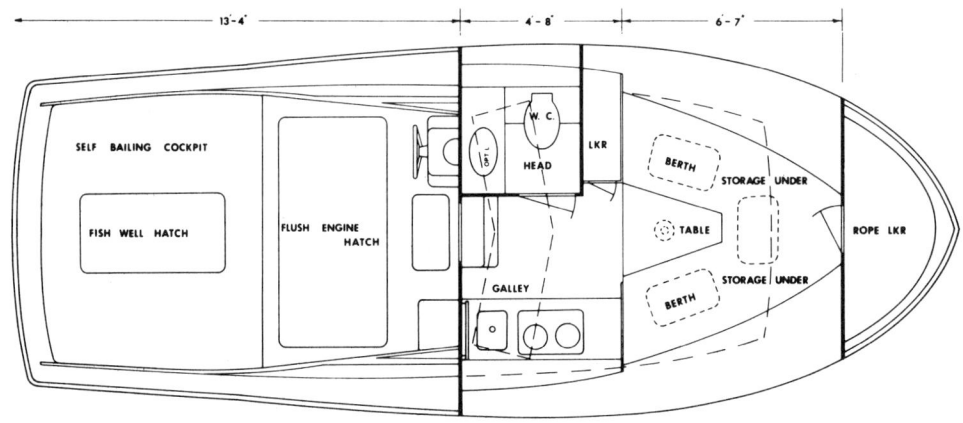

Owners' Evaluations

Three owners have provided evaluation reports on the 28-foot Uniflite Salty Dog. They are John Trulin, Huntington Beach, California; Everett Firth, Dover, Massachusetts; and John P. O'Neal, Groves, Texas. This brings in opinions from the Pacific, the Atlantic, and the Gulf of Mexico. Their comparative evaluations follow.

	Trulin	*Firth*	*O'Neal*
Fuel economy	Good	Good	Super
Handling qualities	Good	Super	Super
Seaworthiness	Super	Super	Super
Overall design	Super	Super	Good
Cruising comfort	Good	Super	Good
Fishing efficiency	Super	Super	Super
Ease of maintenance	Super	Super	Super
Investment value	Super	Good	Good

Trulin's boat is powered with twin 225-hp Chrysler gasoline motors for a top speed of 38 mph and cruising speed of 27 mph. He estimates maximum range at 200 miles at 20 mph, with a usable fuel capacity of 210 gallons. He operates an average of 120 hours per year, 40 percent cruising and 60 percent game-fish trolling, fishing Catalina and the ocean areas off southern California.

In a covering letter he states, "I feel that the Uniflite Salty Dog is one of the finest small sportfishing boats on the market. My boat is three years old and, with a bucket of soap and water and an hour's work, it looks like the day I took delivery. This means no rust in the engine compartment and no corrosion topside. At the end of three years, my boat is worth more than I paid for it, so at least this investment has kept up with inflation."

Firth's Salty Dog is used primarily in the Boon Island region of the coast of Maine. It is powered with twin 270-hp Crusader gasoline motors for a top speed of 37 mph and a cruising speed of 28 mph. Firth estimates a cruising range of 200 miles at 28 mph with 150 gallons of fuel available. Asked how he evaluates this boat in comparison with others he has owned, he states, "Best yet — in its class."

At the time of this writing, John P. O'Neal of Groves, Texas, had just taken delivery of a 1979 Salty Dog and noted that he had not had time to make a long-term evaluation. He claimed a top speed of over 25 mph and a cruising speed of 20 mph with a single Caterpillar Model 3208 diesel of about 210 hp. He had not had time to estimate ultimate cruising range. His boat is used in the Gulf of Mexico for game fishing and family cruising. He regards the Salty Dog as his ultimate fishing machine. Quite interesting is the detailed list of qualities that he seeks in a boat, ranked in order of priority.

1. Seaworthiness	5. Ease of maintenance
2. Fishing efficiency	6. Fuel economy
3. Handling ability	7. Cruising range
4. Personal comfort	8. Investment value

In his report, O'Neal is careful to explain that the list of priorities is not a scorecard of his evaluation of the Salty Dog (his score was given earlier), but rather his personal outlook on the qualities that make up any good boat. To him, seaworthiness is the single most important quality. Investment value happens, in his opinion, to fall at the bottom of the list.

Standard Equipment

Hull

Gunwale guard, heavy-duty
Hull drain plug
One-piece, hand-laid, fire-retardant hull
Shipping cradle

Deck

Anchor combination package
    Danforth anchor, 20-ft chain
    Deck pipe and chocks
    200-ft, ½-in nylon anchor rode
Bow rail
Cleats (4), chocks (2), SS
Emergency escape hatch, forward
Flagstaff with socket
Fuel deckplates with chains
One-piece, nonskid deck surfaces
Deluxe handrails, SS

Superstructure

Door hardware, chrome-plated
Windows, tinted safety glass with screens
Windows, cabin, sliding style
Windshield wiper (1)

Interior Furnishings

Carpeting, padded
Cushions, V-berths, foam-filled
Drapes
Hanging locker
Hull liner, deluxe
Vinyl headliner
Paneling and joinerwork, teak
Table, V-berth

Galley-Dinette

Countertops, heat- and stain-resistant
Dish and food lockers
Large galley counter
Icebox
Sink, SS
Stove, 2-burner alcohol
Utensil and cutlery drawers

Head

Marine toilet, Handi-Head
Mirror
Carpeted floor covering

Safety Equipment

Bilge blower (gasoline only)
Bilge pumps, automatic electric (2)
Fire extinguishers (2)
International navigation lights
Ship's bell, trumpet horn
Shutoff valves on all underwater through-hull fittings

Propulsion and Controls

Alternators, 12 v. DC
Approved all-copper-line fuel system with selector valves and filter

Controls, Morse
Compass, 4-in
Propellers, cupped
Engines, as per order (see options)
Engine mounts, vibration-eliminating
Fuel filters and gauges
Heat exchanger, freshwater cooling
Mufflers, watercooled exhaust
Instruments
    Oil-pressure gauges
    Tachometers
    Voltmeters
    Water-temperature gauges
Reduction gears, as required

Seawater strainers, cooling system
Self-aligning stuffing boxes
Shafts, 1¼- or 1¾-in, SS

Electrical-Mechanical

Battery, 60-amp, heavy-duty
Battery boxes with hold-downs
Circuit breakers on AC and DC systems
Color-coded and marked wiring harness
Electrical system fully grounded
Freshwater system, 30-gal capacity
Lighting, 12 v. DC throughout
Zinc sacrificial electrodes

Optional Equipment

Deck and Hull

Boarding platform
Cleats, springline (2)
Fishbox, cockpit type
Rodholders, flush-mounted
Stern mooring-line hawsepipes (2)
Outriggers, Lee's Jr., with 18-ft poles
Rails, SS, cockpit
Bow roller
Hardtop
Seat, companion, with footrest
Windshield wiper, extra

Interior Furnishings

Cushion, V-berth, fill-in
Refrigerator, Norcold #704 AC/DC,
    4.5 cu ft
Stove, 2-burner alcohol/electric, takes
    shore power
Stove, 3-burner propane with oven
Marine toilet, Microphor, with Raritan
    water closet
Marine toilet, Handi-Head, discharge kit
Head vanity cabinet, sink, Formica top

Electrical-Mechanical-Propulsion

Hour meters, gas or diesel
Trim tabs
Battery isolator system (twin-screw)
Battery switch-over control (twin-screw,
    gas)
Cigar lighters
Dockside power, 30-amp, 115 v. AC,
    50-ft. cable

Fan, defroster
Heater, space, hot-water
Heater, space, electric (115 v. AC, dock
    power)
Washdown pump, seawater
Pressure water system
Hot-water system, 6-gal (must have
    pressure water system and 115 v. AC
    dockside power)

Safety, Navigation, Communication

Alarm, Uniflite Monitor for gas, TS
    (fumes, water temperature, oil pressure,
    gear oil)
Fathometer, Raytheon, DE-738
Hailer, Ray 250 with intercom horn
Radio, VHF/FM, Ray 50A, 25-watt, with
    antenna
Radio, VHF/FM, Ray 48A, with antenna
Stereo, AM/FM, 8-track, with 2 speakers

Miscellaneous

Convertible softtop
Clear backdrop with 4 zippers
Side curtains
Water delivery kit
Mooring lines, 30-ft (4)
Life jackets (6 adult)
Life ring (1)
Emergency flares
Fenders (3)
First-aid kit

DYER 29 OFFSHORE BASS BOAT

Designer	Nicholas Potter
Builder	The Anchorage Inc. 57 Miller Street Warren, RI 02885
Construction	Fiberglass hull and deck, teak/mahogany trim.

Specifications

Length overall	28 ft 6 in	8.69 m
Length, waterline	26 ft	7.93 m
Beam, maximum	9 ft 5 in	2.88 m
Draft	2 ft 6 in	0.76 m
Cockpit area	100 sq ft	9.30 m²
Freeboard forward	4 ft 9 in	1.45 m
Freeboard aft	3 ft 3 in	1.00 m
Height, waterline to windshield top	6 ft 6 in	2.00 m
Weight (approx)	6,700 lb	3,045 kg
Fuel capacity	90 gal	340 l
Water capacity	(optional)	
Sleeping accommodations	2	
Power options (see performance data)		
Gasoline 170 to 330 hp		
Diesel 115 to 210 hp		

Performance

The following comparative data are from Dyer specifications, speeds in knots converted to mph. All are single-screw.

Power (gasoline)	*Top Speed*	*Cruising Speed*
Chrysler, 318 cu in, 225 hp	21.66 mph	18.80 mph
Chrysler, 360 cu in, 250 hp	23.37 mph	19.95 mph
MerCruiser, 350 cu in, 250 hp	22.80 mph	19.38 mph
MerCruiser, 454 cu in, 330 hp	26.22 mph	22.80 mph
Power (diesel)		
Ford 6, 380 cu in, 120 hp	15.96 mph	13.68 mph
Detroit 4-53, 2-cycle, 140 hp	20.52 mph	18.24 mph
Perkins 6, turbo, 160 hp	22.23 mph	19.38 mph
Perkins 6, turbo, 185 hp	23.94 mph	20.52 mph

Single-engine economy with speeds to 26 mph is an attractive quality of the Dyer 29 Offshore Bass Boat. This model sports a light fighting chair, outriggers, and a gin pole mounted through the port covering board. (Photo by Bill Harwell)

The following data are from Dyer "as reported by owners of Dyer 29-footers" (knots converted to mph).

Power (gasoline)	*Cruising Speed*	*RPM*	*GPH*
Crusader 308, 220 hp	17.10 mph	2800	6
Chrysler 318, 225 hp	17.10 mph	2800	8
Crusader 454	20.52 mph	2800	8.5
Crusader 454*	15.96 mph	2450	6.5

Power (diesel)			
Lehman Ford 380, 120 hp**	"Used 220 gal in 100 hr = 2.2 gph"		
Perkins 354, 185 hp***	20.52 mph	2250	4-4½
Perkins 354, 185 hp	17.10 mph	2000	3
Volvo TAMD60, 192 hp	17.10 mph	2500	4
Volvo TAMD60, 192 hp	15.96 mph	2400	3

*"He used 94 gal in 15.6 hr = 6.03 gph: 65% @ 2800 rpm, 35% trolling @ 1500 rpm."

**"GPH quoted is "average for all kinds of running."

***"On any given day, averaged under 3 gph in combination fast cruising, trolling, and slow cruising."

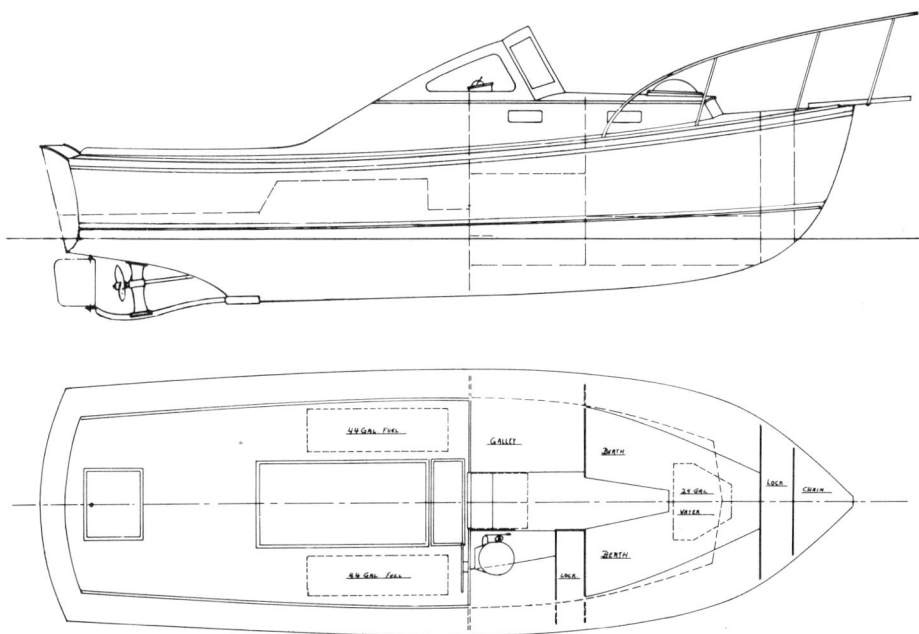

From the data supplied, it can be seen that at the average cruising speed of 17.10 mph (15 knots as quoted by Dyer), the average fuel consumption for gasoline power is about 7 gph, and for diesel about 3½ gph. This suggests that, with a single diesel of the types states, an average cruising speed of 15 knots would provide a maximum range of 385 nautical miles on 90 gallons of fuel, with an endurance of more than 25 hours at that speed.

The fuel ratio of 2:1 for gasoline versus diesel power at the same speed in the Dyer 29 may sound optimistic to some readers. The author can state from his own experience in switching from gasoline power to diesel in a boat of generally the same speed and power requirements that the diesel installation did prove to consume exactly 50 percent of the previous gasoline rate under identical conditions of hours, load, and speed.

Description

The Dyer 29-foot Offshore Bass Boat is one of those great nautical mutations — a small, economical fishing boat that can perform well in both the bass rips inshore and along the 40-fathom curve, looking for big game. Its hull, perfected by The Anchorage under the guidance of the late Nicholas Potter, takes advantage of the inherent efficiency of the traditional single-screw power installation. Down East influence is strong in the sharp, deep forefoot, lively sheer, and generous transom, but the fiberglass construction is strictly modern, reflecting rugged simplicity in design and execution.

The long, built-down keel gives unusual directional stability and a good "grip on the water." The Dyer 29's ability to handle head seas is legendary, and the hull is essentially level-riding at all speeds. The boat is ideal for an experienced angler who likes to fish singlehanded, yet large enough to have earned popularity as a small fishing charter boat licensed for up to six passengers.

Two versions of the standard boat are available. One is a traditional New England bass boat with flush forward deck, minimal cruising accommodations, and maximum fishing space. The other features a small cabin trunk forward with two V-berths, a toilet enclosure, and a tiny but efficient galley. Both models come with an open windshield that can be protected with a sun or Bimini top. Either will take outriggers, two fishing chairs or one light fighting chair, and even a low tower. Enclosing the space under the tower with clear plastic curtains provides an excellent, fully transparent "deckhouse" for weather protection at little cost of weight or capital outlay.

The single engine is placed in a generous box in the center of the cockpit, with plenty of walk space on either side. Marine engines appear to receive attention in direct relationship to their accessibility. The Dyer owner and his engine are on very friendly terms. Fuel tanks are located amidships, port and starboard, placing this variable load at the center of buoyancy. The fuel load of 90 gallons represents less than 10 percent of the normal weight of the boat, yet it is good for at least 30 hours of continuous, variable-speed operation at better than planing speed.

Owners' Evaluations

Captain Jack Reynolds of Westport, Massachusetts, has operated a 1972 Dyer 29 as a charter fishing boat for several years. His performance evaluation is:

Fuel economy	Super
Handling qualities	Good
Seaworthiness	Super
Overall design	Good
Cruising comfort	Good
Fishing efficiency	Super
Ease of maintenance	Fair
Investment value	(not stated)

Captain Reynolds gives his top speed as 21 mph with a 255-hp, 351-cubic-inch Ford conversion gasoline motor. Cruising speed is 15 or 16 knots. Annual use averages 2,000 hours and 15,000 miles or more. Maximum range is given as 250 miles at 15 mph for a fuel rate of less than 5½ gph, or slightly under 3 mpg at that speed.

Captain Reynolds says, "For personalized, intricate bass fishing, the boat is very good." He states that he is primarily a commercial fisherman using hook and line under Massachusetts laws to take striped bass and other fish.

Another owner, Saul S. Feinstein of East Greenwich, Rhode Island, gives this evaluation report:

Fuel economy	Super
Handling qualities	Super
Seaworthiness	Super
Overall design	Super
Cruising comfort	Good

A low tower and fighting chair make an efficient big-game fisherman of the Bluebill. *The side-mounted ginpole can be shipped when not needed. (Photo by Staff Carroll, courtesy of The Anchorage, Inc.)*

Fishing efficiency	Super
Ease of maintenance	Super
Investment value	Super

Feinstein's boat, *Fein Time*, does 25 knots top speed and 18 knots cruising with a 350-hp Crusader gasoline engine, operating 200 to 250 hours on the average and 1,500 to 2,000 miles per year. He spends 20 percent of his time running and 80 percent trolling for game fish. He gives his maximum range as 120 miles at 18 knots. He calls the boat his ultimate fishing machine, but he would trade up in size and price range if he were to sell it.

Dyer bass boat High Noon *is wide open and has a cuddy cabin under a flush forward deck. The hull is dry and level-running, with excellent dynamic stability. (Photo by John Hopf, courtesy of The Anchorage, Inc.)*

He rates the boat's qualities of seaworthiness and handling ability as exceptional. He says that if fuel is available in the future, he will continue to fish at his present rate.

Standard Equipment

Mechanical and Electrical

Chrysler V-8, 318-cu-in, 225-hp,
  1.9:1 reduction gear
Water intake and strainer
Bronze rudder, propeller, shaft, strut
  with ball-joint bearing
Full pipe skeg and inboard stuffing box
Twin mufflers, risers, wet exhausts
45-gal Monel fuel tanks (2)
U.L.-approved shutoffs, fuel filter,
  fuel gauge
Morse Command II steering, 20-in
  destroyer-type wheel

Morse Twin S clutch and throttle controls
12 v. DC electrical system, alternator,
  bonded ground
12 v. DC batteries, master switch,
  instrumentation (2)
Bilge exhaust fan, manual bilge pump,
  windshield wiper

Cabin Equipment

6 ft 6 in V-berths, vinyl cushions,
  stowage under (2)
Enclosed head with portable-type WC

Galley with Formica counter, 4.5-cu-ft
   icebox, dish bins, SS sink, water pump,
   24-gal water tank
Electric cabin lights
Translucent hatch over bunks

Deck Equipment

Marinium bow chocks, bow cleat, spring
   and stern cleats
12-lb Danforth Hi-Tensile anchor and
   hawsepipe
150-ft, ½-in nylon yacht anchor warp

Docking lines (4), fenders (2)
Safety glass in windshield
SS bilge ventilators
Sound-insulated engine box with backrest
   and vinyl cushions
International running and anchor lights
Bell, freon horn, boathook, life vests (3),
   Type IV preserver (1)
2½-lb dry-chemical fire extinguishers (2)
All wooden trim, teak
Companionway lock

The Anchorage does not mass-produce its boats, although the hulls are identical units from the molds. Because of low unit production and close attention to detail work, they are able to build a large portion of personalized finish work into each vessel. There is a considerable variety of power available within the single-screw arrangement, both gasoline and diesel. The result is a fleet of generally similar but highly individual boats of excellent efficiency, good speed for the power, and very good operating economy.

Cockpit of a Pacemaker 38-foot tournament fisherman. (Morris Rosenfeld from Yachting)

SECTION TWO
Boats 31 to 50 feet

BERTRAM 31-FOOT SPORT FISHERMAN

Designer	Bertram Yacht/C. Raymond Hunt
Builder	Bertram Yacht 3663 N.W. 21st Street Miami, FL 33142
Construction	Fiberglass hull, decks and superstructure.

Specifications

Length overall	30 ft 7 in	9.33 m
Length, waterline	28 ft 3 in	8.62 m
Beam, maximum	11 ft 2 in	3.42 m
Draft, propeller	2 ft 8 in	0.82 m
Cockpit area	100 sq ft	9.30 m²
Freeboard forward	3 ft 11 in	1.19 m
Freeboard aft	2 ft 6 in	0.76 m
Heights above waterline		
Flying bridge windshield	9 ft 9 in	2.97 m
Bimini top	12 ft 8 in	3.91 m
Weight, normal	10,300 lb	4,672 kg
Fuel capacity	222 gal	840 l
Water capacity	18 gal	68 l
Sleeping accommodations	4	

Power options

Twin 233-hp MerCruiser gasoline
Twin 330-hp MerCruiser gasoline
Twin 140-hp GM 4-53N diesel
Twin 195-hp Cummins V-504 diesel
Twin 210-hp Caterpillar 3208 diesel

Performance

Power option	Speed	Range
Twin 233-hp MerCruiser gasoline	33 mph (49 kph)	250 mi (375 km)
Twin 330-hp MerCruiser gasoline	40 mph (60 kph)	235 mi (350 km)
Twin 4-53N GM diesel	27 mph (40 kph)	420 mi (626 km)
Twin V-504 Cummins diesel	31 mph (46 kph)	375 mi (560 km)
Twin 3208 Caterpillar diesel	31 mph (46 kph)	375 mi (560 km)

Typical fuel rates at full speed

Fuel rate @ 33 mph (gasoline)	1.13 mpg (0.45 km/l)
Fuel rate @ 27 mph (diesel)	1.89 mpg (0.75 km/l)

A classic in its own time, the trim, slim Bertram 31 is unmistakable whether you find it in Biscayne Bay or French Polynesia. The deep-V hull has great directional stability and easy motion in rough water. Speeds to 40 mph are possible with twin 330-hp engines. (Photo by Jim McNitt)

Speeds and cruising range are test averages and may vary among similar boats depending on weight, engine condition, and bottom condition. Recommended cruising speeds average 70 percent of top speed for gasoline power, and 80 percent to 85 percent of top speed for diesel power. Cruising ranges are calculated on cruising speed.

Description

The temptation was strong, when planning this book, to put the Bertram 31-foot Sport Fisherman in a special category for classic boats. Certainly it has the qualifications — popularity, longevity, durability, and a unique, almost personal, image. Over 2,000 31-footers have been launched in the past 20 years. But the Bertram 31 is also a current best-seller in the Bertram line, still very much alive as a working sportfishing model.

Four versions of the basic 31-foot hull are now being offered. The slight variations in weight and superficial measurements show up in the following table.

	Hardtop	Sport Fisherman	Flying-Bridge Cruiser	Bahia Mar
Length	30 ft 7 in	30 ft 7 in	30 ft 7 in	30 ft 7 in
Beam	11 ft 2 in	11 ft 2 in	11 ft 2 in	11 ft 2 in
Draft (propeller)	2 ft 7½ in	2 ft 8¼ in	2 ft 9 in	2 ft 9 in
Waterline to cockpit deck	11½ in	11 in	11 in	12 in
Maximum height	6 ft 3 in	9 ft 9½ in	9 ft 9 in	7 ft 5 in
Weight (approx)	9,400 lb	10,300 lb	10,600 lb	9,400 lb
Cockpit	110 sq ft	110 sq ft	110 sq ft	147 sq ft
Fuel capacity	222 gal	222 gal	222 gal	222 gal
Water capacity	18 gal	18 gal	18 gal	18 gal
Berths	4	4	4	2

The method of fiberglass construction has remained relatively unchanged, although improvements have been made with respect to glass material, resins, curing, and finish. When asked if hull changes were contemplated to cure the boat's tendency to be a bit wet in head-sea conditions, a Bertram Yacht official smiled and said, "We'd like to, but every time we plan a change we find ourselves back-ordered to the point that we just cannot shut down the production."

That the Bertram 31-footer is highly competitive in today's market can be seen from the 1979 price schedule for the Sport Fisherman model.

Power	Price
Twin 330-hp MerCruiser gasoline	$47,515
Twin 140-hp GM 4-53N diesel	$60,340
Twin 195-hp Cummins 504 diesel	$66,830
Twin 210-hp Caterpillar 3208 diesel	$75,595

When the first Bertram 31-foot Sport Fisherman came out in the early 1960s it was considered a very advanced small offshore boat. The radical deep-V hull required more power for the same speed than some conventional V-hulls, but performance in head and following seas was outstanding. Equally important was the

Low to the water, the cockpit of the Bertram 31 is ideal for light-tackle sailfishing where the emphasis is on tagging and releasing fish not intended for the taxidermist. Chrome cockpit safety rail is unique. Some owners add a padded strip to the rail for comfort. (Photo by Jim McNitt)

boat's quickly proved ability to raise and hold game fish behind the baits. The boat very soon proved its worth in tournament fishing as well as its growing popularity with a rapidly expanding host of family fishermen, who saw the boat as the answer to their prayers.

Seakeeping ability, together with good looks, ease of maintenance, and a realistic price, won the Bertram 31 high regard among professional charter fishermen and owners of high-quality fishing resorts. The famous club at Piñas Bay, Panama, for example, maintained a fleet of Bertram 31-footers from its inception. Over the years, the model has had great appeal to first-time, offshore-boat owners, being big enough to cruise four friendly people, yet small enough to bring initial and operating costs within reason. For many it has proved the "ultimate fishing machine."

One such owner is Ernest "Bud" Swenson Jr., of Fort Lauderdale, Florida. Swenson reports:

> I bought my present 31-foot Bertram in 1973 and have no intention of selling it in the near future. Recently I turned down offers of $6,000 more than I paid for the boat, so, as you can see, the investment in the boat is like having money in the bank and collecting interest.
>
> One of the most important assets of a good fishing boat is a large, roomy cockpit. With 110 square feet of area, the Bertram 31-footer has more cockpit in

proportion to overall size than most larger boats. Another point I like is the low freeboard, which allows me to slide a very large fish over the side of the boat with no great problem.

Another very important point is safety. The Bertram 31 is a tremendous rough-water boat with slow, easy motion and absolute mechanical control. Finally, it is a wonderful boat for raising game fish. I don't mean just one freak hull out of production. I mean all the 31-footers that come off the line.

Swenson gave what looked like an unbiased performance evaluation, checking eight major factors for the scores of Super, Good, Fair, and Poor.

Fuel economy	Good
Handling qualities	Super
Seaworthiness	Super
Overall design	Super
Cruising comfort	Fair
Fishing efficiency	Super
Ease of maintenance	Super
Investment value	Super

Swenson reports a top speed of 40 mph and cruising speed of 28 mph with twin 325-hp MerCruiser gasoline motors. He claims an average of 150 hours of annual use, with 60 percent of the time spent cruising and 40 percent spent trolling. His area is South Florida and the Bahama Islands. Against other sportfishing boats he has owned, he rates this one "the finest."

Writing in the January 1971 issue of *Yachting* in celebration of the tenth anniversary of the original Bertram *Moppie* production, the author had this to say about the Bertram 31-footer when the late Captain Tom Gifford brought one of the new boats to the fishing port of Montauk, New York:

> Aristotle Onassis bought one, some say, because Maria Callas wanted to go fishing. Dan Topping ordered one so he could go striper fishing after the World Series was finished and cure himself of talking like Casey Stengel. A canny old charter skipper, Tom Gifford, bought one because in his business he needed a fast, able, rough-water boat.
>
> Let me tell you what happened when Gifford brought his Bertram to Montauk. I was running a charter fishing boat then, and Tom had spent several summers at the eastern Long Island port with a small, fast, racing type of fisherman called *Stormy Petrel*. Tom liked speed and his name around Montauk before he acquired the Bertram was "Captain Kidney-Killer" because of the way he pounded around offshore.
>
> The day he arrived at the Deep Sea Club marina with the new *Stormy Petrel*, all decked out with a tuna tower, Bob Darenburg, the dockmaster, said, "What the hell do you expect to do this summer, Tom, go drilling for oil?"
>
> Of course Darenburg knew better, but a few of the clam diggers swore the tower was some sort of portable osprey's nest. The way the Bertram tamed the rough water off Montauk Point gave us local fishermen food for thought. A bunch of us would be rolling home from offshore in the late afternoon. An ebb tide would be racing out against the usual 25-knot summer sou'wester. We'd be twisting the spokes out of our steering wheels trying to hold a straight course in those short, steep following seas.

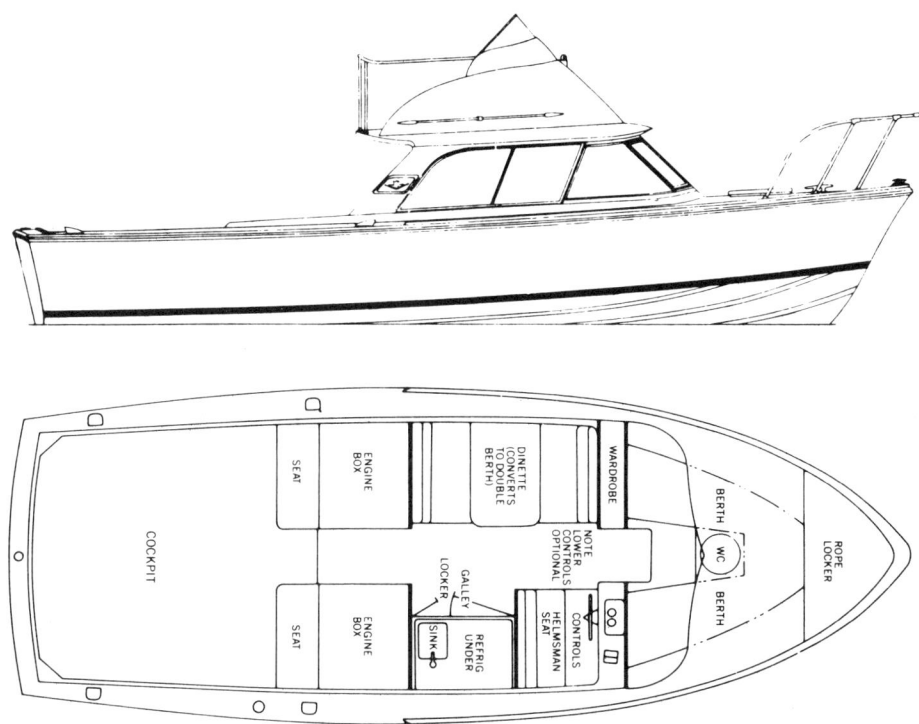

Along would come Gifford, barreling home like Valenzuela booting in a winner at Tropical Park. When he felt charitable he'd tip his cap and give us a bow as he went whizzing by. Once, when several of us were struggling to get our boats through the dangerous Elbow Rip off Montauk Light with a big groundswell running, he roared through at full throttle, combing what was left of his hair, just to show us that the Bertram could run that white water without a hand on the wheel. From our viewpoint it was pretty awful. . . .

But from the viewpoint of literally thousands of boat owners, Dick Bertram's original *Moppie* was the best thing that had happened to offshore fishermen since the invention of the outrigger.

The word "prepotency" describes what happened when a great-hearted little Vermont stallion named Justin Morgan left his indelible genetic stamp on a new breed of superior American work and saddle horses. It could be said that the rare, valuable gift of prepotency was at work when the original Bertram 31-foot Sport Fisherman was created.

A low profile and a saving of weight are achieved by placing the twin engines under slightly raised engine boxes in the forward end of the cockpit, boxes that also serve as seats. There is a step-down in deck level between the engine boxes, providing stepless entry into the low deckhouse. In the Sport Fisherman model, as in the Hardtop and Flying Bridge Cruisers, the deckhouse has a small galley to starboard and a dinette-berth to port. The galley has a refrigerator unit beneath the counter.

Lower controls are to starboard, forward of the galley area. These are optional, although a helmsman's seat is provided in this control space as a standard feature. A V-berth under the forward deck sleeps two, and the W.C. is located in the forward compartment. There is a small vertical wardrobe to port, opposite the lower helmsman's seat. Admittedly spartan, the accommodations of the Bertram 31-foot Sport Fisherman are intended primarily for daysailing and short weekend trips.

The cockpit is large enough to accommodate a fighting chair and two fishing chairs. Normal practice is to fish big game with the fighting chair alone and to fish small to medium game with two fishing chairs or a "rocket launcher" multiple rodholder where light tackle is used. A few Bertram 31-footers have been fitted with towers. Most owners prefer a Bimini top on the bridge and outriggers of untrussed or single-trussed type. The Bertram 31 is susceptible to weight-gain and adverse windage, as are most smaller sportfishing boats. The hull has plenty of reserve buoyancy, but there can be perceptible loss of speed if normal full-load limits are exceeded.

But with all its minor drawbacks, the Bertram 31 remains one of those rare, outstanding small fishing boats that set the style and tone of boats that follow. Like the Morgan horses of Vermont, the offspring of this boat, legitimate and illegitimate, bear an almost equine stamp that replicates from generation to generation.

Standard Equipment

Standard and optional equipment lists are essentially the same for the four models of the Bertram 31-footer.

General

Aft cleats (2)
Anchor, 13-lb, chock, deck pipe and line,
   ½-in × 150 ft
Batteries (2), 12 v., 140 Ah, GM and
   MerCruisers
Batteries (2), 12 v., 200 Ah, Cummins
   and Caterpillar
Battery paralleling switch
Bilge blowers (2)
Bilge pump, electric, automatic
Bow rail
Burgee staff with burgee
Cushions in forward cabin,
   6 ft 4 in bunks
Dinette with cushions, converts into
   double berth 6 ft 2½ in × 40 in
Docklines, nylon, ½-in × 25 ft (2)
Electric fuel gauge
Electric horn, dual trumpet
Engine hour meters (2)

Ensign staff and socket
Fire extinguishers (2)
Foredeck hatch
Fuel filters (2)
Galley with sink and 12 v. refrigerator
Hanging locker in forward cabin
Helmsman's seat
Hydraulic clutches
Instrumentation
   Ammeters (2)
   Oil pressure (2)
   Tachometer (2)
   Water temperature (2)
Life jackets (4)
Life ring
Manganese-bronze rudders
Manganese-bronze struts with Cutless
   rubber bearings
Mufflers, fiberglass, with Veloci-jet,®
   gasoline only

Nonskid deck
Opening cabin windows and windshield
Safety glass windshield and side windows
Ship's bell
Springline cleats (2)
SS and chrome hardware throughout
SS shafts
Stern chocks through deck (2)
Storage compartments in cockpit side
    liners
Toilet, Monomatic, dockside discharge
Valves on all through-hull fittings

Electrical

12 v. system with 2 alternators
Color-coded electrical wiring
Control panel with circuit breakers
Lighting
    Interior: 2 lights in forward cabin,
                2 lights in main cabin
Navigation lights

Other Special Features

Diesel power includes engine alarm
Sound-insulated engine boxes with
    maximum accessibility to engines

Optional Equipment

Deck Hardware

Anchor, 13-lb, extra
Cleat, bow, extra
Fender hooks, 4 each

Electrical

Alarm system, fire, bilge, oil pressure
    (diesel)
Alarm system, fire, bilge, oil pressure
    (gasoline)
Batteries, heavy-duty (2 each), in place
    of standard (standard with Cummins
    and Caterpillar)
Bilge pump, 12 v., automatic, additional
Converter, 40-amp
European shore power, with converter
Shore power, with line, 120 v., 30-amp,
    with 2 outlets
Windshield wipers (2 each)
Lights
    Docking lights, forward, flying bridge
        control
    Searchlight, portable
Electronics
    Radio ground plate, dual
    Synchronizer, Judson, diesel
    Synchronizer, Judson, gasoline

Interior

Equipment
    Controls, lower
    Holding tank, 10-gal (for use with
        standard toilet)
    Overboard discharge (for use with
        standard toilet)
    Toilet, Groco, electric with Lectra San
Furnishings
    Bulkhead with door
    Cushions, engine box, 3208 CAT (2)
    Cushions, engine box (2)
    Draperies, aft bulkhead
    Draperies, complete set (without aft
        bulkhead)
    Screen, foredeck hatch
    Screens, side windows
    Screens, windshield
    Screens for aft bulkhead
    Stove, alcohol, 2-burner, aluminum

Fishing Equipment

Fishbox, curved to fit transom, with or
    without circulating water
Fish chair, Pompanette, Q4
Fish chair, Pompanette, Q4L
Fish chair, Pompanette, Sailfish R-3
Outriggers, 4-ft, with 21-ft aluminum
    poles
Rodholders, flush-mounted (2 each)

Canvas

Bimini top, Dacron
Bimini top, vinyl
Cockpit cover, hardtop to transom
    (Vivatex)
Cover, compass, 3½-in, vinyl
Cover, compass, 5-in, vinyl
Cover, instrument, vinyl
Drop curtain, vinyl
Flying bridge cover, Dacron

Flying bridge cover, vinyl
Shipping cover, canvas
Sun awning, Dacron
Sun awning, vinyl
Windscreen, Bimini top to bridge,
  Dacron
Windscreen, Bimini top to bridge,
  vinyl
Windshield cover, Dacron

General

Anchor line, nylon, ½ in × 150 ft
Boathook, 8-ft, with holder
Cockpit steps, port and starboard mount
Compass, 3½-in, flush-mounted

Compass, 5-in, flush-mounted
Cradle
Dockline, nylon, ½ in × 25 ft
Dockline, nylon, ½ in × 38 ft
Fire extinguisher, 20-lb, CO_2, automatic
Freshwater cooling, 330 Merc
Paint, bottom, antifouling (blue only)
Propellers (2 extra)
Shaft, diesel (1 extra)
Shaft, gasoline (1 extra)
Transom steps
Trim tabs, 18-in
Washdown pump, with 10-ft hose
Zincs on shafts

PERFORMER 32-FOOT "STUART ANGLER" TOURNAMENT AND RAISED BRIDGE FISHERMEN

Designer	Stuart Angler
Builder	Performer Boats
Allfin Industries
1003 S.E. 17th Street
Fort Lauderdale, FL 33316
Construction	Hand-layup fiberglass hull, deck, and superstructure.

Specifications

Length overall	32 ft	9.76 m
Length, waterline	28 ft 1 in	8.57 m
Beam, maximum	11 ft	3.36 m
Draft	2 ft 6 in	0.76 m
Cockpit area	140 sq ft	13.0 m²
Freeboard forward	4 ft	1.22 m
Freeboard aft	3 ft	0.92 m
Height above waterline	6 ft	1.83 m
Weight, lightest version	6,000 lb	2,727 kg
Weight, heaviest version	10,000 lb	4,545 kg
Fuel capacity	200 gal	765 l
Water capacity	15 gal	57 l
Sleeping accommodations	2	

Continued

With speeds to 50 mph, Performer's 32-foot Stuart Angler Tournament Fisherman is designed to meet the needs of the competitive angler who fishes light tackle against time limits. (Photo by Performer Boats)

Specifications *continued*
   Power options (owner's selection, single- or twin-screw)
      270- to 350-hp Crusader gasoline
      210- to 240-hp Renault diesel
      260-hp Detroit diesel
      250-hp Caterpillar diesel
      270-hp Volvo diesel
      250-hp Cummins diesel
      196- to 277-hp SS diesel

Performance

Detailed performance data were not available for these two closely related models, but builder's literature cites a single-diesel model with a top speed of over 30 mph, and twin-engine boats with top speeds of 40 to 50 mph. From this information it can be deduced that the faster twin-screw models probably have a top-speed endurance of 4 to 5 hours and top-speed range in the neighborhood of 200 miles. Cruising speed of, say, 30 mph would probably give a cruising endurance of 8 to 10 hours and a cruising-speed range of 250 to 300 miles.

The single-diesel model mentioned could be considered to have a top-speed endurance of 13 to 15 hours and top-speed range of 400 to 450 miles. Cruising-speed endurance at 25 mph would be in the neighborhood of 20 hours with an ultimate range of nearly 500 miles at that speed.

At trolling speed, the wide, flat wake is the kind that sailfish seem to find attractive. This model's single chair could be replaced by a "rocket launcher" for tournament work. (Photo by Performer Boats)

Naturally, speed and range will depend considerably on the boat's load and wind resistance. Wind resistance of a low tower might cut top speeds by several knots, as would the weight of a full-sized fighting chair and other big-game fishing equipment. The Raised Bridge Fisherman model can be expected to weigh more than the Tournament model, as is shown by the normal weight span of 6,000 to 10,000 pounds.

Description

This remarkable fishing machine was first manufactured by the Stuart Angler Corp. and is now built by the Performer Company, which bought the original molds. Both the Stuart Angler Tournament and Raised Bridge Fisherman models are built around the same modified V-hull with sharp entry forward and flatter deadrise aft. The bow has lots of flare and molded-in spray deflectors, resulting in a smooth, dry ride.

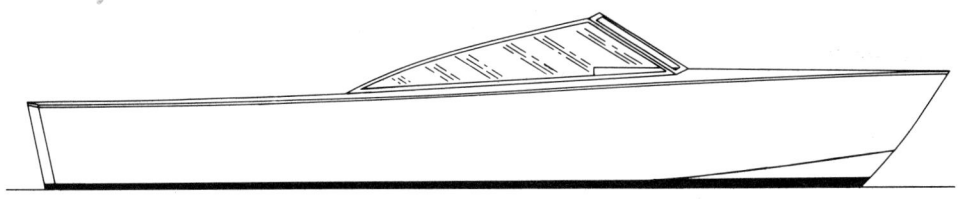

LOA 32' • BEAM 11' • DRAFT 2'6"

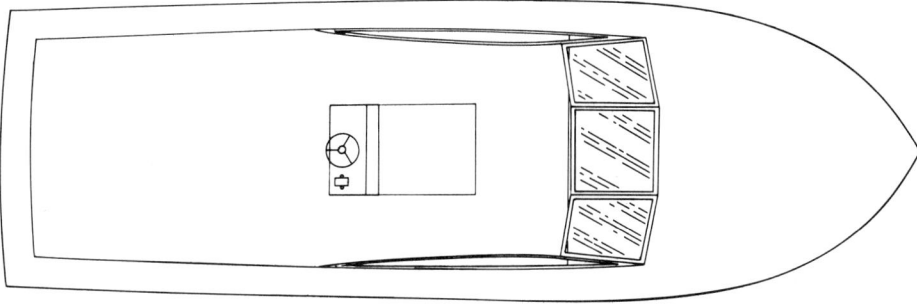

SINGLE SCREW

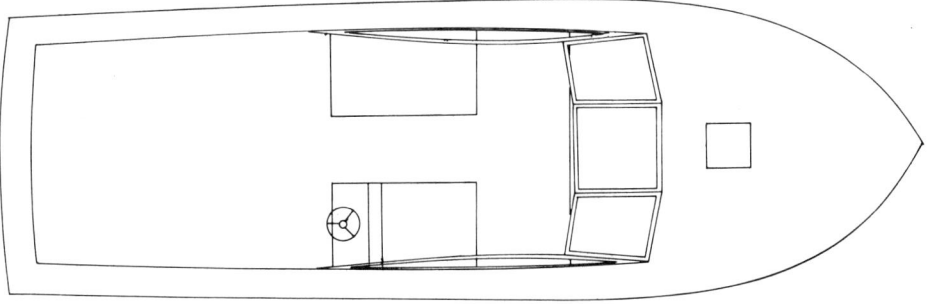

TWIN SCREW

The Tournament Fisherman has moderate beam and is available with single- or twin-screw power. The interior layout can be customized to meet individual owners' requirements. (Courtesy of Performer Boats)

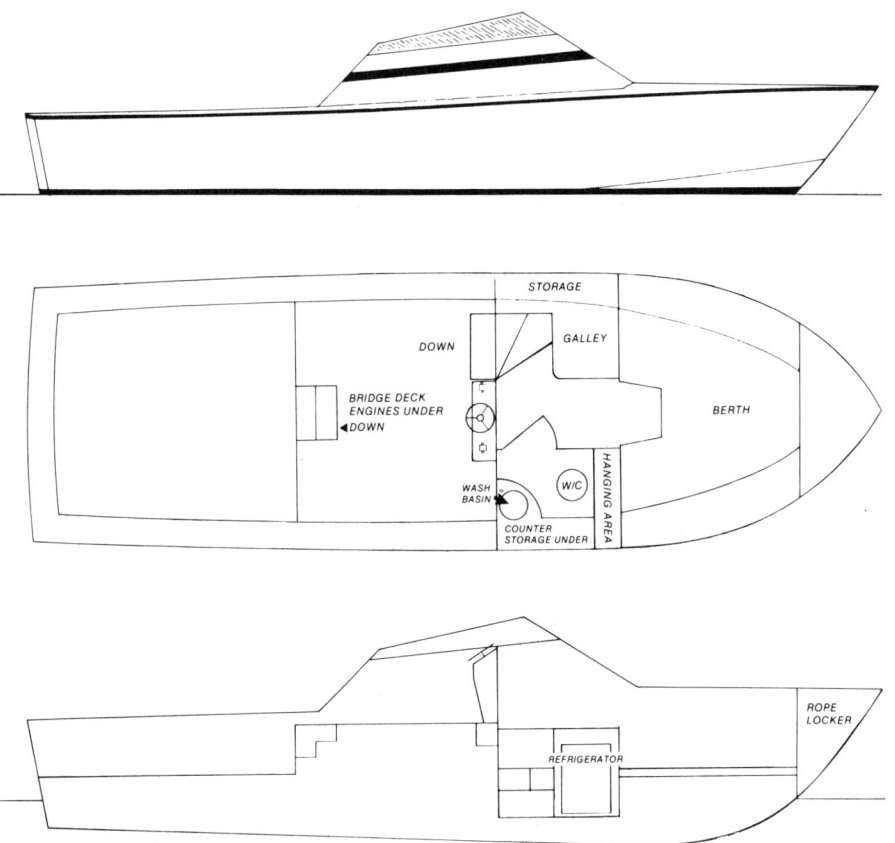

Raised-Bridge model has a raised deck instead of boxes over the motors. Cuddy cabin has full headroom in the galley-head area and V-berths under the forward deck. (Courtesy of Performer Boats)

These boats are quite frankly light-tackle tournament racers. In the Bimini racing start, the fastest boats get to the distant fishing grounds first after the sound of the starting gun. When the grounds are 50 miles away, a high top speed (in reasonable weather) very often commands early strikes from the fish.

The Stuart Angler model carries its cockpit deck flush forward to the windshield. Motors are under the amidships center-control console. Deck space is maximum. The addition of a low tower permits the installation of sun canvas over the lower control station. Operator's eye level at the tower station is about equal to that of a helmsman in the average 40-footer's flying bridge, but it is still a distinct advantage over cockpit-level vision.

Perhaps the most versatile all-around cockpit arrangement is to install a single, light, fishing-chair mount near the stern. This can be used for medium and heavy big game when needed, or the chair can be left ashore and a "rocket launcher" multiple rodholder substituted on the chair's mounting tube for light-tackle, time-limit tournament angling.

Outriggers should be capable of being rigged back flat over the stern to reduce windage at top speed. Electronics will probably be held to a single sensitive flasher-recorder, VHF/FM and/or CB radiotelephone, portable RDF or miniaturized Loran-C, and possibly a commercial receiver.

While the hull is stock, the builder is able to give considerable attention to the purchaser's desires in power selection, equipment, and installation. These can include a transom door, live-bait wells, padded coamings, choice of outriggers, and interior decor. Interior layout of the Raised Bridge Fisherman is shown in the accompanying sketches. Two friendly people should be able to weekend in relative comfort. The boat is essentially a high-performance dayfisherman, yet it is capable of fishing in any fishable weather along with the bigger boats.

Hull, forward and side decks, battery boxes, and hatches are hand-laminated fiberglass with gelcoat finish. The longitudinal stringers and bulkheads are molded in for strength. Cockpit is nonskid and self-bailing. Accessibility to engines is quite good. The live-bait well is molded into the hull. Fuel and water tanks are aluminum for strength and light weight. The windshield is tinted safety glass. The V-berths measure a full 6 feet 7 inches and have 4-inch cushions. The headliner and hull liner are vinyl. These essentials are present, but no attempt is made to overcrowd the boat with frivolous junk.

Standard Equipment

Fiberglass exhaust and muffler system
Bronze strut and steady bearing
Bronze rudders, rudder ports, stuffing boxes
SS shafts
Bronze sea valves and strainers on all underwater through-hull fittings
Fuel filters
Reinforced engine beds
Bronze propellers
Panish controls
Freshwater cooling
Engine space sound-insulated
Mechanical steering
12 v. DC electrical system
150-Ah battery for gasoline, 200-Ah battery for diesel, in fiberglass boxes
Battery disconnect switches, breaker panel
Bonding system
Automatic bilge pumps (2)
Full engine instrumentation
Electric fuel gauge
Air/electric horn

Cockpit lights
Bilge blower (gas only)
Battery parallel switch on twin installations
8-in Marinium cleats (6)
Hawsepipes (2), bow chocks (2), deck pipe
Running and anchor lights
Aluminum rubrail
Welded aluminum handrail and windshield frame
Hatch in forward deck
Large rope locker
6 ft 7 in V-berths with 4-in cushions
Coast Guard–approved head
SS sink with hand pump
Vinyl overhead and hull liner
Formica counters
Teak trim throughout
200-gal aluminum fuel tank
15-gal water tank
Docklines (4)
Life preservers (4)
Fire extinguishers (2)

Tower, outriggers, chairs, and other specialized gear as per owner's selection.

STEBER 32-FOOT SPORT FISHERMAN

Designer	Cresta
Builder	Stebercraft Pty. Ltd. P.O. Box 90 Taree, N.S.W. 2430, Australia
Construction	Fiberglass hull, deck, and super-structure with hardwood trim.

Specifications

Length overall	32 ft	9.75 m
Length, waterline	28 ft	8.54 m
Beam, maximum	11 ft	3.35 m
Draft	3 ft	0.91 m
Cockpit area	110 sq ft	10.23 m²
Freeboard forward	4 ft 6 in	1.37 m
Freeboard aft	3 ft 6 in	1.07 m
Height, waterline to windshield top	10 ft 2 in	3.11 m
Weight	NA	
Fuel capacity	200 Imp gal	907 l
Water capacity	60 Imp gal	272 l
Sleeping accommodations	6	

Power options

Twin 200-hp Chrysler CM6-55TI diesels
Twin 165-hp Fiat 806 SM diesels
Twin 190-hp Baudoin DF3SM diesels
Twin 145-hp Perkins HT6.354 diesels
Twin 175-hp Perkins HT6.354 diesels
Twin 130-hp Volvo AQD sterndrive diesels
Other motors by arrangement

Performance

The only performance information available from the Australian builder is a statement that a pair of 200-hp diesels, driving through V-drive units, can provide a top speed of 30 mph. From a different source, Australian journalist Peter Webster's Powerboat Tests (April 1978), we have this evaluation:

The Steber 32 is close to the traditional concept of a deep-V sportfishing boat. It is a very deep V with an estimated deadrise of 20 degrees. By modern standards this must be considered unusual, as most sportfishing boats in the international sphere such as the Merritt, Rybovich, and Hatteras are today heading back to moderate deadrise angles of 10 to 12 degrees.

In the case of the Steber 32, there is no doubt that this is a very together fishing boat. Powered by two 6-cylinder turbocharged Chrysler diesels of 200 hp

From Australia comes this trim 32-footer built on the former Cresta deep-V hull. The engines are placed well aft and drive through V-drives. The fiberglass hull is offered with a variety of twin gasoline and diesel power options. (Photo by Stebercraft Pty. Ltd.)

each, the Steber 32 gets along in great fashion, moving onto plane almost as quickly as a high-powered petrol engine runabout.

The engineering of the Steber 32 is quite interesting. The Chryslers drive forward to Twin Disc V-drives, running back to emerge from the hull almost under the engines. The V-drives have given Steber the ability to place the engines exactly where he wants them, in this case well aft of the centre. The result is one of the neatest balancing tricks we have seen in a cruiser for some time. The Steber 32 is one of the very rare boats that is so well balanced it runs quite satisfactorily without trim tabs. Running angle is surprisingly flat and there is virtually no pitching in a seaway. It is a very well-mannered boat with the weight of the engines and fuel tanks thoughtfully placed to achieve the best running trim and balance.

Description

According to Peter Webster, Bruce Steber (the builder) purchased the original molds of the well-known (in Australian circles) Cresta 32 and eventually developed a new sportfishing model using the proven Cresta hull. The boat has

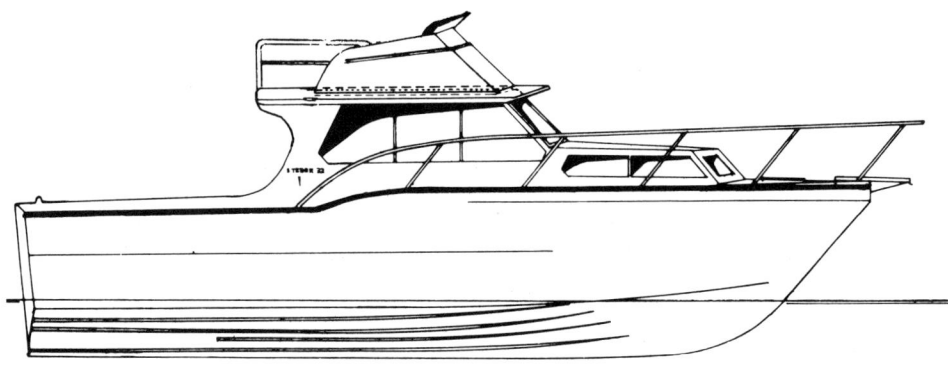

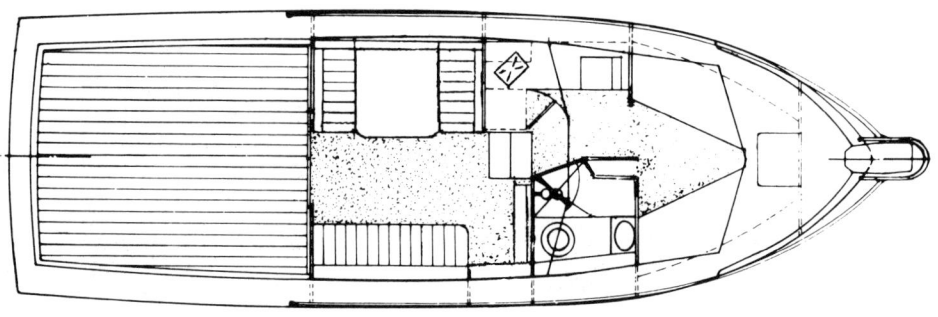

evidently found a ready market among sports-loving Aussies, who have developed one of the world's most spectacular big-game fisheries along the Queensland Coast, pursuing gigantic black marlin.

From the sketches and plans, the boat appears to be an archetype of the American family fishing cruiser of a few years ago. There is a step-up from the cockpit deck to the deckhouse level to accommodate the engines under flush hatches. The deckhouse features a dinette to port that converts into a double berth, and a Pullman-type seat to starboard that makes up into upper and lower single bunks. These, combined with the V-berths in the forward sleeping space, provide accommodations for up to six.

Down below, there is a galley to port and a comfortable head to starboard. No attempt is made to crowd an apartment's trimmings into this boat's interior. The effect is of well-planned space. Peter Webster describes the accommodations:

> One of the nicest features of the Steber 32 is the planning of this area [the deckhouse]. Seated at either the dinette or the sofa, one is able to converse with the cook, and vice versa. It makes the salon seem much bigger than normal too, yet because it [the galley] is on a different level two steps down, there is suffi-cient separation from the hassle of meal preparation. On the starboard side op-

posite the galley is the beautifully appointed head, complete with ceramic-tile sole, shower recess, toilet, basin, and well-designed vanity unit. The shower has pressure hot and cold water.

The builder offers a fully equipped fishing platform onto which he and the owner can install agreed-upon equipment. This includes the owner's choice of outriggers, chairs, electronic gear, communications instruments, etc. The large, uncluttered cockpit is ideally laid out for heavy-duty fishing. From the available photos and sketches, it would seem an advantage to place the flying-bridge control station farther aft in the bridge instead of all the way forward, as seems to be indicated. The after position is preferred by leading amateur and professional skippers, who realize the advantage of being able to view the entire cockpit from the bridge control station.

But the Australian fishermen have excellent original ideas of their own, as Peter Webster points out.

> Another handy touch in the cockpit is provision of a small hand basin in the starboard corner, located over a cupboard housing the gas bottle for the galley. The basin is a boon for the crew for washing hands after handling bait or bloody fish.

His comments about the flying bridge echo the sentiments expressed above.

> On the bridge the helmsman's vision is outstanding, although we were not too happy about the traditional bench seat arrangement. We would have preferred the new American layout where two seats are run fore and aft on either side of the bridge, with a central, fully adjustable swivel chair for the helmsman.

Regarding availability of Steber boats, the builder says:

> Each of our models may be purchased in various stages for owner completion, or complete with owner's choice of power and other equipment. Construction may be done to Maritime Survey status (for licensing of boats to carry passengers for hire) if required.

Standard Equipment

Heavy-duty hull, Klegecell sandwich construction, deck and superstructure
Electric anchor capstan with deck foot switch
6½-in cross bollard (bow)
Bowsprit with heavy-duty anchor rode roller
Forward anchor hatch, chute to storage compartment
Heavy-duty SS, 1¼-in bow rail

Anodized aluminum-tinted windows, armor glass (4 sliding)
Dual hand throttles
Helm console and instrument panel (dual station)
Navigation lights
Bronze-anodized sliding doors (2 fixed, 1 sliding)
90-gal aluminum fuel tanks (2), with equalizing cocks and sumps, inspection ports

6-micron fuel filters/water traps (2)
Fuel and water deck fillers and breathers
Heavy-duty after cross bollards
Self-draining cockpit
Nonskid deck
Solid fiberglass molded rudders with SS
 shafts
Aft fiberglass hull beltings (port and
 starboard)
Lower wheel, 24-in dia.; bridge wheel,
 14-in dia.
Dual-station hydraulic steering
Engine air intakes, baffles, ducts
Propeller shafts, 1½-in, SS
Shore-power system, 240 v. AC
Main cabin roof, hardtop with roof
 liner, cockpit overhang, sun visor
Port and starboard windscreen wipers
SS flying-bridge handrail
Flying bridge, 8 ft wide, with port and
 starboard lockers and side panels
Tinted bridge windscreen
SS bridge ladder, teak steps
30-gal, SS freshwater tanks (2)
Continuous-fed, 8-gal, pressurized hot-
 water tank
Pressurized hot-water system
Built-in bait tank and lid
V-berth skylight ventilation hatch

V-berths with storage under, shelves
 above, closet
Galley cupboards, cocktail cabinet
Settee and convertible dinette, storage
 under
Cockpit storage compartments
Galley steps
Teak-faced, waterproof, plywood trim
 with solid teak edging
Toilet storage cupboards, sliding mirror,
 shelves
SS sinks, galley, and toilet, storage under
Crockery storage racks
Cutlery drawers with storage under
Marine toilet, chemical
2-burner gas stove, oven, gas bottle,
 regulator
12 v. DC, 1.5-cu-ft refrigerator
 (also 240 v. AC)
Hand-set shower in toilet room
Upholstered bridge seat with SS rail
Vinyl-ease, 3-inch-thick upholstery
 throughout
Waterproof carpeting throughout
PVC curtain tracks
Complete exhaust system, plumbing
Complete wiring system, including
 3 banks of 12-v. batteries, isolating
 switches, bilge pumps, lighting
Engine installation to owner's choice

Special Options

Safety equipment
Teak landing platform
Additional built-in live-bait tank with lid
Cockpit shower

Sink in cockpit
Curtains throughout
Radio, sounder, etc.

STAMAS 32-FOOT SPORT FISHERMAN

Designer	Peter G. Stamas
Builder	Stamas Boats Inc. 300 Pampas Avenue Tarpon Springs, FL 33589
Construction	Fiberglass hull, decks, and super-structure, with full-length fiberglass hull liner; wooden transverse bulkheads.

Thoroughly workmanlike is the design of the Stamas 32-footer. The hull rides dry and level at speeds to 32 mph with twin 255-hp gas motors. There are comfortable cruising accommodations for up to four persons. The boat will easily take outriggers and a moderate tower. (Photo by Stamas Boats Inc.)

Specifications

Length overall	32 ft 3 in	9.75 m
Length, waterline	28 ft	8.83 m
Beam, maximum	12 ft	3.67 m
Draft	2 ft 9 in	0.84 m
Cockpit area	100 sq ft	9.30 m²
Freeboard forward	4 ft 6 in	1.37 m
Freeboard aft	3 ft	0.91 m
Height above waterline	11 ft 6 in	3.54 m
Weight (normal)	11,000 lb	5,000 kg
Fuel capacity	250 gal	945 l
Water capacity	50 gal	189 l
Sleeping accommodations	2-4	

Power options
   Twin 255-hp MerCruiser V-8 gasoline, 350 CID (5.735 l)
   Twin 255-hp OMC V-8 gasoline, 350 CID (5.735 l)
   Twin 200-hp Chrysler 6-cyl diesels, 331 CID (5.425 l),
      1.58:1 reduction gear

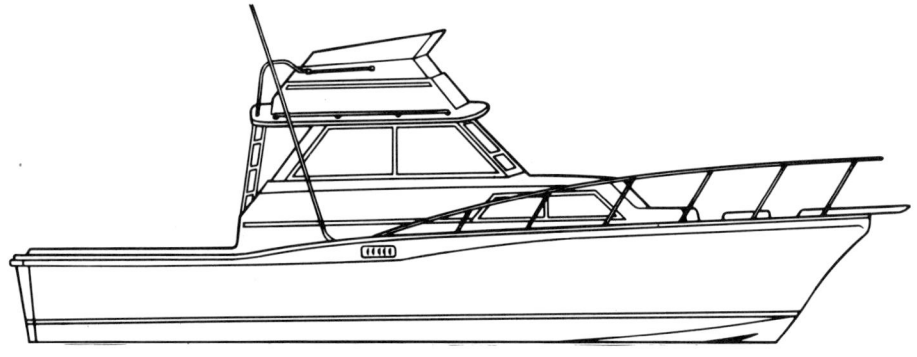

Performance

With twin 255-hp MerCruiser or OMC gasoline motors

Top speed	32.2 mph (48.0 kph)	@ 4000 rpm
Cruising speed	27.2 mph (40.5 kph)	@ 3500 rpm
Cruising range	245 mi (365 km)	@ 3500 rpm

With twin 200-hp Chrysler 6-cyl diesels

Top speed	28.0 mph (41.7 kph)	@ 3125 rpm
Cruising speed	24.4 mph (36.4 kph)	@ 2800 rpm
Cruising range	270 mi (402 km)	@ 2800 rpm

Tabulated performance, twin 255-hp MerCruiser engines*

RPM	MPH	GPH	MPG	Trim Angle
1000	6.4	3.6	1.78	0.3°
1500	8.4	5.6	1.50	0.9°
2000	10.2	10.3	0.99	3.7°
2500	16.5	17.2	0.96	6.0°
3000	19.5	22.8	0.98	5.9°
3500	27.2	28.0	0.97	5.1°
4000	32.2	34.2	0.94	4.6°

Fuel flow measured in hundredths of a gallon; speed measured to 1/10 mph by K-band Doppler radar. Test information courtesy of Motor Boating & Sailing magazine, October 1977.

The tabulated speed/fuel data suggest an interesting situation. From the data, the boat's most efficient long-range speed appears to be 6.4 mph at 1000 rpm with an mpg rate of 1.78. This suggests an endurance of 140 hours at normal off-shore trolling speed and an ultimate range of 445 miles at that slow speed. The displacement speed of 8.4 mph is reached at 1500 rpm with an mpg rate of 1.5, for an endurance of about 166 hours and a range of 375 miles.

At 2000 rpm the boat is trying to get up on plane with the fuel rate suddenly down to 0.99 mpg, for a speed of 10.2 mph. At this speed the endurance would be just a hair under 25 hours for a range of about 245 miles. From here on up to the top speed of 32.2 mph at 4000 rpm, the fuel rate drops by infinitesimal degrees to 0.94 mpg. The endurance at full speed looks like 7.3 hours, but the range at full speed is a surprising 235 miles. This suggests that wetted-surface friction drag with increasing speed is offset by the dynamic rise of the hull out of the water and the lowering of the trim angle with increasing speed.

In any event, an owner can push the throttle right up to hammer-down if he has to, without having to worry about a horrendous decrease in fuel economy.

Description

This smart 32-foot fisherman is the top of the line for Stamas Boat Inc. of Tarpon Springs, Florida. The look is lean, angular, and, despite the generous 12-foot beam, not boxy. The cockpit is entirely adequate for a pair of fixed or portable fishing chairs and a large portable fishbox, or for a single full-sized fighting chair. The bridge controls are placed well aft, affording a clear view of the entire cockpit. There is a molded-in relaxing seat at the forward end of the low cabin trunk. The side decks are up to 19½ inches wide, a blessing in rough water or when docking at night.

The deckhouse features lower control station to starboard and an optional convertible dinette to port. Down below, there is a small galley to port and a head with toilet, basin, and shower to starboard. Lockers separate this space from the forward stateroom with a deep V-berth sleeping two. There has been no attempt to cram the contents of a five-room apartment into this 32-footer. The result is a boat with comfort in essentials for two couples on cruise, and adequate space for dayfishing parties of up to six. The after end of the deckhouse is open but can be fitted with a suitable drop curtain, charterboat style.

The author remembers vividly a salmon trip on Lake Michigan out of Portage Lake in an early version of the Stamas hull. It was blowing 40 knots out of the nor'west and the little Stamas was one of no more than a dozen boats that ventured out that windy day. We limited on coho salmon in four hours while the boat rode like a duck in the trough of the short, steep seas. Then the owner smoked it for home, running like a quarterhorse across the seas. The feeling of controlled speed and power was tremendous.

Owner's Evaluation

Jack Wells of Brielle, New Jersey, reports on his 1978 Stamas 32-footer, averaging 300 hours of use per season. Power is a pair of 330-hp, 454-CID, OMC gasoline engines. Wells claims a top speed of 40 mph and 230 to 250 miles cruising range at 27 mph. He spends 10 percent of his time cruising and 90 percent fish-trolling. Here is his evaluation score.

Fuel economy	Good
Handling qualities	Good
Seaworthiness	Super
Overall design	Super
Cruising comfort	Good
Fishing efficiency	Super
Ease of maintenance	Super
Investment value	Super

Wells considers the Stamas 32-footer to be his ultimate fishing machine, "now restricted to the summer season." He adds, "For its size it's one of the finest boats available." He concludes by saying that if he decides to buy a new boat, he will trade up in size and price range, hoping that when he is ready, Stamas will have a larger model ready for him.

BERTRAM 33-FOOT SPORT FISHERMAN

Designer	Bertram Yacht Div. Whittaker Corp.
Builder	Bertram Yacht 3663 N.W. 21st Street Miami, FL 33142
Construction	Fiberglass hull, decks, and super-structure. Wood and vinyl decor and trim.

Specifications

Length overall	33 ft	10.00
Length, waterline	28 ft 4 in	8.54 m
Beam, maximum	12 ft 8 in	3.86 m
Draft	3 ft 3 in	1.01 m
Cockpit area	120 sq ft	11.16 m²
Freeboard forward	5 ft 3 in	1.60 m
Freeboard aft	3 ft 4 in	1.03 m
Height above waterline	11 ft	3.36 m
Weight (approx)	18,000 lb	8,182 kg
Fuel capacity	255 gal	946 l
Water capacity	70 gal	264 l
Sleeping accommodations	4	

Continued

This trim 33-footer from Bertram blends modern design with the now-classic Bertram deep-V hull. Four can cruise and fish in comfort in a vessel that claims speeds of up to 32 mph with twin 330-hp gasoline motors. Turbo diesels are an option. (Photo by Bertram Yacht)

Specifications *continued*

Power options
Twin 330-hp MerCruiser gasoline
Twin 270-hp Caterpillar Turbo diesels

Performance

Builder's reported figures are based on a projected 325-gallon tank.

With twin 330-hp MerCruiser gasoline engines

Top speed	32.0 mph (47.7 kph)	@ 4000 rpm
Cruising speed	25.6 mph (38.4 kph)	@ 3200 rpm
Cruising range	224 mi (334 km)	@ 3200 rpm

With twin 270-hp Caterpillar Turbo diesels

Top speed	31.5 mph (47.0 kph)	@ 2800 rpm
Cruising speed	28.1 mph (41.9 kph)	@ 2500 rpm
Cruising range	403 mi (600 km)	@ 2500 rpm

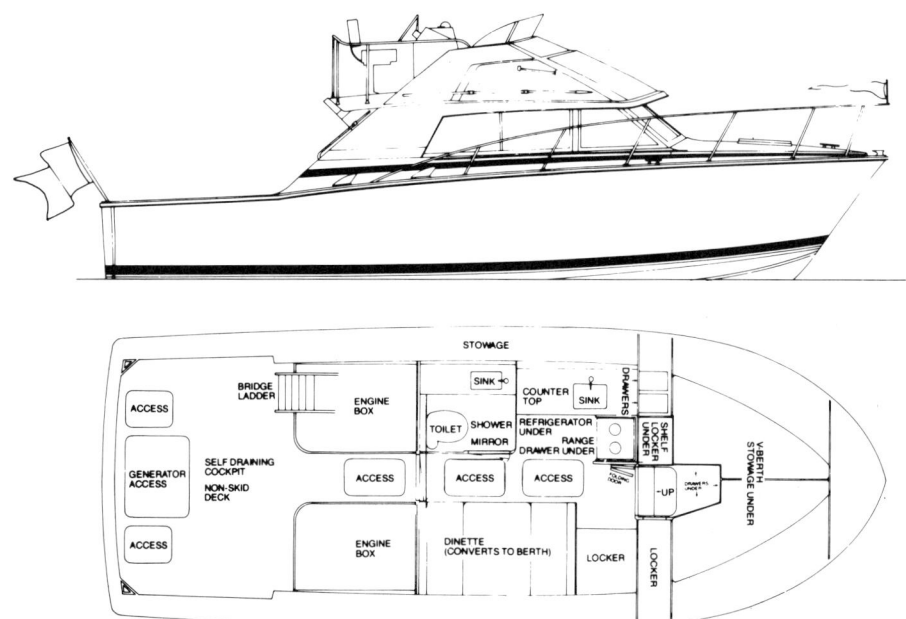

Speeds and cruising ranges are test averages and may vary among similar boats depending on weight, hull trim, and engine and bottom condition.

Description

Thoroughly modern in design and appearance, the Bertram 33-footer has the distinctive reverse sheer of its larger sister models and retains the equally distinctive forward slope of deckhouse and flying-bridge front. Excessive height of deckhouse is avoided by keeping the cockpit deck low and continuing the cockpit deck level between the two engine boxes situated in the forward end of the cockpit, following the pattern of the 31-footer.

The Bertram 33 is "fatter" than the 31-foot model, having a length-beam ratio of 2.6, as compared to the smaller boat's length-beam ratio of 2.73. This, plus the slightly larger overall and waterline lengths and hull depth, adds up to a displacement averaging 18,000 pounds against the 31-footer's 10,300 pounds. This is reflected in slightly lower top and cruising speeds for what is, in effect, identical gasoline or diesel power.

Literature supplied by Bertram at the time of this writing described the fuel capacity as 255 to 260 gallons, but speed and range test data were described as "projected with 325-gallon tank." The present trend in deep-V hulls in the popular 30- to 50-foot range is toward length-beam ratios considerably smaller (wider-hulled) than was the case just a few years ago. This appears to be an attempt to attain two important objectives: (1) to overcome the tendency of some deep-V hulls to be slow in recovering stability in a rough beam sea, and (2) to provide the greatest possible interior cubic capacity in a relatively short hull, taking advantage of the availability of high-output gasoline and diesel engines to drive the relatively short, wide hull.

Boats of this type sell remarkably well, which seems to indicate that the powerboat-buying public likes the type of hull and accommodations that modern builders offer. The literature describes the model as a "very tough, very fast, very big, little sportfisherman. . . a boat you can take 50 or 60 miles offshore in very messy stuff, fish all day, and not feel beat to death when you get back."

The bridge is particularly well laid out for competitive fishing. The helmsman's seat is practically at the after edge of the bridge deck, giving him a complete and unobstructed view of the entire cockpit. This is particularly important when fighting or gaffing a very large fish. It also means that the helmsman or lookout can get down into the cockpit in a flash to lend a hand in an emergency. The bridge is well protected by an adequate metal ladder and handrail. A Bimini top is usually fitted, unless a tower is required, in which case a canvas sun-dodger may protect the bridge, stretched between the tower legs. Most well-designed towers have hold-fasts, or framing, for carrying such a canvas.

The deckhouse features a convertible dinette to starboard on entering from the cockpit, forward of which is a locker. The head, with shower, toilet, and sink, is located to port at the after end of the deckhouse. Just forward of this is an L-shaped galley with sink, cupboards, stove, and built-in refrigerator. Optional lower controls can be fitted in lieu of the deckhouse locker space to starboard.

The forward cabin contains a large V-berth sleeping two, plus lockers and a chain locker in the forepeak. It is separated from the deckhouse by a folding door for privacy. Reverse-cycle air conditioning is available as an option and is extremely popular in warmer climates. Another popular option is a 6.5 kw (gasoline) or 7.5-kw (diesel) auxiliary generator, placed under the after deck with access by a deck hatch in the stern.

The interior of the Bertram 33 reflects the modern trend toward decorator-styled color and texture combinations. Rubbed teak and mahogany trim is evident, with panels done in a light, durable, wood-grain finish. Special attention is paid to necessities like the head, where the finish is laboratory white and chrome. A Monomatic toilet with dockside discharge is standard. An optional feature is either one of two Groco toilet models, or a 10-gallon holding tank with the Monomatic unit.

The effect is that of a very modern cottage or apartment away from home, preshrunk to the dimensions of this 33-foot boat. Old shellbacks may bridle at what to them is the new effete nauticalism. This shellback does not agree. Having slept in too many wet bunks, existed on too many makeshift meals of cold beans and warm beer, and suffered claustrophobia from too many tiny, musty cabins, the so-called effete comforts of the modern fishing cruiser are a very welcome change.

The general interior aspect is open, airy, light, and surprisingly spacious. Cockpit space is ample for either family or tournament fishing, and the comfortable bridge station makes a happy social center as well as a base for more serious fishing operations. A North Carolina owner who wishes to remain anonymous gives this performance evaluation.

Fuel economy (diesel)	Good
Handling qualities	Good
Seaworthiness	Super +

Overall design	Super
Cruising comfort	Good
Fishing efficiency	Super
Ease of maintenance	Good
Investment value	Good

Admittedly critical, this owner says that the Bertram 33-footer is not his ultimate fishing machine but is a very good interim vessel until he becomes wealthy enough to trade up in size and cost. Any new boat, however, will have to change three of his four "Good" ratings to "Super." He averages 250 hours a year on the water and estimates that 250 available gallons of diesel fuel will take him 300 miles at 27 mph (2450 rpm). Compared with other boats he has owned, he rates this one "the best — so far."

Standard Equipment
General

Adjustable pedestal helmsman's seat on bridge

Anchor, 13-lb, with deck pipe, chock and line, ⅝ in × 150 ft

Battery paralleling switch

Batteries, 220 Ah (2)

Bench seat forward, bridge console with cushions

Bilge blower

Bilge pumps, automatic (3)

Bow rail

Burgee staff with burgee

Cleats, bow (2), stern (2)

Coaming padding, flying bridge

Cockpit steps, port and starboard mounts

Combination bow chocks and running lights

Docklines, nylon, ½ in × 25 ft (3)

Electric horn, dual trumpet

Electrical bonding system

Electrical outlets, duplex (4)

Electrical panel with circuit breakers

Engine hour meters

Ensign staff and socket

Fire extinguishers (3)

Flying bridge with lockers, controls, and rails

Freshwater gauge

Fuel filters

Fuel gauge, electric

Hot-water heater, 115 v. AC, and engine heat

Hydraulic steering

Life jackets (4)

Life ring

Lighting, 12 v. throughout

Mufflers, fiberglass, with Veloci-jet, gas only

Navigation lights

Nonskid deck

Raw-water sea strainers

Ship's bell

Shoreline, 30-amp

Shower with sump pump

Springline cleats, port and starboard

Toilet, Monomatic, with dockside discharge

Trim tabs, hydraulic

Water-pressure system

Deckhouse

Aft bulkhead with hinged door

Carpeting

Dinette with cushions (converts to double berth)

Drapes, throughout

Locker storage

Sliding cabin windows with screens

Galley

Combination electric/alcohol stove, 2-burner

AC/DC electric refrigerator

Drawer and locker storage

SS sink

Forward Stateroom

Carpeted hull sides

Carpeting

Drawer storage under berths

Forward cabin cushions

Hanging lockers

Storage under berths

Telephone shower in head
Vanity with locker and sliding mirrors
in head

Optional Equipment

Deck Hardware

Anchor, 13-lb, extra
Cleats, fenders (4 each)
Windlass, anchor, 12 v.

Electrical

Alarm system, fire, bilge, oil pressure
and heat (gasoline/diesel)
Converter, 40-amp, automatic
DC power monitor
Electronic power supply for flying
bridge, 30-amp, 6 circuits
European shore power
Generator, 6.5-kw (gasoline)
Generator, 7.5-kw (diesel)

Lights

Docking lights, transom, single-control
Docking lights, bow, single-control
Docking lights switch at lower station,
bow or transom
Searchlight, 1-mile, single- or dual-
control
Searchlight, portable

Electronics

Radio ground plate, dual
Wiring and fuse for autopilot
Synchronizer, Judson, gasoline

Interior Equipment

Air conditioning, reverse-cycle,
throughout
Controls, lower, diesel, include 2 windshield wipers, washers, and 4-in
compass
Controls, lower, gasoline, include 2 windshield wipers, washers, and 4-in
compass
Holding tank (for use with standard
Monomatic toilet), 10-gal
Toilet, Groco, electric, with Lectra San
Toilet, Monomatic, with dockside and
overboard discharge

Diesel power includes:

Freshwater cooling
Oil and water alarm system
Oil coolers
Sound insulation

Fishing Equipment

Fighting chair, Rockaway
Fishbox, curved to fit transom, with
or without circulating water
Gin pole, with rigging
Outriggers, 4-ft, with 21-ft aluminum
poles
Rodholders, flush-mounted (4 each)

Canvas

Bimini top, Dacron or vinyl
Cockpit cover, hardtop to engine box
Cockpit cover, hardtop to transom,
Dacron or vinyl
Flying-bridge cover, Dacron or vinyl
Flying-bridge instrument panel cover,
Dacron or vinyl
Shipping cover
Sun awning, Dacron or vinyl
Windscreen, Bimini top to spray shield,
Dacron or vinyl
Windshield cover, Dacron or vinyl

General

Anchor line, nylon, ⅝ in × 150 ft
Boathook, 8-ft, chocked
Cockpit coaming padding
Compass, 4-in, flush-mounted (upper
only)
Cradle
Dockline, nylon, ½ in × 38 ft
Fire extinguisher, Halon
Flying-bridge companion seat
Freshwater cooling, 330 Merc (standard
with diesel)
Fuel tank, 75-gal, extra (NA with
optional generator)
Paint, bottom, antifouling (blue only)
Propellers (2 extra)
Shaft, extra, diesel (1 each)
Shaft, extra, gasoline (1 each)
Swim platform
Transom steps
Washdown pump with 10-ft hose
Water inlet, dockside supply
Zincs on shafts

BRUNO & STILLMAN SPORTCRUISER 35

Designer	Bruno & Stillman
Builder	Bruno & Stillman One Dover Road Newington, NH 03801
Construction	One-piece fiberglass with teak trim. Hard-chine V-hull.

Specifications

Length overall	35 ft	10.68 m
Length, waterline	33 ft 4 in	10.16 m
Beam, maximum	11 ft 6 in	3.51 m
Draft	2 ft 10 in	0.88 m
Cockpit area	90 sq ft	8.37 m²
Freeboard forward	5 ft 7 in	1.71 m
Freeboard aft	3 ft 4 in	1.01 m
Height, waterline to windshield	11 ft 3 in	3.43 m
Weight	NA	
Fuel capacity, standard	115 gal	435 l
Fuel capacity, optional	180 gal	680 l
Water capacity	60 gal	227 l
Sleeping accommodations	4	

Power options

Perkins 130-hp diesel
Perkins 160-hp diesel
Caterpillar 3208 NA diesel
Caterpillar 3208 Turbo diesel
Other models by arrangement

Performance

The following data are converted to miles per hour from the builder's speeds given in knots and should be considered relative, not absolute.

With Perkins 130-hp diesel (115-gal fuel capacity)		With Perkins 160-hp diesel (115-gal fuel capacity)	
Top speed	16 mph	Top speed	18.3 mph
Cruising speed	12 mph	Cruising speed	15.0 mph
Cruising fuel rate	2.5 gph	Cruising fuel rate	3.5 gph
Cruising endurance	46 hr	Cruising endurance	33 hr
Cruising range	552 mi	Cruising range	495 mi

With Caterpillar 3208 NA diesel (115-gal fuel capacity)		With Caterpillar 3208 Turbo diesel (115-gal fuel capacity)	
Top speed	25.0 mph	Top speed	28.6 mph
Cruising speed	21.7 mph	Cruising speed	24.0 mph
Cruising fuel rate	8.5 gph	Cruising fuel rate	8.5 gph
Cruising endurance	13.5 hr	Cruising endurance	13.5 hr
Cruising range	293 mi	Cruising range	324 mi

Description

The Bruno & Stillman Sportcruiser 35 is described as a direct development of this firm's 35-foot workboat hull, a hull designed for good speed and carrying capacity with moderate power. One such workboat with a 100-hp diesel made the passage from Portsmouth, New Hampshire, to Bermuda in 63 hours, averaging 10 knots while burning only 4 gph, for a fuel-mileage rate of 2.5 mpg. Later the same boat made the longer open-water passage from Bermuda to the Florida Keys.

The beam of 11 feet 6 inches is generous but not excessive and gives the hull excellent stability in rough water. Layout is conventional, avoiding extremes of design or construction. The only difference between the workboat and sport-cruiser is 4 inches greater freeboard in the cruiser model. This makes for a drier boat with more cockpit depth. Basic plans call for a single-engine installation, with the power plant under a slightly raised, flush deckhouse deck. The deckhouse steering station is forward, to starboard, remote-connected to the flying-bridge station. The bridge station is placed to give the operator a clear view of the cockpit.

Down below, the cabin arrangement is conventional with a large V-berth sleeping two in the bow, separated by a bulkhead from the main cabin. A twin-seat dinette to starboard converts into a double berth. There is storage space under the dinette seats and a locker forward. The head, with sink, lockers, and toilet, is forward, to port. The galley with sink and refrigerator is aft, also to port.

Deckhouse furnishings may be installed to owner's specifications. The after end can be enclosed with a drop curtain, or a half-bulkhead with sliding panel door may be installed. There is provision for a permanent bridge ladder from the cockpit. While the general design is not in any way extreme, it is good-looking in a functional way — the work of designers who understand both boats and fishing.

Owner's Evaluation

Thomas J. DePersia of West Suffield, Connecticut, reported on his 1979 Bruno & Stillman Sportcruiser 35. He gave the normal top speed as 20 mph and cruising speed as 15 to 18 mph with a Caterpillar 3208 220-hp diesel. He estimates the cruising range at 360 miles at 18 mph on 180 gallons of fuel. His fishing area extends from Montauk Point, New York, to Maine, with primary interest in the giant bluefin tuna of the Massachusetts Bay and Gloucester regions. DePersia uses the boat about 400 hours per year, averaging 4,000 miles, and spends half his time cruising and the other half fishing. His evaluation score is as follows:

Fuel economy	Super
Handling qualities	Good
Seaworthiness	Super

The Sportcruiser 35 is a typical Down East hull with a pleasing if conventional layout. The large cockpit can accommodate a fighting chair and a pair of fishing chairs, as well as a fishbox, a tackle locker, and a bait freezer. Speeds are claimed to 28 mph with a single diesel. (Photo by Bruno & Stillman)

Overall design	Super
Cruising comfort	Super
Fishing efficiency	Super
Ease of maintenance	Super
Investment value	Super

Standard Equipment

Safety/Navigational

Automatic electric bilge pump
Approved ventilation system
Heavy-duty bronze seacocks
Grabrails
Complete running lights
Nonskid surface on all decks
Self-bailing cockpit

Forepeak

V-berths, 6 ft 6 in (2)
Full-length shelves
5-in bunk cushions
Overhead fabric liner
Carpeted sole
Overhead light
Storage compartments
Reading lamps (2)

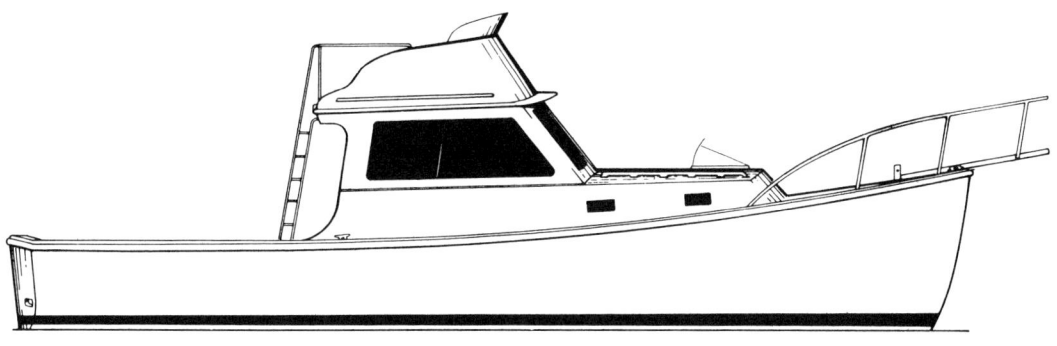

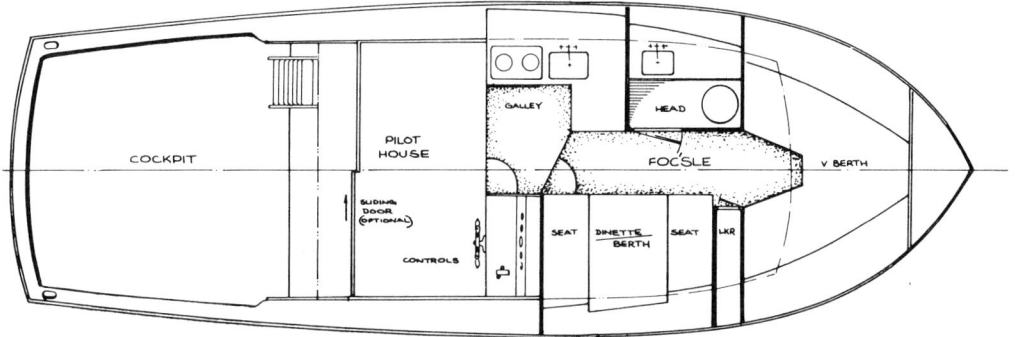

Galley

SS sink, hand pump
Two-burner stove
Refrigerator
Storage compartments

Cabin

Forward hatch
Opening portlights with screens (4)
Convertible dinette with table
5-in cushions throughout
Hanging locker/door
Carpeted sole
Overhead fabric liner
Overhead light
Storage compartments

Electrical

Engine alternator
12 v. DC, heavy-duty marine batteries (2)
Battery safety switch
Wiring harness
Engine alarm system
Electrical panel with circuit breakers

Flying Bridge

Side seats (2)
Full bench seat
Wind deflector
Ladder and railing
Hydraulic power steering
Engine controls
Full engine instrumentation
Compass
Grabrails

Head Enclosure

SS sink with hand pump
Vanity
Head, Type 1
Door
Overhead light
Molded shower pan

Deckhouse

Overhead light
Standard bulkhead
Drop curtains, aft
Windows
Flush engine access hatch

Hardware/Outfitting

Heavy-duty, solid-PVC rubrails
Opening hatch in forward deck
Bow bitt, bow chocks
Recessed stern hawse tubes, recessed stern
  cleats
Spring cleats
Boot stripe
Bottom, 2 coats antifouling paint
Docklines, 40-ft (2)
Insurance during construction

Launch and commission at Newington,
  New Hampshire, or load onto owner's
  truck

Engine/Drive System

Perkins 6-365 130-hp diesel, or option
Heat-exchanger cooling
Reverse/reduction gear
Wet exhaust/muffler
Insulated engine hatch
SS shaft, 1¼-in
Zinc shaft collar
Bronze stern tube assembly
Bronze propeller, 4-blade
SS skeg
Fiberglass rudder
Exhaust port flapper

Optional Equipment

Perkins T6-354 160-hp diesel
Caterpillar 3208 V-8 210-hp diesel
SS bow rail with anchor pulpit
Complete lower helm assembly and
  station
Pressurized hot and cold water system,
  shower

Name and hailing port painted on
  transom
After deckhouse bulkhead with sliding
  doors
Shore electric power system with charger-
  converter
Flying-bridge helmsman's chair
Other options by arrangement

HARRIS 36-FOOT SPORTFISHERMAN

Designer	Royal Lowell, Pownal, ME
Builder	Canyon Corp. 194 Main Street Amesbury, MA 01913
Construction	Fiberglass edge-grain core laminate hull, fiberglass superstructure. Full-length stringers. Mahogany trim.

Viewed bows-on, the Harris 36-foot Sportfisherman is an impressive vessel with accommodations for four or six people and top speeds to 33 knots with twin 330-hp gasoline motors. Diesels are optional. (Photo by Kirk Williamson, Studio North)

The tall tower carries a radar antenna, a must for fog navigation. The cockpit control station is one of the attributes of the true tournament fisherman. The low cockpit makes gaffing easy. (Photo by Kirk Williamson, Studio North)

Specifications

Length overall	35 ft 10 in	10.93 m
Length, waterline	33 ft 4 in	10.17 m
Beam, maximum	12 ft 3 in	3.74 m
Draft	2 ft 8 in	0.81 m
Cockpit area	120 sq ft	11.16 m²
Freeboard forward	5 ft 6 in	1.68 m
Freeboard aft	3 ft 4 in	1.02 m
Heights above waterline		
Bridge windshield	11 ft 10 in	3.63 m
Tower top	27 ft	8.24 m
Weight, nominal	14,500 lb	6,590 kg
Fuel capacity		
(variable option)	250 gal	945 l
Water capacity		
(variable option)	40 gal	150 l
Sleeping accommodations	6	

Power options (single- or twin-screw)
   Chrysler 330-hp gasoline
   Caterpillar 3208 diesel
   GM 4-53, 4-71, 6-71
   Cummins VT 555
   Others by arrangement

Performance

Builder's Speed/Fuel/Range Data *(250 gallons of fuel)*

Power	RPM	Speed	GPH	Range*
Twin Caterpillar 3208	2800	24 kn	11.6	465 nm
	2400	20 kn	7.2	625 nm
Twin Cummins VT 555	3000	27 kn	15.9	382 nm
	2600	22 kn	10.2	485 nm
Twin GM 4-53	2800	18 kn	7.8	519 nm
	2400	15 kn	4.9	689 nm

Range computed at 90% fuel available (225 gal).

Estimated Comparative Engine Data*

Power	Fuel/Gal	Top Speed	Cruise
Single GM 4-53	100	14 kn	12 kn
Single GM 4-71	200	17 kn	15 kn
Single GM 6-71	250	21 kn	19 kn
Single Caterpillar 3208 VT 555	250	19 kn	17 kn
Twin GM 4-71	250	24 kn	20 kn
Twin Chrysler 330-hp gasoline	250	33 kn	25 kn

Ranges are not included because fuel rates were not available.

Description

The 36-foot Harris Sportfisherman is available in three basic designs, a Sport-fisherman with cruising-style deckhouse and accommodations, an Express Fisherman with open bridge in lieu of enclosed deckhouse, and a Charter Fisherman with deckhouse designed to accommodate daysailing fishing parties. All three models may be equipped with a tower. The Charter Fisherman and Sportfisherman have flying bridges designed for competitive fishing.

According to the builders, the concept behind the Harris 36 is "a low-cost, economical sportfishing boat ideally suited to the charter fisherman or cruiser/fisherman. With a cruising speed of 20 knots and exceptional seakeeping qualities, the Harris 36 has a hard-chined, modified deep-V configuration with a full keel and soft entry forward. It provides an exceptionally stable fishing platform with safety and comfort."

A glance at the plan and profile drawings will reveal a boat with graceful, lively sheer and the clean look of a boat engineered by fishermen for fishermen. The cockpit measures 120 square feet of useful surface, large for a boat of this size. There is no attempt at making the boat a floating dormitory. Standard sleeping arrangement is for four persons, although two more can be accommodated in optional overhead bunks in the forward compartment. The simple galley is designed

The reverse-curve sheer is pleasing. The centerline outrigger from the tower deck is a Florida touch, important for fast, light-tackle competitive angling for sailfish and white and blue marlin. (Photo by Kirk Williamson, Studio North)

for putting together pick-up meals and is located in the deckhouse in the two enclosed models. An optional shower may be installed in the Sportfisherman at the cost of a little locker space.

The hull skin is formed by sandwiching an edge-grain balsa core between two fiberglass skins. Engine beds are fastened directly to full-length longitudinal stringers. The engine compartment is insulated against heat and noise. An interesting feature of Harris manufacture is that the basic hull is available in various stages of completion. While the prices quoted in the following breakdown are those for 1978, the list gives a good comparative idea of how the basic hull can be bought and what additional features will cost. Both the Sportfisherman and the Express Fisherman are available under this arrangement.

Feature	*1978 Price**
Hull with 2 bulkheads, 4 stringers for twin-screw	$9,975
Hull with 2 bulkheads, 2 stringers for single-screw	9,800
Forward deck, house, side aft decks, windows	
Sportfisherman	5,975
Express Fisherman	6,600
Cockpit floor with molded hatches	1,700
Flying bridge with center console, side seats	2,200
Assembly of all molded parts (except bridge) and installation	
of deckhouse windows	1,050
PVC rubrail, spray rail, quarter guards	1,080
Full-length spray rails (including rail above)	925
Installed flying bridge, console, seats, trim, doors	1,250
Aft bulkhead with windows, door, teak trim, finish	1,850
Drive train, twin-screw: engine beds, shaft log struts, rudders, rudder ports, hydraulic steering, 5-in exhaust lines with mufflers, raw-water strainers, seacocks, 22-in props, 1½-in shafts 9 ft long (SS)	5,800
Drive train, single-screw: essentially the same, including single 1½-in SS shaft 10 ft long	4,600

Present prices and availability of features may be obtained from the builder.

Owners' Evaluations

Three owners submitted comments and evaluation reports at the request of the author: Joseph D. Kirn of Metairie, Louisiana; A.C. Toegemann of Cranston, Rhode Island; and Al Magliozzi of Winchester, Massachusetts. Their reports of operating conditions and performance evaluation are remarkably consistent.

Operating Conditions

	Kirn	*Toegemann*	*Magliozzi*
Power	Single J&T 6-71	Twin Cat 3208	Twin GM 4-53
Top speed	20 mph	24 mph	18 mph
Cruising	18 mph	19 mph	16 mph
Usable fuel	250 gal	225 gal	232 gal
Range/speed	360/18	350/18	400/16
Annual use	300 hr	200 hr	500 hr
Time running	40%	40%	85%
Time trolling	60%	60%	15%

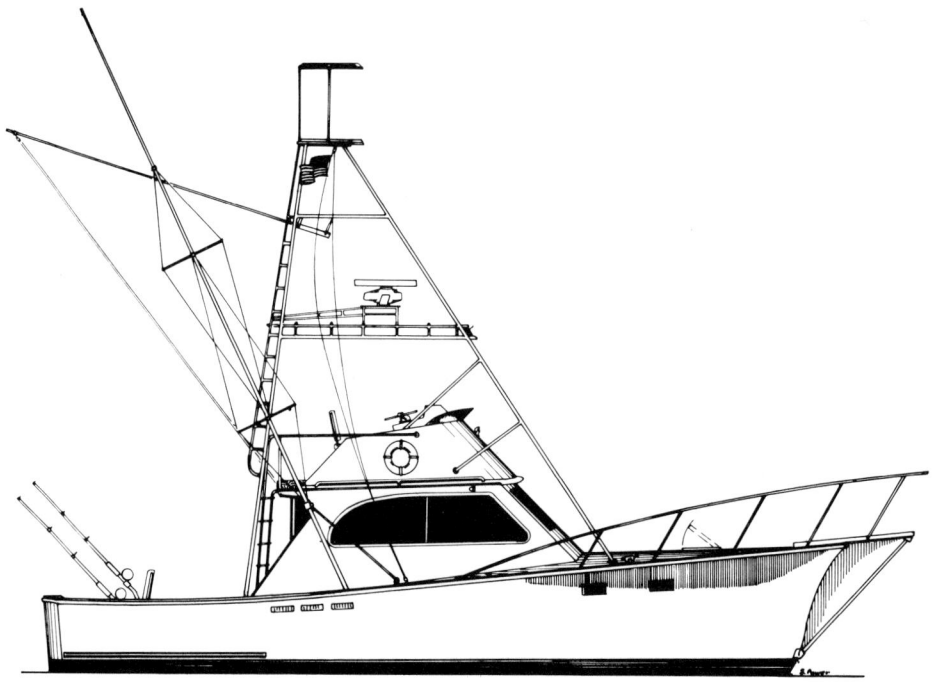

OUTBOARD PROFILE

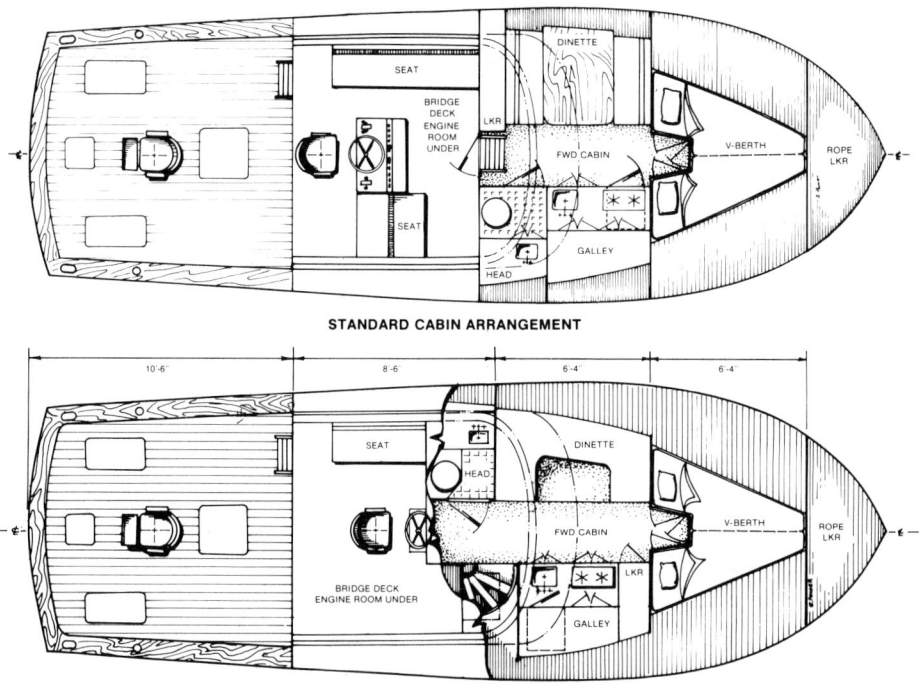

STANDARD CABIN ARRANGEMENT

ALTERNATE CABIN ARRANGEMENT

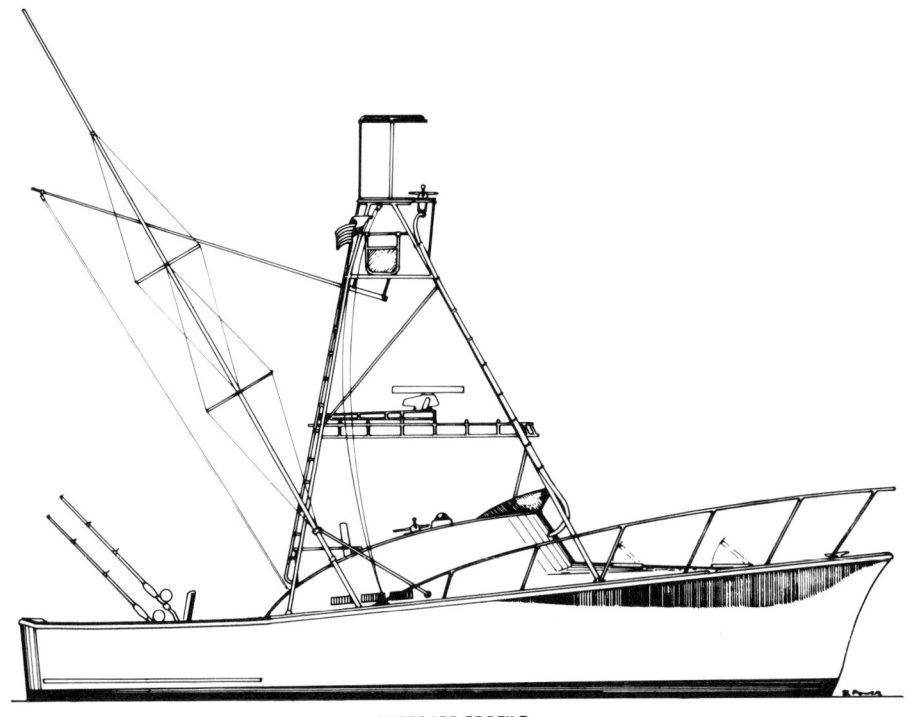

OUTBOARD PROFILE

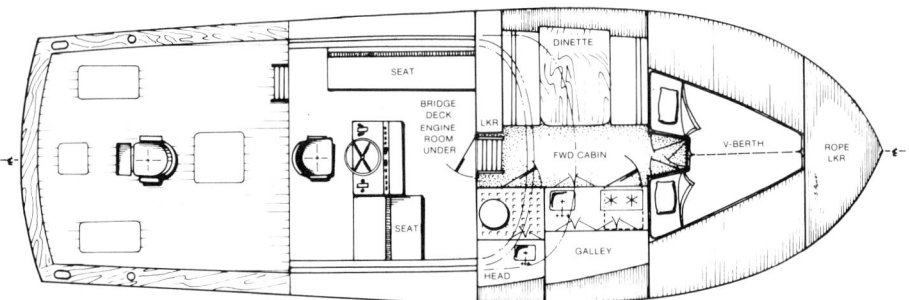

STANDARD CABIN ARRANGEMENT

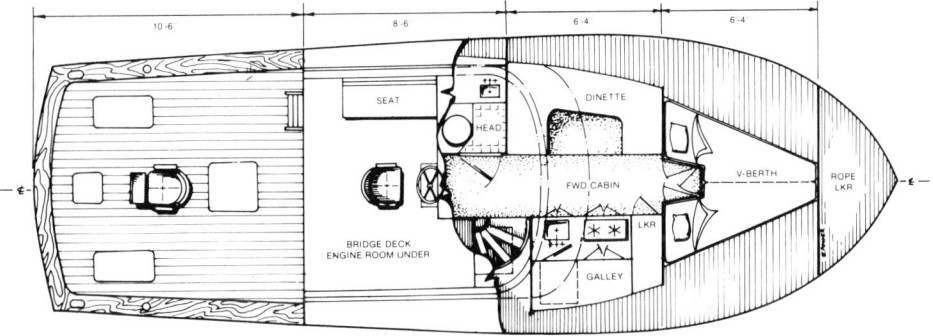

ALTERNATE CABIN ARRANGEMENT

Areas Fished

Kirn — Louisiana Coast, Gulf of Mexico
Toegemann — Atlantic, Block Island to Nantucket
Magliozzi — Massachusetts Bay, Ipswich Bay, Cape Cod,
    Nantucket

Owners' Evaluations

	Kirn	*Toegemann*	*Magliozzi*
Fuel economy	Super	Super	Super
Handling qualities	Good	Super	Super
Seaworthiness	Super +	Super +	Super
Overall design	Good	Good	Super
Cruising comfort	Super	Good	Good
Fishing efficiency	Super	Super	Super
Ease of maintenance	Good	Super	Super
Investment value	Good	Super	Super

Owners' Comments

Kirn: "This hull will take any head-on sea . . . compared to other sportfishing
    boats I have owned, I rate this one superior."

Toegemann: "My ultimate fishing machine . . . I rate its seaworthiness at the top
    of the performance list."

Magliozzi: "I'm in the charter business. Before buying this boat, I checked from
    Maine to Florida. This is the best in my opinion . . . good boat plus
    good clientele equals good pay."

Standard Equipment

Engine Systems

Engine alarm system for low oil pressure
    and high water temperature
Engine compartment, fully insulated
Filters, fuel, primary and secondary
Fuel system, 300-gal capacity (two
    150-gal tanks) aluminum or SS with
    crossover manifold
Freshwater cooling
Raw engine water strainers
Vibration-dampening engine mounts

Electrical

Batteries, 12-v., 100-Ah (4)
Battery boxes
Battery switch, 4-way
Bilge pumps, 12-v. (2)
Bonding system with ground plate

Dual 12-v. system
Lighting, 12-v., interior, bilge, cockpit,
    international navigation
Panel, 12-v. with circuit breakers in
    salon, auxiliary 12-v. panel on bridge,
    110-v. panel with circuit breakers in
    salon
Shore power, 30-amp, 110-v., with volt-
    meter and 50-ft shore cord
Wiring, color-coded
Zinc collars, one per shaft, one per
    rudder

Mechanical

Exhaust system, 5-in, with 5-in fiber-
    glass muffler
Rudders, manganese bronze

HARRIS 36-FOOT SPORTFISHERMAN RANGE/FUEL CURVE

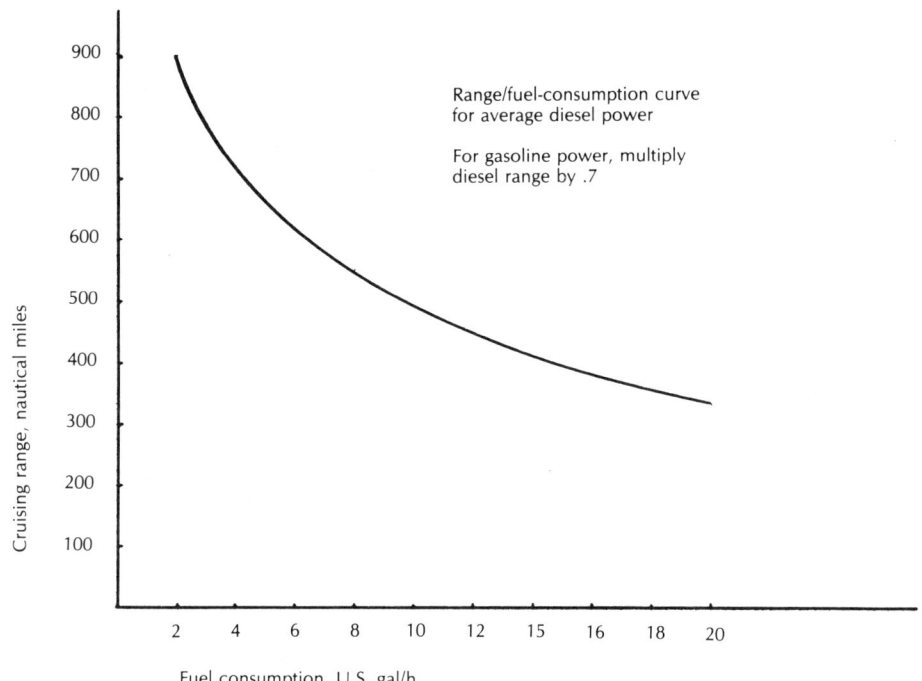

Range/fuel-consumption curve
for average diesel power

For gasoline power, multiply
diesel range by .7

The relationship of cruising range to fuel consumption can be expressed graphically. This curve gives approximate cruising ranges for various rates of fuel consumption with typical diesel power in the Harris 36-foot hull. It can be interpolated as being fairly typical of similar hulls of the same size and weight. Because the data base used to construct the curve was obtained from planing speeds, the graph should not be considered accurate for the same hull at displacement speeds (usually under 12 knots). Accuracy should be considered as plus or minus 10 percent. Source of data: Builder's speed/fuel/range information based on standard 250-gallon fuel capacity. Low cutoff point for planing is probably about 4 gph.

Sea valves on all underwater intake and
   discharge fittings
Shaft logs, manganese bronze
Shafts, 1½-in SS
Steering, manual hydraulic
Struts, manganese bronze

Deck Hardware and Exterior

Anchor, 22-S
Anchor line, 500-ft, ½-in nylon
Anchor chain
Anchor chocks
Bow rail, SS
Chocks, 6-in skene type

Cleats, 12-in bow, 10-in springline,
   10-in stern
Docklines (4)
Fog bell
Hatch forward, smoked Lexan
Hawsepipes for stern cleats
Horn, twin trumpet air
Paint, bottom, antifouling
Rope pipe deck plate (for anchor line)

Water Systems

Dockside freshwater connection
Freshwater tank, molded, 75-gal

Hot-water heater, 12-gal, 110-v. and off
  heat exchanger
Water system, pressurized hot/cold, with
  expansion tank

Flying Bridge

Compass, 5-in, flush-mounted
Engine controls, dual-lever
Helm console
Helm seat, adjustable, swivel
Helm wheel, SS
Horn, 12-v., dual trumpet
Instrumentation: oil pressure, water
  temperature, ammeters, tachometers,
  hour meters
Ladder, SS with teak steps
Safety rails, SS
Seats, box-type with cushions (2)
Windshield, tinted Venturi-type

Salon

Aft bulkhead with sliding doors
Bulkhead finish, high-pressure laminate
Carpeting throughout
Cushions, on dinette and engine boxes
Draperies
Furniture, convertible dinette
Overhead, perforated headliner
Trim, varnished teak
Windows, sliding side windows, fixed
  forward windows

Galley

Cabinets, varnished teak
Counter, high-pressure laminate
Refrigerator, 12-v./110-v.
Sink, SS
Stove, 2-burner, alcohol

Head

Exhaust fan
Medicine cabinet
Mirror
Toilet, electric
Trim, varnished teak
Vanity, varnished teak with high-
  pressure laminate countertop
Wall coverings, finished with high-
  pressure laminate

Forward Stateroom

Carpeting throughout
Cushions, 4-in Polyfoam, upholstered
Dresser
Hanging locker
Trim, varnished teak
V-berths with storage under
Wall coverings, finished with high-
  pressure laminate

Miscellaneous

Fire extinguishers, 2½-lb, dry-chemical
  (3)
Life jackets, adult (6)

Optional Equipment

Tuna tower and controls
Cockpit controls
Cradle, shipping and storage
Transom and bow lettering
Bow pulpit
Constavolt, 30-amp, 12-v.
Shower with curtain
Teak cockpit floor
Transom door
Gin pole
Live-bait well
Generator, 3-kw, diesel

Air conditioning, electric heat
Autopilot, Unipas 2000, 2nd station
Windlass
Bimini top, bridge
Tackle locker, cockpit
Cooler and storage unit, cockpit
Saltwater washdown
Colored hull
Trim tabs, 36-in Bennet, molded into
  hull
Launch and make-ready (plus fuel)

Comparative Prices with Standard Equipment
(1978 list*)

Harris 36-foot Sportfisherman

Power	Base Price
Twin 330-hp Chrysler gasoline	$ 82,900
Twin Caterpillar 3208 diesels	97,900
Twin GM 4-71 TI diesels	103,500
Single GM 6-71 diesels	87,900

Harris 36-foot Express Fisherman

Power	Base Price
Twin 330-hp Chrysler gasoline	$77,900
Twin Caterpillar 3208 diesels	92,900
Twin GM 4-71 TI	97,500
Twin GM 6-71	98,500

Harris 36-foot Sportfisherman

Power	Base Price
Single GM 6-71	$44,900

*Prices quoted are for comparison only. For current prices, consult manufacturer.

EGG HARBOR
36-FOOT TOURNAMENT FISHERMAN

Designer	Egg Harbor Boat Company
Builder	Egg Harbor Boat Company Egg Harbor City, NJ 08215
Construction	Fiberglass hull, decks, and super-structure. Mahogany interior trim, teak exterior trim.

Specifications

Length overall	36 ft	11.00 m
Length, waterline	NA	NA
Beam, maximum	13 ft 3 in	4.00 m
Draft	2 ft 9 in	0.84 m
Cockpit area	100 sq ft	9.30 m²

Continued

Functionally modern in design, the 36-foot Tournament Fisherman from Egg Harbor packs cruiser accommodations into a hull that many consider an ideal size for competitive fishing. (Courtesy of Egg Harbor Boat Co.)

Specifications *continued*

Freeboard forward	5 ft 5 in	1.65 m
Freeboard aft	3 ft	0.92 m
Height above waterline	NA	NA
Weight	NA	NA
Fuel capacity	356 gal	1,346 l
Water capacity	75 gal	283 l
Sleeping accommodations	6	

Power options
    Standard: Twin 330-hp Chrysler gasoline, 2.5:1 reduction gear
    Other power by arrangement with builder

Performance

While performance data were not available at the time of this writing, comparison with generally similar hulls seems to indicate top speed of at least 30 mph at full throttle and cruising speed of 25 mph at 80 percent throttle. Using the latter as a guide and assuming a fuel rate of 25 gph, or 1 mpg, cruising range at 25 mph would be slightly over 350 miles.

Description

Many serious anglers regard the size range of 36 to 40 feet as ideal for competitive tournament fishing. The Egg Harbor 36-foot Tournament Fisherman fits in the lower end of this category yet includes adequate beam for stability and cruising

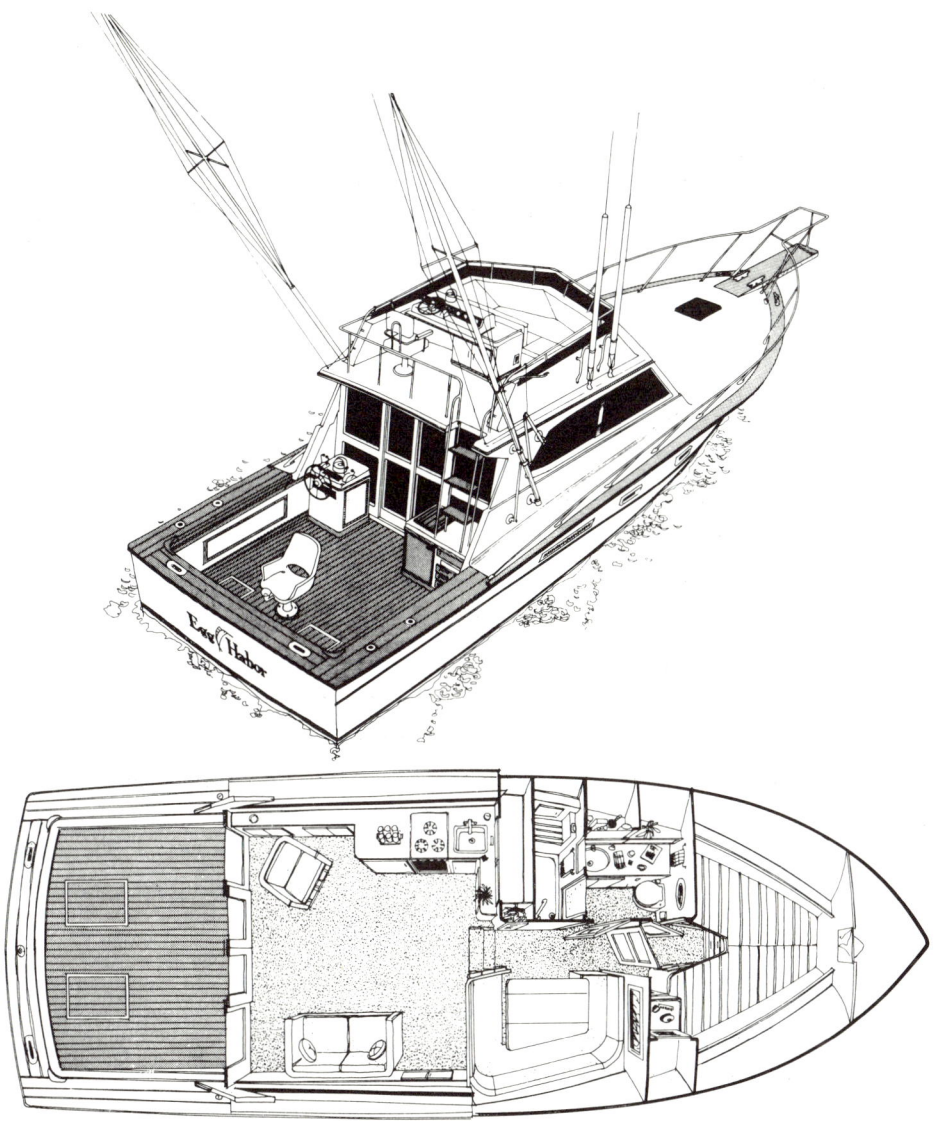

accommodations for up to six persons. Layout is conventional for this type of service, with plenty of room in the cockpit for a full-sized fighting chair and two light fishing chairs. A control station can be placed to port and a bait-tackle center, to starboard behind the deckhouse bulkhead.

The flying bridge is well thought out, with the helmsman's station located far aft for a good view of the cockpit and a large array of weathertight instruments and controls. A bench-style seat along the forward edge of the control console doubles as a tackle locker, with access from the deckhouse, below. This is clever use of available space. This bench also provides seating for four or more, who may be extra lookouts or guests.

Interior appointments rival those of a well-found cruising yacht. Mahogany paneling is used throughout, with meticulous attention to detail. The fairly small deckhouse features a galley to port and a two-seater lounge to starboard. A U-shaped luxury lounge below, to starboard, features a hydraulically operated single-pedestal table that lowers to become part of a 7-foot double bed.

An alternative floor plan provides a separate guest stateroom in lieu of the luxury lounge. The master stateroom (so described by the builder) is located forward with two large V-berths, drawers and lockers, and a screened, opening hatch to the forward deck. The head, located to port, has a stall shower and the usual furnishings.

TOLLYCRAFT 37-FOOT CONVERTIBLE SEDAN

Designer	Edward Monk, Jr. Seattle, WA
Builder	Tollycraft 2200 Clinton Avenue Kelso, WA 98626
Construction	One-piece fiberglass hull, decks, and superstructure.

Specifications

Length overall	37 ft 4 in	11.4 m
Length, waterline	33 ft 5 in	10.2 m
Beam, maximum	13 ft 2 in	4.0 m
Draft	3 ft	0.9 m
Cockpit area	90 sq ft	8.4 m²
Freeboard forward	6 ft	1.83 m
Freeboard aft	4 ft 2 in	1.28 m
Height above waterline	12 ft 6 in	3.75 m
Weight (average, gasoline)	22,000 lb	10,000 kg
Weight (average, diesel)	24,000 lb	10,910 kg
Fuel capacity	300 gal	1,134 l
Water capacity	138 gal	484 l
Sleeping accommodations	4-6	

Power options
  Twin 330-hp MerCruiser gasoline, 1.9:12 reduction gear
  Twin 3208 Caterpillar diesels

Performance

With twin 330-hp MerCruiser gasoline motors, full fuel and water tanks

Top speed	28.5 kn (32.5 mph) @ 4000 rpm
Top fuel rate*	40.0 gph
Top fuel economy	0.71 nmpg (0.81 mpg)
Top-speed endurance	7.50 hr

Solid comfort while on a fishing cruise is the hallmark of this West Coast fisherman. She has accommodations for four to six. Twin 330-hp gasoline motors drive her to 28.5 knots and twin Caterpillar diesels can provide 21 knots and a 328-nautical-mile cruising range at 17.5 knots. (Photo by Tollycraft)

Top-speed range	214 nm (244 mi)
Cruising speed	22.0 kn (25.1 mph) @ 3000 rpm
Cruising fuel rate*	24.0 gph
Cruising fuel economy	0.92 nmpg (1.05 mpg)
Cruising endurance	12.5 hr
Cruising range	275 nm (313 mi)

With twin 3208 Caterpillar diesels, full fuel and water tanks

Top speed	21.0 kn (24.0 mph) @ 2800 rpm
Top fuel rate*	24.0 gph
Top fuel economy	0.92 nmpg (1.05 mpg)
Top-speed endurance	12.5 hr
Top-speed range	275 nm (313 mi)
Cruising speed	17.5 kn (20.0 mph) @ 2500 rpm
Cruising fuel rate*	16.0 gph
Cruising fuel economy	1.09 nmpg (1.25 mpg)
Cruising endurance	18.75 hr
Cruising range	328 nm (374 mi)

Fuel rates are builder's estimates.

Description

With a distinctive West Coast look, the Tollycraft 37-foot Convertible Sedan is a very comfortable, medium-range power cruiser easily adapted to light-, medium-, or big-game sportfishing. Emphasis is on cruising comfort and easy

37' CONVERTIBLE SEDAN

ENGINE: TWIN 330
FUEL: FULL
WATER: FULL

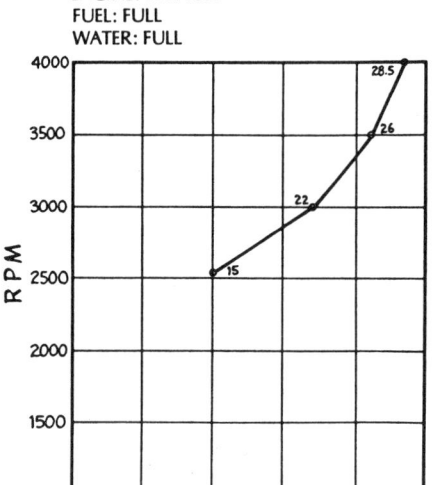

37' CONVERTIBLE SEDAN

ENGINE: TWIN 3208 CAT DIESELS
FUEL: FULL
WATER: FULL

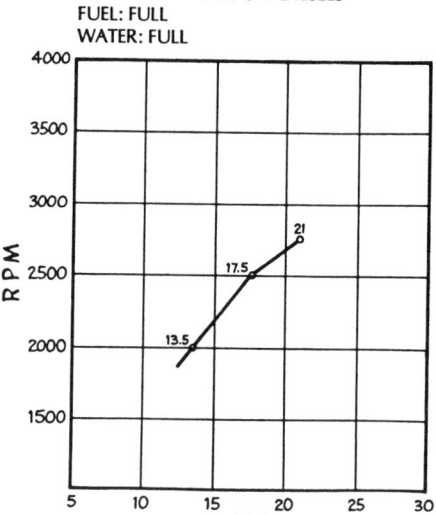

Comparing the gasoline and diesel speed curves, it is apparent that the Tollycraft 37-foot hull displays most efficient cruising speeds between 15 and 22 knots.

operation and maintenance without professional help. The 90-square-foot cockpit is quite adequate for family game fishing. The ogee sheer of the flying-bridge wings is aesthetically pleasing, but placement of the operator's station far forward on the bridge makes it difficult for him to observe cockpit activities while fishing. This may be no great handicap while slow-trolling for fish like salmon, but it would be a distinct disadvantage in Mexico, Southern California, or Hawaii, where marlin, swordfish, and large, active yellowfin tuna abound.

Two interior layout plans are offered. Plan A places the galley on the starboard side of the commodious deckhouse. In this plan the deckhouse carries an L-shaped settee to port with high-low table and an extra comfortable chair. There is a stateroom to port, below, with upper and lower berths and another cabin in the bow with V-berths. To starboard, below, are a large shelf-top wardrobe and a commodious head with W.C., sink, shower, lockers, etc. Berthing arrangements under Plan A can accommodate six.

Plan B has the galley below, to port, in the space of the upper-lower stateroom of Plan A. The bulkhead between galley and deckhouse is cut away so the galley is entirely visible from the deckhouse, a modern treatment that enhances the feeling of open space. The deckhouse layout offers a double-bed settee to port, with an optional arrangement of other furniture to starboard. Forward, the V-berth stateroom is identical with Plan A, as is the head arrangement.

Both plans provide for a permanent, lower-deckhouse steering station to starboard in addition to the bridge station. A cockpit steering station is not offered, since this is seldom a requirement for West Coast fishing. Decor is nautical rather than modern-designer style with emphasis on hand-rubbed hardwood surfaces and trim. Large and pleasingly distributed windows add to the feeling of interior space. The overall effect is that of a boat designed and equipped for gracious on-the-water living, with fishing as an important adjunct.

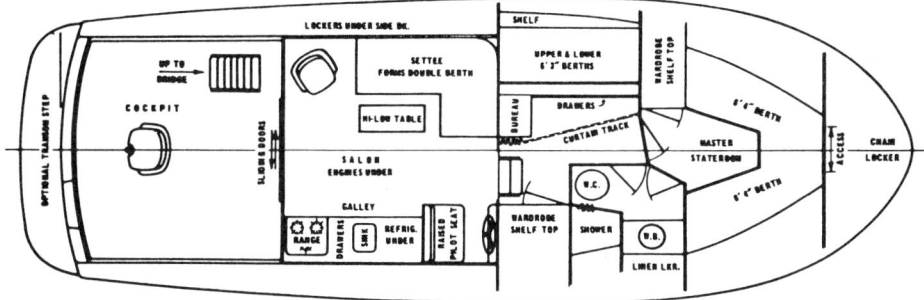

Upper Galley "Plan A"

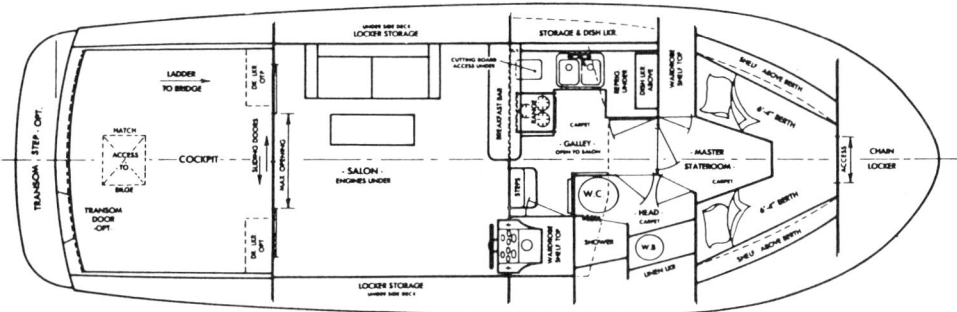

Lower Galley "Plan B"

Owner's Evaluation

From Mr. and Mrs. Steve Wilcox of Longview, Washington, there is an owner's evaluation of two Tollycraft 37-foot Convertible Sedans used for professional charter fishing work out of Maui and the Kona Coast of Hawaii. The Wilcoxes report an annual working period of 1,500 hours and 12,000 miles, with 20 percent of the time spent in cruising and 80 percent in game fishing. Power is a pair of Model 3208 Caterpillar diesels rated at 210 hp per engine. Here is their performance evaluation:

Fuel economy	Good
Handling qualities	Super
Seaworthiness	Super
Overall design	Good
Cruising comfort	Super
Fishing efficiency	Good
Ease of maintenance	Good
Investment value	Good

The Wilcoxes put their ultimate cruising range at about 400 miles at 15 mph with 300 gallons of fuel. Mr. Wilcox says of the boats' flying bridges, "Bridge controls could be relocated farther aft for better visual contact between skipper and cockpit, but the large bridge is excellent for professional charter fishing work. The hull is very seaworthy, dependable, and for its price a good investment."

Captain Dave Padgett, the Wilcoxes' professional skipper, makes this personal observation:

> *No-Ka-Ai V* [a third 37-foot Tollycraft owned by the Wilcoxes] is a 1977 model and has been used only on the Columbia River for salmon, and for albacore fishing in the Pacific off the Columbia River. So far the annual use is about 200 hours, with about 40 percent of the time in trolling and 60 percent cruising. We feel that besides being a good sportfishing boat, it is also built for cruising comfort. To date [October 15, 1979], the two boats in Hawaii have logged 5,700 and 3,600 hours, respectively, and we have had to replace only one Cutless shaft bearing.

Steve Wilcox rates ease of maintenance and seaworthiness as the two qualities of greatest importance in a boat for charter. He rates fishing efficiency, handling ability, and investment value as the next most important qualities. Third priority goes to fuel economy and personal comfort, with cruising range in fourth and final place.

Standard Equipment

Mechanical

Twin 330-hp MerCruiser freshwater
   cooled gasoline engines, 1.97:1 reduc-
   tion gear
Twin 3208 Caterpillar freshwater cooled
   diesels
Alarm system, audio, temperature and oil
Batteries, 12 v. DC (3)
Battery switches, vaporproof
Bearings, Cutless rubber, propeller shafts
Belt guards on engines
Bilge blowers, 12 v. DC (2)
Bilge pumps, 12 v. DC (3)
Circuits individually fused, color-coded
Compasses (2)
Electrolysis bonding system
Engine hour meters (2)
Full instrumentation, both control
   stations
Lights, engineroom, 12 v. DC
Mounts, engine, adjustable
Mufflers, engine
Oil change pump system, 12 v. DC
Propeller shafts, heavy-duty, SS, 1½-in
Steering, hydraulic
Through-hull fittings, bronze below
   waterline, nylon above

Transmissions, hydraulic
Underwater gear, high-test bronze
Shore power system, 120 v. AC, with
   outlets
Shore power cable, 50-ft
120 v. AC circuit-breaker panel
12 v. DC circuit-breaker panel
12-gal hot-water heater

Exterior

Anchor with rode
Bell
Command bridge with control station,
   seats, covers
Cover, cabin windshield
Deck hardware, SS
Ensign staff, teak
Handrails, 1-in SS
Horn, freon, 12 v. DC
Ladders, cockpit, teak
Ladder, bridge, 1-in SS
Lights, anchor, dash, bridge, 12 v. DC
Lights, international running, 12 v. DC
Mooring lines (3)
Toe rails, teak
Tollycraft pennant with bow staff
Transom door and step

Venturi windshield, bridge
Window screens on opening windows
Windows, tinted glass
Windshield wipers (3)

Interior

Breakfast bar
Cabinet, dish
Carpet, cabin sole, interior hull sides
Carpet pad, all cabins
Chain locker in forepeak, with door
Decor, color-coordinated
Doors, privacy
Draperies
Drawers, wood
Fire extinguishers (3)
Formica countertops
Forward cabin hatch with screen
Heads, self-contained, 12 v. DC
Headliner, cabin, perforated vinyl
High-low table
Insulation, engineroom

Interior cabinetry, teak-accented
Ladders, cabin, teak
Lights, cabin, 12 v. DC/120 v. AC
Lockers, hanging
Lower control station
Mattresses, cushions, Polyfoam and
  Dacron
Mirrors, head and stateroom
Owner's manual
Pastry board
Portlights with screens
Propane tank with regulator
Range, propane, 3-burner, with oven,
  cover
Refrigerator, 12 v. DC/120 v. AC
Settee, convertible
Shower with drain pump, 12 v. DC
Sinks, SS, head and galley
Sliding doors, salon to cockpit
V-berth filler pad
Water system, pressure hot and cold

Optional Equipment

Mechanical

Automatic bilge-pump switches
Batteries, 205-amp (exchange)
Battery charger, 40-amp
Battery isolator switch
Engine synchronizers
AC outlet, exterior, extra
Gas detector (sniffer)
Generator, 7.5-kw, gasoline
Generator, 12.5-kw, diesel
Engine hour meter, generator
Spare shaft-storage tube
Strainers, intake water, gasoline
Trim tabs, dual station

Exterior

Anchor windlass, 12 v. DC, with chain,
  bow roller
Anchor windlass, 12 v. DC, with chain,
  bow pulpit
Bottom paint, antifouling
Deck box with cushion

Seawater washdown pump, 12 v. DC
Transom step, swim ladder

Interior

Air conditioning, reverse-cycle
AM/FM stereo tape, 8 speakers
Head, Vacu-Flush, Mansfield
Heater, 120 v. AC
Heater, propane
Icemaker*
Lower-station helm seat*
Lower-station helm seat with cabinet
Power ventilator, head, 12 v. DC
Range, 120 v. AC, with oven
Refrigerator, extra, 12 v. DC/120 v. AC*
Trash compactor, 120 v. AC*

Must be purchased with lower-station helm seat with cabinet (lower-galley model only).

Miscellaneous

Shipping cradle, bridge
Shipping cradle, hull

HATTERAS 37-FOOT CONVERTIBLE

Designer	J.B. Hargrave, N.A., Inc. 205½ Sixth Street West Palm Beach, FL 33401
Builder	AMF — Hatteras Yachts 2100 Kivett Drive P.O. Box 2690 High Point, NC 27261
Construction	Fiberglass hull, deck, and super-structure, with teak and hardwood trim and decor

Specifications

Length overall	37 ft	11.29 m
Length, waterline	32 ft 2 in	9.82 m
Beam, maximum	14 ft	4.27 m
Draft	3 ft 3 in	1.00 m
Cockpit area	100 sq ft	9.30 m²
Freeboard forward	6 ft 4 in	1.93 m
Freeboard aft	3 ft 8 in	1.12 m
Headroom, interior	6 ft 6 in	2.00 m
Height, waterline to windshield	13 ft 5 in	4.10 m
Weight, normal load	29,000 lb	12,955 kg
Fuel capacity	330 gal	1,247 l
Water capacity	135 gal	510 l
Sleeping accommodations	4-6	

Power options
  Twin 310-hp GM 671N diesels
  Twin 360-hp GM 671TI diesels

Performance (normal full loads of fuel and water)

With twin GM 671N diesels
(310 hp × 2 = 620 total hp)

Top speed	25 mph @ 2500 rpm
Top fuel rate	40 gph, or 0.63 mpg
Cruising speed	20 mph @ 2300 rpm
Cruising fuel rate	30 gph, or 0.67 mpg

With twin GM 671TI diesels
(360 hp × 2 = 720 total hp)

Top speed	30 mph @ 2500 rpm
Top fuel rate	34 gph, or 0.88 mpg
Cruising speed	26 mph @ 2300 rpm
Cruising fuel rate	27 gph, or 0.96 mpg

The word "convertible" suggests a boat of several purposes, and the Hatteras 37-footer combines cruising comfort with a high degree of tournament-quality fishing efficiency. Twin diesels promise speeds to 30 mph. (Photo by AMF — Hatteras Yachts)

The builder notes that "speed and consumption figures are attained by measuring under ideal weather and sea conditions, with substantially full water and fuel tanks. Performance above can be expected under similar conditions but is not guaranteed."

Calculated endurance and range (from builder's data, 330 gal)

	Twin 671N	*Twin 671TI*
Top-speed endurance	8.25 hr	9.71 hr
Cruising endurance	11.00 hr	12.22 hr
Top-speed range	208 mi	290 mi
Cruising range	221 mi	317 mi

The builder's performance data and the endurance and range figures derived from these data suggest that in this boat we have an interesting combination of relatively high, most-efficient planing speed and higher engine efficiency with turbocharging and intercooling of the engines.

The TI diesels, for instance, cruise the boat 1 mph faster than the top speed available with engines under natural aspiration. The difference in fuel rates is startling: 0.63 mpg at 25 mph for the naturally aspirated engines and 0.96 mpg at 26 mph for the TI engines. This represents an increase of propulsive efficiency of

*Opposite top: A well-appointed galley is to port in the deckhouse. Rod stowage is in overhead racks. **Opposite bottom:** The saloon is spacious with excellent visibility. **Left:** The master stateroom in this plan has upper and lower berths. **Below left:** The interior of the master head is well arranged. A separate door secludes the shower. **Below right:** Twin V-berths are fitted in the forward stateroom. (Photos by AMF — Hatteras Yachts)*

better than 50 percent at that speed. A gain of efficiency of even half this amount would thoroughly justify the added expense of installing TI engines in a new boat or a vessel that is being repowered.

Description

The Hatteras 37-foot Convertible is an excellent example of that popular class of powerboat, the family fishing cruiser. It is small enough to be owned and operated by a family unit without professional help, yet large enough, fast enough, and well enough designed and equipped to be highly competitive in tournament-style game fishing. Styling is strictly modern, but it is not allowed to interfere with normal efficient installation of fishing equipment.

The cockpit is not large by some standards, but it is easily sufficient for a full-sized fighting chair or a pair of smaller fishing chairs. The influence of fishermen is noted in the placement of the bridge control station well aft on the flying bridge, where an unobstructed view of the cockpit is essential to successful game fishing. The vessel pictured sports a low tower, but a taller tower can be handled easily. The very generous beam of 14 feet represents a beam-length ratio of 1:2.64, close to what may be considered the practical limit of ratio for a boat of this length. The generous beam, however, does not seem to detract from the boat's ability to get up and go under the push of a maximum of 720 hp.

Construction in fiberglass is contemporary. The hull is laid up in solid fiberglass, while decks and cabin are of sandwich construction. Cabins are equipped with a vinyl perforated headliner, and hull sides exposed in compartments are covered with sponge-backed vinyl for heat-sound insulation. An unusual practice is to cover exterior gelcoated surfaces with polyurethane paint for greater durability and easier maintenance.

Interior finish is hand-rubbed and oiled teak paneling. Particular pains are taken to match grain and color. Carpeting is supplied throughout in the interior. The raised flush forward deck is unusual in a boat of this size and creates a great deal of useful room below. The strong reverse sheer is distinctive and is repeated in other Hatteras models.

Handling qualities have been described as a mixed bag. The double-chine underbody minimizes wetted area and maximizes interior space but produces a rougher ride than the straight deep-V hull. Stability, however, is outstanding both underway and while motionless in rough water. The boat tracks true in rough water and the manual-hydraulic steering system makes steering almost effortless.

In truth, the Hatteras 37-foot Convertible is a very successful compromise between the sometimes-conflicting requirements of a stylish, family power cruiser and a boat capable of true competitive fishing. Its rating among the cognoscenti of sportfishing is quite high.

Standard Equipment

The standard equipment listed for the 37-foot Convertible is essentially the same for other Hatteras models presented in this book. The complete list will not be repeated for other Hatteras models, but significant changes in standard and optional equipment will be given for other models.

Hardware and Miscellaneous

All hardware chrome-on-brass or SS
Anchor with chocks (1) and deck
  hawsepipe
Stern cleats and hawsepipes (2 each)
Springline cleats, bow cleats and chocks
  (2 each)
SS bow, side-deck, and flying-bridge
  handrails
SS bridge ladder, boarding step with teak
  steps
Fog bell, dual electric fog horn, boat-
  hook
Zincs on rudders and shafts
Nonskid exterior decks
Bow and stern staffs with ensign and
  pennant
Life jackets and life ring
Mooring lines
Portable fire extinguishers
Trim tabs

Engineroom and Bilge

12 v. DC caged lights, 12 v. DC bilge
  blowers
Twin diesels, freshwater-cooled
  Mufflers
  Hour meters
  Heavy-duty alternators
  Fuel filters
  Raw-water strainers
Automatic, remote-manual
  fire-extinguisher system
7.5-kw diesel generator, freshwater-
  cooled
Fuel-tank selector manifold
Automatic bilge pumps (4), hand bilge
  pump (1)
Portable fire extinguisher
Sea valves on all underwater through-
  hull fittings
Electrical bonding throughout
1¾-in SS propeller shafts
Bronze struts with rubber strut bearings
Bronze rudders and 4-blade propellers
Reinforced fiberglass fuel tanks
Sewage holding tank with dockside
  pumpout
DC battery panels

Electrical System

Two banks, heavy-duty, 12 v. DC
  batteries with auto-charger

Battery paralleling system, switch at
  control console
Transformer-connected shoreline
12 v. DC and 120 v. AC lighting fixtures
120 v. AC duplex outlets
Control and distribution panels with
  circuit breakers
Visual-audio engine-temperature, oil-
  pressure systems
Full engine instrumentation at main
  control station
AC power loss with ground-fault
  interruption, AC circuits
Navigation lights
SSB ground screen laminated in hardtop

Deckhouse and Galley

Carpeting, vinyl headlining, draperies
High-pressure laminate countertops
Access hatch to engineroom
Storage cabinets, one with damp-chaser
Refrigerator with freezer
3-burner, 120 v. AC range with oven
SS sink
Tinted safety glass, sliding side windows
12 v. DC and 120 v. AC fixtures and
  outlets
Windshield cover for privacy

Flying Bridge

Bench seat with vinyl-covered cushions
Storage lockers
SS rails and stanchions
Tinted acrylic windshield
Control station with instrumentation,
  lighted gauges
Dual-lever clutch and throttle controls
Compass with light
Hydraulic steering
Adjustable helmsman's seat

Cockpit

Molded fiberglass deck and sides
Hatches to lazarette and fuel-tank
  connections
Scuppers in cockpit and cockpit hatches
Ladder to flying bridge
Transom gate
Shoreline electrical inlet
Shore water connection

Bow Stateroom

Carpeting, padded vinyl hull-side
  covering and headlining

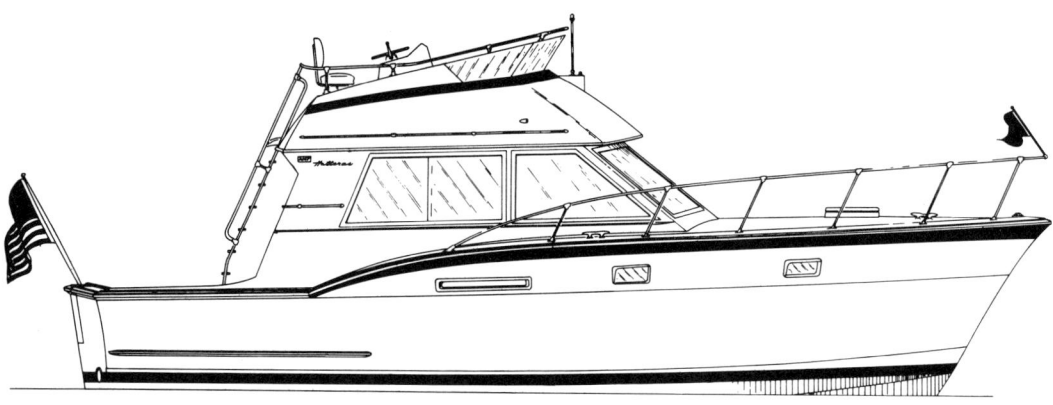

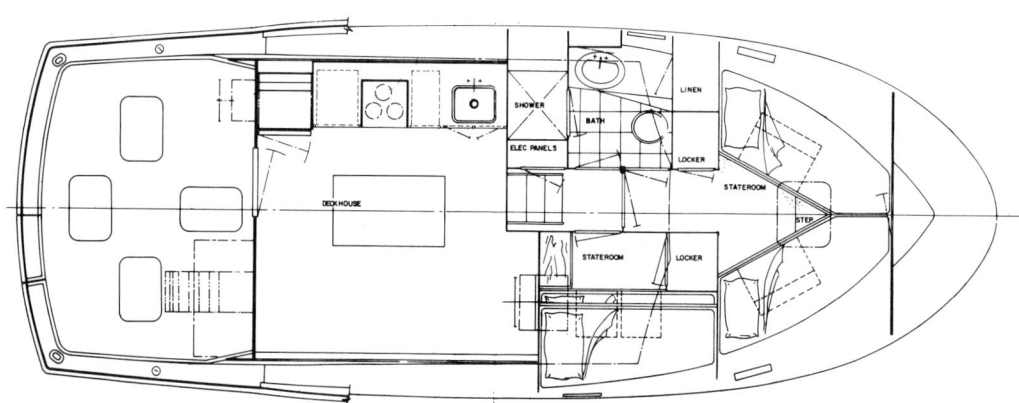

V-berths with Polyfoam mattresses
Storage under berths
Rope storage locker, hanging locker
Door to head
Ventilating frosted portlights
Screened overhead hatch
12 v. DC and 120 v. AC light fixtures,
    120 v. AC outlets
Full-length mirror

Head

Vinyl flooring, wall covering, headlining
High-pressure laminate countertop
Stall shower with seat, automatic sump
    pump
Vitreous china lavatory (electric)

Linen locker, medicine locker with
    mirror
Towel bars, retractable clothesline
Exhaust blower, 12 v. DC and 120 v. AC
    lights, outlets
Ventilating portlight with draperies

Guest Stateroom

Carpeting
Upper and lower berths with Polyfoam
    mattresses
Storage under lower berth
Nightstand with drawers, hanging locker
Portlight with draperies
12 v. DC and 120 v. AC light fixtures,
    120 v. AC outlets
Full-length mirror

Optional Equipment

Base Options

Cockpit or salon controls

Air conditioning, reverse-cycle
Icemaker

Swim platform on transom
Curved convertible deckhouse lounge
AM/FM stereo receiver with tape deck
Tackle center with bait freezer, sink,
   work surface
Cradle, heavy-duty
Water-delivery kit*

*Includes AT fluid, 1 case oil, oil spout, assort-
ment of screws, bulbs, fuses, etc.; deck mop and
brush, hose, nozzle, fenders, belts, impellers,
solenoids, etc.*

Mechanical Options

Pulpit, fiberglass
Windlass (two models available)
Extra anchor with chocks
Dunnage box, fiberglass
Air-box reservoir drains
Helm chair, additional, for bridge
Oil-changing system (GM)
Oil-changing system (generator)

Water Systems and Plumbing

Toilet, Raritan Crown
Washdown, freshwater, cockpit
Washdown, freshwater, foredeck
Washdown, saltwater, cockpit
Washdown, saltwater, foredeck

Fishing Equipment*

Rodholders, flush-mounted
Fighting chair, Pompanette R3RC
Fighting chair, Pompanette Y2QRC
Fighting chair, Pompanette Q4L

*Outriggers and/or tower by customer's special
order.*

Electronics

Raytheon Flashing Sounder F-360D
Raytheon Flashing Sounder F-720D
Raytheon Recording Sounder DE-936G
Raytheon Digital Sounder DE-750Digital
VHF/FM radiotelephones
   Raytheon 50A (remote control extra)
   Raytheon 48A
SSB radiotelephones
   Raytheon 1209C
Intercom, Bogen, 120 v. AC, 2-station
   (maximum 7)
Loran, Raytheon Model 6000
Radar
   Decca 110
   Raytheon 3900

Autopilot, Wood-Freeman Model 500B

Propulsion Equipment

Propellers for 671N or 671TI
Propeller shafts for 671N or 671TI

Canvas

Bimini top, bridge, folding
Flying-bridge cover
Flying-bridge enclosure, 3 or 4 sides
Bridge instrument-panel cover
Bridge helmsman-seat covers
Cockpit sun shade
Cockpit coaming padding
Searchlight cover, canvas front
Depth-sounder cover

Gauges and Instruments

Speedometer-odometer, Signet
Rudder-angle indicator, Yachtsman
Glendenning engine synchronizer
Compass compensation (1 or 2 units)

Decor and Furnishings

Carpeting for nonstandard areas
Sheets, standard berth
Mattress pads, all berths
Pillows, Dacron-filled
Upholstered helm seat, inside controls

Electrical and Appliances

Telephone inlet, 1 or more outlets
TV antenna, RCA rotating, 1 jack
TV outlets, additional
Receptacle, waterproof, 115 v. AC
Cockpit lights (2)
Engineroom light, additional
Searchlight, hand-held, 6-in
Searchlight, remote-control, 10-in
Additional searchlight, control station
Docking lights, bow and transom, pairs
Docking-light switches, additional
Garbage disposal

Paint

Boottop, other than standard black,
   including double colors
Feature stripe, optional single or double
   colors
Transom lettering, name and port
Registry number lettered on bow
Name lettered on bow

RYBOVICH 37-FOOT CUSTOM SPORTFISHERMAN "VAL JEAN"

Designer	John Rybovich & Sons
Builder	John Rybovich & Sons West Palm Beach, FL
Construction	Wood: Longitudinal cedar planks over sawn and bent white oak frames. Bottom double-planked with marine plywood and Philippine mahogany. Decks and superstructure fiberglass over marine plywood. Teak cockpit sole and covering boards, teak and Honduras mahogany trim.

Specifications

Length overall	37 ft	11.29 m
Length, waterline (approx)	35 ft	10.68 m
Beam, maximum	11 ft 4 in	3.46 m
Draft	2 ft 6 in	0.76 m
Cockpit area	100 sq ft	9.30 m²
Freeboard forward	NA	
Freeboard aft	NA	
Weight	NA	
Fuel capacity	270 gal	1,020 l
Water capacity	40 gal	151 l
Sleeping accommodations	5	

Power (as of rebuilding, 1978)
    Twin 1974 MerCruiser gasoline, 350 hp each @ 4200 rpm
        2.1:1 reduction gears
    Propellers: 20-in dia. × 22-in pitch, cupped, 3-blade Dyna-Jet

Performance

From data supplied by Florida yacht broker Bill Dunne, after her rebuilding in 1978, *Val Jean* gave the following performance:

Top speed	28 kn @ 4200 rpm
Top-speed fuel rate	50.0 gph, or 0.56 nmpg
Cruising speed	20 kn @ 3000 rpm
Cruising fuel rate	23.5 gph, or 0.85 nmpg
Cruising-speed range	204 nm
Cruising endurance	10.2 hr

Val Jean *runs quite level.*

Description

Val Jean is an example of a quality wooden hull that, with care and proper maintenance, has increased considerably in value with the passage of time. Built originally as *Suzi* by the Rybovich boatyard of West Palm Beach, Florida, in 1938, she underwent overhaul and rebuilding in 1978 after 40 years of active campaigning in southern waters. Bill Dunne lists *Val Jean* as Number 7 in the distinguished Rybovich line of custom-built sportfishermen.

Some observers have compared the early Rybovich boats to classic cars like the Cord, the Marmon, the early Packards, and the Pierce-Arrow. The difference is that an owner of one of the beautiful old classic cars is content to display his treasure a few times a year at parades and antique car shows, whereas the owner of a vintage Rybovich thinks nothing of competing head-to-head in tournament work, month after month, year after year, taking on the newest and fastest of the modern sportfishermen.

The semi-open deckhouse is rigged with drop curtains across the after end for maximum hot-weather ventilation. A full-length settee-berth occupies the port side, with a large tackle locker built into the space under the windows. To starboard is a dinette-berth with folding table, lockers, and a lower control station at the after break of the deckhouse.

Top left: The cockpit control station. Top right: The deckhouse rod locker holds six rigged rods. Center left: The uncluttered cockpit has a single fighting chair. Center right: The view forward into the deckhouse from the cockpit. A large storage locker is beneath the portside settee, which becomes a berth at night. Bottom left: The bridge control station is centerline. Just visible at the right of the photograph is the Loran unit. Bottom right: The galley and forward cabin are spacious and airy.

Below, there is a small, open galley to starboard and a head to port. Twin V-berths occupy the bow. Emphasis is on economy of space and reduction of unessential weight to increase performance. The boat is designed primarily for dayfishing with modest cruising accommodations.

The cockpit is equipped with a single fighting chair placed centerline, well aft. Baitwell and fish tank are underdeck. The bridge has the pilot seat located centerline with good visibility of the cockpit. Electronics, such as the sounder and radar console, swing out of the bridge console on door-backs. While the boat did not have it at the time of this evaluation, the bridge had been enclosed in a light plastic and aluminum canopy for protection against northeastern fog and inclement weather.

Interior below is mainly painted, maximizing the feeling of space and light. Hardwood-finish trim is hand rubbed. Natural teak cockpit and forward decks complete the nautical effect and provide excellent nonskid surfaces. The hull exterior was fiberglassed during the 1978 refit.

The V-bottomed hull form is in no way extreme or unconventional. The beam of 11 feet 4 inches was considered rather wide at the time of her building, but its 3.09:1 length-beam ratio is consistent with modern design and provides great stability when trolling at low speeds in rough water. All of the custom Rybovich models are noted for their comfort and easy motion in a seaway. The hull runs level and remarkably dry at cruising and maximum speeds.

Standard Equipment

The following equipment list is from the Bill Dunne listing and represents the equipment present at that time.

Benmar Model MR12, 12-mi radar
Modar Model Triton 15-channel, 25-watt
    VHF/FM radio with bridge remote
E.F. Johnson Messenger 5-watt CB
    radio transceiver
Northstar Model 2000A dual automatic
    tracking Loran-A
Furuno Model FE500 recording depth
    sounder
Datamarine digital depth sounder
Dytek digital sea-temperature gauge
Benmar automatic pilot
J.W. Sniffer fume detector
Fi-Quench Halon fire-control system
Rybovich hot/cold water-pressure system
Sendur hot-water heater

Rybovich outriggers, 28-ft, telescoping
Rybovich fighting chair
Bimini top, full enclosure
Enclosed 6-rod storage locker
Rybovich rod hangers (6)
Danforth Model 22S anchor, 300-ft, ¾-in
    nylon anchor line
Cockpit cover
Bow rail
Auto-electric bilge pumps (3)
Manual bilge pump (1)
Spare propellers (2)
Spare engine parts
Freshwater washdown connection
Pioneer AM/FM stereo cassette player
    with speakers in cabin and on bridge

BERTRAM 38-FOOT III CONVERTIBLE

Designer	Bertram Yacht Division, Whittaker Corp.
Builder	Bertram Yacht 3663 N.W. 21st Street Miami, FL 33142
Construction	Fiberglass hull, decks, and superstructure.

Specifications

Length overall	38 ft 6 in	11.74 m
Length, waterline	33 ft	10.07 m
Beam, maximum	13 ft 3 in	4.04 m
Draft	3 ft 7 in	1.09 m
Cockpit area	100 sq ft	9.30 m²
Freeboard forward	5 ft 6 in	1.68 m
Freeboard aft	3 ft 4 in	1.02 m
Height above waterline	12 ft	3.66 m
Weight, with generator		
Gasoline, dry	22,000 lb	9,979 kg
Diesel, dry	24,000 lb	10,886 kg
Gasoline, cruise	26,000 lb	11,794 kg
Fuel capacity	399 gal	1,510 l
Water capacity	100 gal	379 l
Sleeping accommodations	6	

Power options
Twin MerCruiser 330-hp gasoline
Twin Cummins 270-hp 555 VT diesels
Twin Caterpillar 270-hp Turbo diesels

Performance

Builder's tests with 399-gallon (1,510-liter) tank capacity.

With twin 330-hp MerCruiser gasoline engines

Top speed	27.5 mph (41.0 kph)	@ 4000 rpm
Cruising speed	22.0 mph (32.8 kph)	@ 3200 rpm
Cruising range	223 mi (332 km)	@ 3200 rpm

With twin 270-hp Cummins diesels

Top speed	25.7 mph (38.3 kph)	@ 3000 rpm
Cruising speed	23.1 mph (34.5 kph)	@ 2700 rpm
Cruising range	350 mi (522 km)	@ 2700 rpm

A well-arranged cockpit, a bridge fitted for fishing efficiency, and a wide, smooth-running hull mark the Bertram 38-foot III Convertible as a real tournament contender and a very comfortable cruising fisherman. The stern door can take fish to 1,000 pounds. Twin 330-hp gasoline engines give speeds to 27.5 mph and a range of over 220 miles at 22 mph. Diesel efficiency suggests speeds to 26.8 mph and a range of more than 350 miles at a cruising speed of 23 or 24 mph. (Photo by Bertram Yacht)

With twin 270-hp Caterpillar diesels

Top speed	26.8 mph (40.0 kph) @ 2800 rpm
Cruising speed	24.0 mph (35.6 kph) @ 2500 rpm
Cruising range	362 mi (540 km) @ 2500 rpm

Speeds and cruising ranges are test averages and may vary among similar boats depending on weight, trim, and engine and bottom condition.

Description

The Bertram 38-foot III Convertible is described as "a combination of comfortable six-berth cruising boat and a serious offshore fishing machine." It is aimed, quite frankly, at the relatively large market of power yachtsmen who also like to fish. The powerful, deep-V hull retains the distinctive Bertram reverse sheer, broken only by a slight knuckle in the sheerline at the after end of the deckhouse.

This model illustrates perfectly the way in which sportfishing-boat design has influenced powerboat construction. The flying bridge is now the logical control station, with lower controls in the deckhouse listed as options at extra cost. A cockpit control station can be fitted on the starboard side of the deckhouse after bulkhead, also an option. This is regarded by many tournament anglers as "must" equipment.

Cockpit space is no larger than in smaller boats of the same general design, measuring about 100 square feet, but this is adequate for all offshore fishing operations with parties of up to six anglers, plus an owner's or professional crew. The general good looks, utility, and efficiency of the sportfishing-boat layout have proved quite congenial for most family and many guest cruising applications.

The spaciousness of the deckhouse interior creates the impression of a much larger boat. On entering from the cockpit there is a forward-facing lounge on the port side. Just forward of this is a spacious high-low table with two movable easy chairs. The lounge converts into a double berth at night. The starboard side of the deckhouse is occupied by a long countertop containing the galley range and oven, refrigerator, and a locker or optional built-in freezer. Paneling is medium-dark, wood-grained material with mahogany trim. Carpet, lounge fabrics, and window drapes are color-keyed for harmony and design.

The deckhouse control station, when fitted, is placed forward to port, and there is a fold-down bench seat along the port bulkhead under the windows to seat diners at the high-low table at mealtime. As in other Bertram models, the windows are tinted safety glass with sprayproof gaskets and drainage for opening or sliding windows.

The port stateroom under the flush forward deck has upper and lower berths. A head with toilet, shower, and sink is located to starboard. A separate toilet and sink serve the forward stateroom, which is given privacy by sliding and hinged doors. Drawers and lockers are built into every available space. There is an emergency and ventilating hatch and skylight in the forward deck.

The Bertram 38-footer has a surprisingly easy motion in short, steep, quartering seas at trolling speed. The effect is more that of a well-ballasted sailboat than a fast powerboat. The author fished a Bertram 38 out of Kailua-Kona, Hawaii, during a recent billfish tournament. Hooked into a Pacific blue marlin, the boat backed into short, steep, following seas with a minimum of discomfort. Captain Bart Miller, the professional skipper, gave this opinion of the boat.

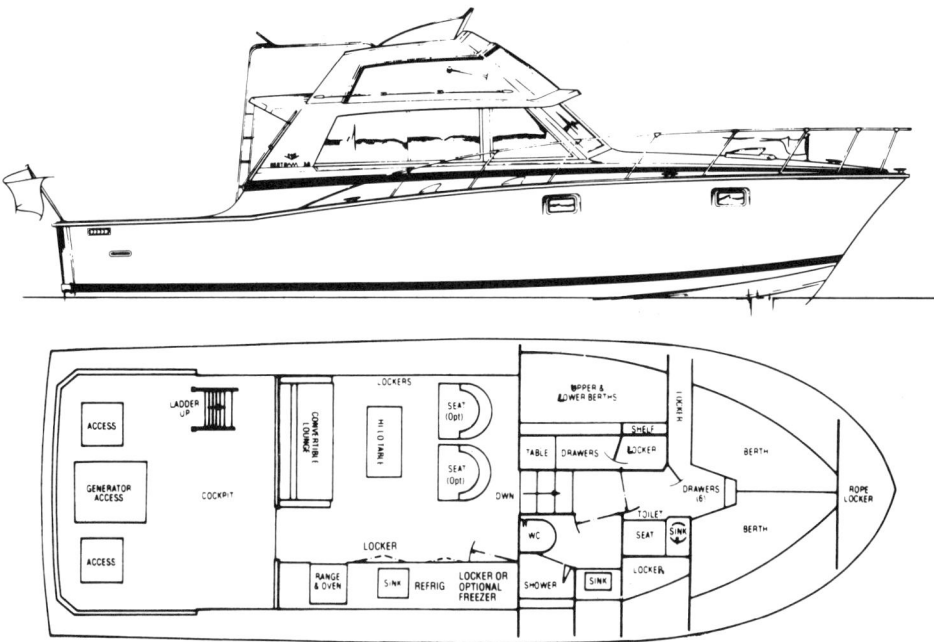

When this Bertram first came to Kona, some of the local skippers swore it would fall apart in the rough seas of the inter-island passages. I took it from Honolulu to Kailua on a hell of a windy day, averaging 18 knots for the trip. Now the same skippers are looking for similar boats for themselves, because the fishing tourists who come here expect speed and comfort as well as fish.

Owner's Evaluation

Bertram 38 owner Peter Nason of Carversville, Pennsylvania, uses his boat an average of 400 hours a year, covering more than 3,000 miles, not counting Intracoastal Waterway north-south delivery runs. With twin 275-hp Cummins 555TI diesels, he averages 375 miles cruising range on 375 gallons of usable fuel at 22 mph, slightly better than the builder's figures given earlier. He gives the boat the following performance evaluation.

Fuel economy	Good
Handling qualities	Super
Seaworthiness	Super
Overall design	Super
Cruising comfort	Super
Fishing efficiency	Super
Ease of maintenance	Good
Investment value	Super

Asked if this is his ultimate fishing machine, Nason replied, "At the present time I would have to say, yes, it is." He has owned four powerboats, three of them sportfishermen, all Bertrams of smaller sizes. He says of his present boat, "The new 38 is the best."

Owners who participated in boat evaluations were asked one special question: "What are the primary satisfactions you get from sportfishing?"

Many different answers were given. Nason's reply touches a crucial point of boat ownership. When asked the question, he responded, "Relaxation, mainly, but also I am in charge of the boat and the fishing."

This is a key satisfaction that motivates many boat owners. It is the sense of being the captain of one's own special little ship, of creating new adventures that can be shared with good companions. A few observers have called this the "Captain Bligh complex." Very few sportfishermen who are their own skippers become Captain Blighs. The wise owner-skipper soon discovers that to be considered a winning skipper, he has to develop and manage a winning team of anglers. A Captain Bligh does not gather to himself the kind of fishing companions who help to fill the freezer or win points in the big tournaments.

Standard Equipment

General

Anchor, 22-lb
Anchor chocks and deck pipe to locker
Anchor line, nylon, ⅝ in × 150 ft
Anchor light, telescopic type
Bell
Bow rail, SS
Burgee staff and burgee
Chocks, stern, with cleats in cockpit
Cleats, foredeck (2), springline (2)
Combination bow chock/navigation light
Docklines, nylon, ½ in × 38 ft (4)
Ensign pole and socket
Fire extinguishers, portable CO_2, 2½-lb (3)
Horn, electric, dual trumpet
Life jackets, adult (6)
Navigation lights
Ring buoy
Thermal and acoustic insulation
Windshield and windows, tinted safety glass

Mechanical

Bilge blower (1)
Bilge pumps, automatic (3)
CO_2 fire-extinguishing system, automatic/manual
Dual-lever engine controls
Freshwater cooling, main engines, diesel
Fuel filters
Fuel shutoff valves
Fuel tank, 400-gal, usable
Hot-water heater, 20-gal, 115 v. AC

Hydraulic steering
Mufflers, fiberglass
Raw-water sea strainers
Seacocks on all through-hull fittings
SS propeller shafts
Trim tabs, electro-hydraulic
Vibration mounts, all engines
Water-pressure system, electric
Water tank, 100-gal, aluminum

Electrical

221-Ah batteries, 2 with paralleling device
55-amp engine-driven alternators (2)
Automatic 40-amp converter
30-amp, 115 v. AC shore-service inlet and 35-ft cable
Engineroom DC lighting and AC outlet
Electric bonding system
Radio ground plates (dual)

Interior

Carpeting throughout
Drapes throughout

Deckhouse

After bulkhead with sliding door
Cocktail table (high-low)
Convertible lounge
DC lighting, AC outlets
Electrical distribution panel
Headliner, soft vinyl
Interior, mica and wood
Screens on side windows

Galley

DC lighting, AC outlet
Exhaust blower
Freshwater-tank supply indicator
Range, 3-burner, with oven and rotobroil
Refrigerator/freezer under counter
Single-lever hot and cold faucet
SS sink

Port Stateroom

Berths, upper and lower, 36 in × 78 in
DC lighting, AC outlet
Drawers under lower berth
Companionway entrance, sliding door
Hanging locker with light
Hull-side ports, ventilating, screens
  and drapes
Overhead vinyl
Night table, lower berth with 2 drawers
  and cushion

Main Bath

China sink with single-lever faucet
DC lighting, AC outlet
Exhaust fan
Portlight in shower
Shower stall with glass door and seat,
  automatic sump pump
Toilet, Monomatic, dockside discharge
Vanity with locker storage under sink
  and sliding mirror

Forward Stateroom

Mirrors, 1 vanity, 1 full-length, on door
6-drawer storage under berths
Carpeted hull sides
DC lighting, AC outlet

Hanging lockers port and starboard,
  with lights
Hull-side ports, ventilating, screens and
  drapes
Pillow shams and bedspreads
Toilet, Monomatic, with dockside
  discharge
V-berths with Polyfoam mattress and
  cover (2)
Vanity, wash basin and sink
Ventilating hatch and skylight with
  screen

Cockpit

Cockpit boarding ladder with port
  and starboard mounts
Cockpit sole, vinyl-covered
Overhead lighting, DC
Reinforcement under deck for fighting
  chair
Scuppers through transom
Stowage lockers, port and starboard,
  with hinged doors

Flying Bridge

Compass, 5-in
Handrail and chart flat
Helmsman seat with footrest
Locker stowage
Padded coaming
Safety monitor system, engines, fire, bilge
Safety rail and ladder
Seating for 6
Steering, engine controls, full
  instrumentation
Tinted Plexiglas sprayshield

Optional Equipment

Deck Hardware

Anchor, 22-lb, with chocks, deck pipe
  and line, extra
Pulpit, bow
Windlass, 12 v. DC
Windlass with wildcat, 115 v. AC

Electrical

Converter, 40-amp, additional
Generator, 6.5-kw, gasoline
Generator, 7.5-kw, diesel

Lights

Docking lights, bow, single-control
Docking lights, transom, single-control

Searchlight, portable
Searchlight, 10-in, remote, single-control
Searchlight, 10-in, remote, dual-control

Electronics

Autopilot, Benmar, single, with hand-
  held remote
Autopilot, Benmar, dual, with hand-held
  remote
Electronic power-distribution panel
  (flying-bridge installation), 12 v. DC,
  60-amp, 10-circuit capacity

Interior Equipment

Air conditioning, reverse-cycle

Deckhouse controls for diesel engines,
with windshield wipers and washers
(NA with cockpit control station)
Deckhouse controls for gasoline engines
(NA with cockpit controls)
Freezer, galley
Garbage-disposal unit
Toilet, Monomatic, with dockside and
overboard discharges
Toilet, Mansfield Vacu-Flush, with
holding tank, dockside discharge only
Toilet, Mansfield Vacu-Flush, with dock-
side and overboard discharges
Toilet, Groco, electric, with Lectra-San

Furnishings

Chair, main salon (1 each)
Radio, stereo, AM/FM with tape and
remote speakers
Sea rails for Princess stove

Fishing Equipment

Cockpit engine controls for diesel
(NA with deckhouse controls)
Cockpit engine controls for gasoline
engines (NA with deckhouse controls)
Fighting chair with cover, F-10
Pompanette
Fishbox curved to fit transom, without
circulating water

Gin pole with rigging
Outriggers, Lee's, 21-ft poles, 8-ft base,
aluminum
Rodholders, flush-mounted (4)
Transom door, starboard side

Covers

Bimini top, Dacron
Bimini top windscreen, front and sides
Cockpit cover, Dacron
Shipping cover
Sun awning, cockpit, Dacron

General

Boathook, 8-ft, chocked
Cockpit coaming padding
Cockpit sole, teak, instead of standard
Cradle, storage
Freshwater cooling, gasoline main
engines
Paint, bottom, antifouling (blue only)
Propellers, extra pair, gasoline or diesel
Shaft, extra (1 each), gasoline or diesel
Swim platform, fiberglass with ladders
Telephone connection with shore line
Transom steps (NA with swim platform)
Washdown pump with 10-ft hose,
cockpit
Water inlet, dockside supply
Zincs, electrolytic, on shafts only

MAGNUM MARINE 38-FOOT SPORTFISHERMAN

Designer	Magnum Marine Corp.
Builder	Magnum Marine Corp. 2900 NE 188th Street North Miami, FL 33160
Construction	Hand-laid and reinforced fiberglass hull, decks, and superstructure.

Magnum Marine's reputation for very fast ocean-racing powerboats is fortified by the performance claims of this sleek 38-footer. Emphasis is on speed, with estimates of 50 to 60 mph for engines totaling 1,000 hp in diesel and 1,240 hp in gasoline. A pair of 300-hp 6V53TI two-cycle diesels are said to provide a top speed of 31 knots (35.5 mph). (Photo by Magnum Marine)

Specifications

Length overall	38 ft	11.59 m
Length, waterline	33 ft	10.07 m
Beam, maximum	12 ft 3 in	3.74 m
Draft to keel	2 ft 4 in	0.71 m
Draft to rudder tips	3 ft 4 in	1.02 m
Cockpit area	100 sq ft	9.3 m²
Heights above waterline		
Hardtop	8 ft 1 in	2.47 m
Bridge windshield top	11 ft 1 in	3.39 m
Weight, normal	19,000 lb	8,636 kg
Fuel capacity	400 gal	1,512 l
Water capacity	75 gal	284 l
Sleeping accommodations	6-8	

Power options

Twin 330-hp, 454 CID MerCruiser gasoline (standard)
Twin 350-hp, 454 CID MerCruiser gasoline
Twin 375-hp, 484 CID BPM gasoline
Twin 620-hp, 730 CID BPM gasoline
Twin 300-hp GM S&S 6V53TI diesels
Twin 500-hp GM S&S 6V92TI diesels

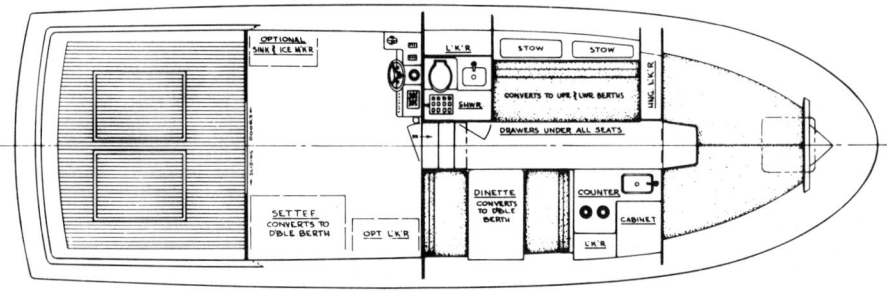

Performance

With twin 330-hp MerCruiser 454 CID gasoline engines

Top speed	30.0 kn (34.2 mph) @ 4000 rpm
Cruising speed	24.0 kn (27.4 mph) @ 3200 rpm
Fuel rates	NA

With twin 300-hp GM 6V53TI diesels

Top speed	31.0 kn (35.3 mph) @ 3000 rpm
Cruising speed	27.0 kn (30.8 mph) @ 2700 rpm
Fuel rates	NA

In a different set of data, the top speed with twin 350-hp MerCruiser gasoline engines is given as 40 mph (64 kph), and cruising range with safety factor as 325 miles. Fuel rates and further speed-range-endurance information should be requested from the manufacturer. The data given do suggest, however, that the cruising fuel rate for a range of 325 miles is 0.81 mpg. This would suggest a cruising range of over 400 miles for a diesel version with equivalent power. Speeds of the 1,000-hp diesel and 1,240-hp gasoline models can be guessed to register in the 50- to 60-mph range.

Description

A direct development from the Magnum line of ocean-racing powerboats, the Magnum Marine 38-foot Sportfisherman is more of a high-speed racer than a true fishing machine. Hull form is deep-V, following the European influence of overhanging, ice-pick bow and extremely clean superstructure. Outriggers are usually installed to lie back almost flat over the stern when underway at high speed to reduce wind resistance and excessive whipping. A high tower would also offer considerable air resistance at speeds of 40 to 60 mph. The low tower depicted complements the hull's suggestion of speed and power.

The boat is offered in at least three standard configurations. One is a conventional hardtop model with flying bridge. Another is the hardtop without the bridge. A third is an open version with folding softtop and open windshield. The latter can be rigged with transparent curtains around the sides and forward part of a tower frame. This arrangement would probably work best in models powered for under 40 mph top speed. A Bimini softtop can be fitted to any bridge model.

Accommodations for six are in the larger main cabin and the smaller forward cabin. Galley and dinette (convertible to a double bunk) are to starboard. To port are the enclosed head with shower stall and upper and lower bunks.

The bow stateroom contains a large V-berth sleeping two friendly people. A convertible settee in the deckhouse provides sleeping space for another couple, bringing the total sleeping accommodations up to 8. While not exactly spartan, the accommodations are simple and understated in style and decor, understandable in a vessel where every extra pound of weight detracts from the primary purpose, getting from here to there as rapidly as possible.

The boat's speed suggests that it would be at home in those tournaments in which a LeMans start places emphasis on a fast getaway to distant grounds. A low tower, coupled with a "rocket launcher" type of rodholder in lieu of a fighting chair, would equip it properly for fast, light-tackle, tournament fishing against arbitrary time limits. The rocket launcher is actually a multiple rodholder that puts up to four pieces of tackle in the center of the cockpit, rather than in side holders, where one, two, or up to four competing anglers can tend the rods. The fishing is done standing up, with each angler wearing a gimbal belt and, if needed, a light fishing harness. It is effective with tackle whose line-test rating is 30 pounds or less.

Standard Equipment

Engines and Machinery

Standard or optional engines as indicated
Dual-control station (cockpit)
1¼-in. dia. SS shafts
Custom struts with rubber bearings
Custom Magnum rudders with rudder ports
Custom Magnum shaft logs
Special Ni-Bral propellers

Custom Magnum water pickups (transom-mounted)
Fuel filters, mufflers (4), seawater strainers
Balanced drive lines (engines to V-drives)
Power-steering system on flying-bridge models

Custom Magnum Flying Bridge

Venturi windshield

Pilot chair with slide attachment
Full instrumentation
Power steering and complete controls
Safety rail
Custom ladder
Custom SS, foam-covered steering wheel
Large storage area with access doors

Deck Hardware

Large mooring bitt
10-in stern cleats (2)
8-in spring cleats (2)
6-in bow chocks (2)
16-lb anchor with chocks, deck pipe
Custom Magnum anodized air vents (4)
Fuel deck filler plates (2)
Water tank filler plate
Custom heavy-duty aluminum rubrail

Tanks and Piping

200-gal fuel tanks, heavy-duty aluminum,
  racing strength, foamed in place (2)
Fuel pickups for each tank (2)
Custom hold-down brackets for each tank
Shutoff valves on all through-hull fittings
75-gal freshwater tank

Electrical Equipment

Custom electric panel with circuit
  breakers
All wiring color-coded and numbered
Heavy-duty, 100-amp, 12 v. DC batteries
  with boxes (3)
Separate 12 v. DC and 115 v. AC systems
Shore powerline with connectors,
  polarity indicator
Electric hot-water heater
Electric head and garbage-disposal unit
Odor-free chlorinator
2-burner electric stove
Electric refrigerator, 4.5 cu ft
Auto-electric-manual bilge pumps (2)
Swivel lights in salon (2)
Electric freshwater pressure system
Electric shower-drain pump
Electric bilge blowers (2)
Heavy-duty parallel battery switch
Battery selector shutoff switch

Overhead cabin lights, 12 v. DC and
  115 v. AC
Swivel reading lights over V-berths
International navigation lights
Complete bonding and grounding harness
Twin trumpet horns

Instruments

Tachometers (4)
Oil-pressure gauges (4)
Ammeters (4)
Water-temperature gauges (4)
Visual-reading fuel gauges (2)
Removable control panel
Oil-temperature gauges (4)
V-drive oil-pressure warning lights (4)

Interior and Cockpit Appointments

Fiberglass cockpit sole
Portlights with screens, balanced, self-
  supporting (8)
Custom stand-up head and macerator-
  chlorinator package
All normal head hardware
Lounge settee, customer's upholstery
  selection
Anchor rope locker
Convertible dinette, seat cushions, etc.
Draperies for all portlights
Carpet (customer's selection), cabin sole,
  stairs, etc.
Berth cushions, complete set
Large hanging locker
Teak step pads (2)
Custom teak boarding ladder
Double helmsman's seat
Custom galley unit
Custom Magnum windshield
All hull colors custom
Custom interior soundproof hull covering

Miscellaneous

Brass bell, mouth foghorn
Adult life jackets (6)
2½-lb, dry-chemical fire extinguishers (3)
150-ft. ½-in nylon yacht anchor line
  with shackle

Optional Equipment

Because a large portion of the boat's finish and equipment is of the customer's
selection, the builder offers a long list of optional equipment, which duplicates

some of the items already mentioned. Options include a wide array of fishing gear, cockpit side padding, electronics, air conditioning, covers, electrical equipment, and ship's hardware and software. Consult the builder for suggestions and details.

PACEMAKER SF38 SPORT FISHERMAN

Designer	Pacemaker Yachts
Builder	Pacemaker Yachts Egg Harbor City, NJ 08215
Construction	Fiberglass hull, sub-decks, and super-structure. Teak cockpit deck and trim.

Specifications

Length, including pulpit	41 ft 11 in	12.78 m
Length, hull, overall	38 ft 5 in	11.71 m
Length, waterline	34 ft 10 in	10.62 m
Beam, maximum	14 ft 5 in	4.39 m
Draft	3 ft 6 in	1.07 m
Cockpit area	80 sq ft	7.44 m²
Freeboard forward	6 ft 3 in	1.91 m
Freeboard aft	3 ft 10 in	1.17 m
Heights above waterline		
Deckhouse	9 ft 9 in	2.97 m
Flying bridge shield	12 ft 9 in	3.89 m
Bimini top	17 ft 2 in	5.23 m
Deadrise	9.5°	
Weight, 2 SF 6V-92TA diesels		
Heavy	26,577 lb	12,055 kg
Light	21,639 lb	9,815 kg
Fuel capacity	512 gal	1,938 l
Water capacity	150 gal	566 l
Sleeping accommodations	6	

Power options
   Twin 350-hp Crusader gasoline, 2.5:1 reduction gear
   Twin 6-71N or TI diesels
   Twin 6V-92TA diesels

Performance

The tables on page 230 are taken from the builder's performance charts shown on page 229. Endurance and range are interpolated from available data and are not guaranteed performance.

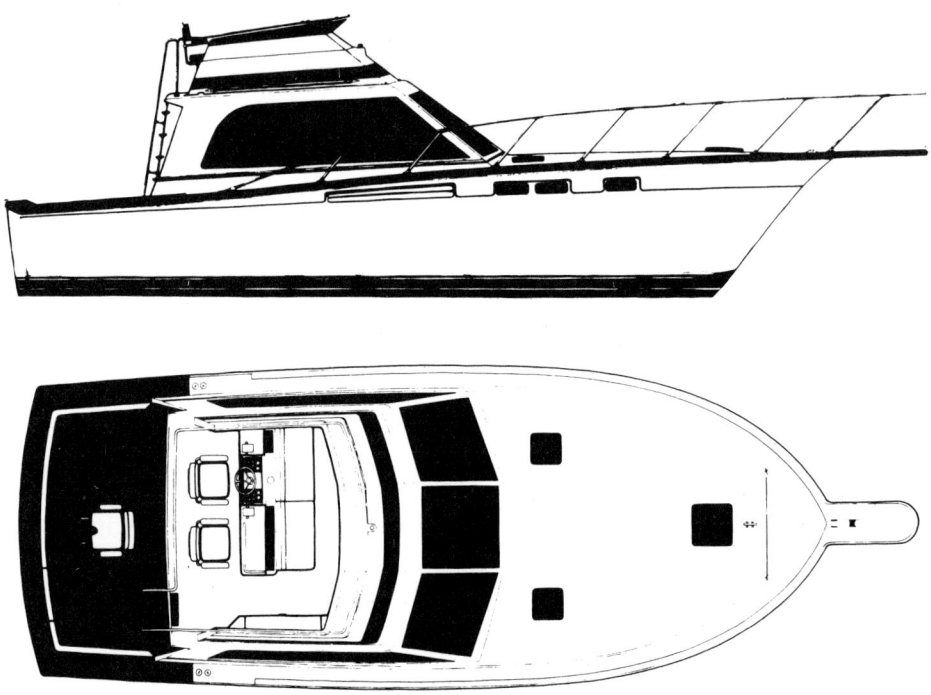

Above: The profile of the Pacemaker SF38 follows the modern trend of reverse sheer to pro-vide maximum cabin space. The long safety rail and short pulpit are valuable safety adjuncts when handling ground tackle or docklines in foul weather. The strong beam-to-length ratio is evident in the plan view. The relatively small bridge has controls located well aft, giving the operator an unobstructed view of fishing action in the cockpit. (Courtesy of Pacemaker Yachts)

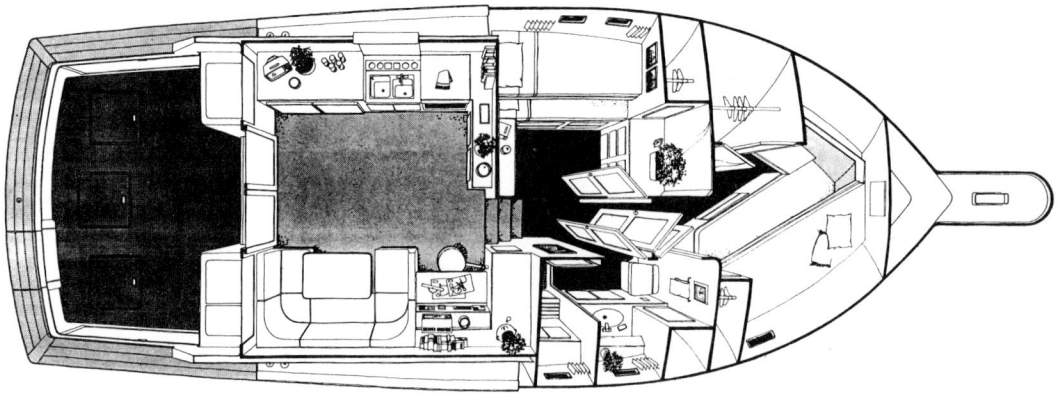

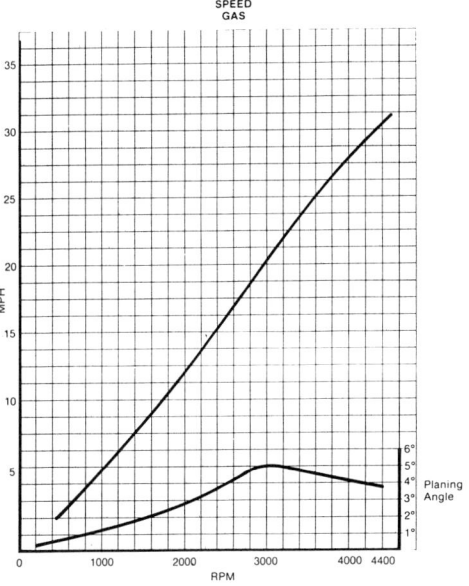

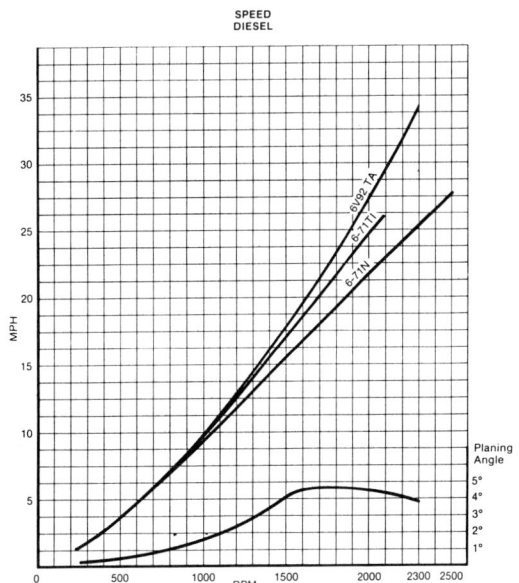

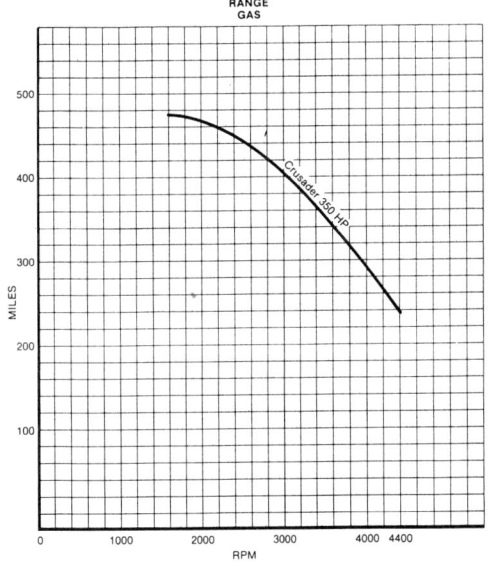

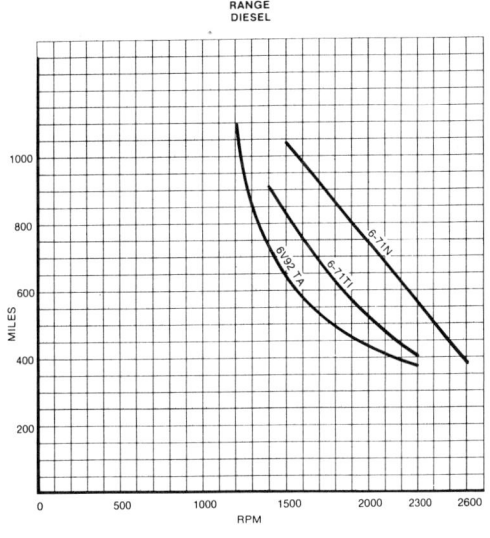

With twin 350-hp Crusader gasoline engines, 2.5:1 reduction gear

RPM	Speed	GPH	MPG	Endurance	Range
2000	12.0 mph	9.0	1.33	38.8 hr	465 mi
2500	16.0 mph	13.3	1.20	26.3 hr	420 mi
3000	20.0 mph	18.4	1.14	19.0 hr	400 mi
3600*	25.0 mph	27.5	0.91	12.7 hr	320 mi
4000	28.0 mph	33.7	0.83	10.4 hr	290 mi
4400	30.4 mph	45.4	0.67	7.7 hr	235 mi

Normal fast cruising speed.

With twin Detroit 6V-92TA diesels

RPM	Speed	GPH	MPG	Endurance	Range
1200	13.0 mph	4.1	3.14	111.4 hr	1,100 mi
1600	19.5 mph	10.7	1.83	32.8 hr	640 mi
2000*	27.5 mph	22.4	1.23	15.7 hr	430 mi
2300	34.0 mph	31.8	1.07	11.0 hr	375 mi

Normal fast cruising speed.

With twin Detroit 6V71N diesels

RPM	Speed	GPH	MPG	Endurance	Range
1500	15.5 mph	5.2	2.97	67.3 hr	1,040 mi
1800	19.5 mph	7.9	2.46	44.3 hr	860 mi
2100*	23.0 mph	11.9	1.94	29.4 hr	680 mi
2300	25.3 mph	15.5	1.63	22.6 hr	570 mi
2500	28.0 mph	21.7	1.29	16.1 hr	450 mi

Normal fast cruising speed.

These tables indicate a medium-sized offshore fishing boat with good speed and greater-than-average range and endurance. Five hundred gallons of fuel is a lot to cram into a 38-footer, but such a supply would make it possible to run at 20 knots water speed from Key West to Cozumel, 400 miles against an average 2½-knot head current, and arrive with 7 or 8 hours of fuel still in the tanks.

For normal day-to-day fishing, one would not need to carry the full load. A 10-hour offshore fishing day can be broken down into about 4 hours of fast running at 20 gph, and 6 hours of trolling at no more than 5 gph. This totals 110 gallons for the day. A total of 200 gallons would leave a generous reserve for emergencies. These observations, of course, apply to diesel power. Gasoline endurance and range appear to average about half of that available with diesel.

It is interesting to note that the fuel economy in miles per gallon does not peak at a particular planing speed but occupies a gradually descending curve from first planing speed (about 15 mph) to top speed. This means that an owner can set his normal fast cruising speed at the engine manufacturer's recommended continuous-duty speed, rather than at a most-efficient hull speed that may or may not coincide with the recommended continuous-duty speed. The result could well be longer engine life.

Description

The Pacemaker SF38 is that company's answer to the need for a high-performance, medium-sized sportfishing boat with tournament handling qualities and completely modern design and decor. The generous beam of more than 14 feet increases stability and interior living space as well as load-carrying ability. The boat is big enough to be worked with at least one professional for serious fishing, yet small enough to be handled by an experienced amateur fisherman and his family.

The cockpit is large enough for a full-sized fighting chair flanked by two lighter fighting chairs, and it comes with a transom door as standard equipment. A transom platform can be added as an option. To port, forward, provision is made for a cockpit control station, and to starboard a tackle locker and bait freezer. The bridge station is far enough aft to give the helmsman full visual coverage of the cockpit. An interesting note is the inclusion of a bridge radar mount as standard equipment. Radar has become increasingly important to off-shore game fishing for navigation and safety.

The deckhouse has a galley and refrigerators to port, with a dinette and navigation table to starboard. The latter is a touch not frequently found in power-boats of this class. The dinette can be converted into a double bunk. Rod stowage is in cockpit side lockers. Windows are tinted safety glass.

Down below, the master stateroom is to port, with upper and lower bunks located along the ship's side, fore and aft. To starboard is the head with shower and lockers. The forward stateroom sleeps two in upper and lower berths. Closet space and lockers are generous. In all, the Pacemaker 38SF is a fisherman that answers many questions in these performance-conscious days.

Standard Equipment

Engine pans, SS
Fuel gauges
Engine stops, manual, sw/o
Engine hour meter
Engine alarm
Engineroom insulation
Mufflers
Trim tabs
Flying-bridge trim-tab control
Bilge pump, auto (3)
Cockpit seawater washdown
Strainer, hull-mounted
Seacocks
Exhaust flapper
Air conditioning, 3-zone reverse-cycle
Horns, dual electric
Zincs, buttons on trim tabs, transom
   plates, collars on shaft
Water connection, dockside
Pressure water, hot and cold
Shower, with telephone head
Holding tank, 80 gal
Blower, bilge (2)
Halon extinguishing system #10
Battery, 6V-105 amp (2 per engine)

Converter, 30-amp
Lights, engineroom, 12-v.
Generator, 6.5-kw, gas
Ground tubes
Split shore service
Pole, with ensign
Hatch screens
Radar pedestal, flying-bridge mounted
Anchor
Tinted glass
Coverboards, cockpit
Exhaust fan
Refrigerator, 110-v.
Stove, Princess, with oven
Sink, SS
Berth cushions, 6-in foam
V-fill cushion, 6-in
Medicine cabinet
Countertop, Corian
Mirror
Head, electric
Shower door
Toothbrush holder
Towel bar
Soap dish

Cocktail bar, in salon
Stereo AM/FM tape, with 2 speakers
TV antenna, with outlet
TV line splitter
Sofa, cruiser only
Cockpit lighting
Switch, DC power relay
Battery boxes
Interior lighting, 12-v.
Flying bridge
Compass, 4-in binnacle
Dacron flying-bridge cover
Steering, hydraulic
Instrumentation
Windshield grab rail, SS
Helm seat
Companion seat
Windshield wipers

Cockpit bait and tackle locker
Bow pulpit, with SS rail
Bow staff
Cleats, springline
Hawsepipes, side aft, port and starboard
Ladder, boarding onto cockpit
Live-bait well
Gate, transom
Anchor lights
Running lights
Anchor line
Fog bell
Dock lines
Life jackets (1 for each bunk)
P.F.D. throwable
Cleats, springline
Chocks
Flying-bridge or cabin-top rail

Optional Equipment

Freshwater cooling (standard with diesel)
Synchronizer light, gasoline only
Freshwater spigot, bilge (standard with
    diesel)
Lectra/San
Gas sniffer
Battery, 12-v., 205-amp (2 per engine)
Converters, 60-amp (standard with
    diesel)
Freshwater-cooled gas generator
Generator hour meter (1 per generator)
Generator, 7.5-kw, diesel
Additional 110-v. outlets

Outriggers, Lee senior
Padded cockpit coaming
Rodholders, flush-mounted
Windlass
Swim platform
Toe rails
Head, Crown
Head, Mansfield
Speakers, additional
Heater, 110-v.
Icemaker, Icerette
Launch and make-ready
Lower helm trim-tab controls

FRANCO HARRAUER
38½-FOOT SPORTFISHING CATAMARAN

Designer	Franco Harrauer, N.A. Via Aurelia or. 286-a 16035 Rapallo, Italy
Builder	Cantiere Navale Sciallino Regione Pineo 17023 Ceriale, Italy
Construction	Hand-layup fiberglass hulls, decks, and superstructure.

Specifications

Length overall	38 ft 6 in	11.75 m
Length, waterline	28 ft 3 in	8.60 m
Beam, maximum	18 ft 4 in	5.60 m
Draft (hulls only)	2 ft 4 in	0.70 m
Cockpit area	160 + sq ft	15 + m²
Freeboard forward	NA	
Freeboard aft	NA	
Height above waterline	NA	
Displacement	NA	
Fuel capacity	317 gal	1,200 l
Water capacity	145 gal	550 l
Sleeping accommodations	8-10	

Power options
  Twin Aifo #806 107-hp diesels
  Twin Aifo CP3 140-hp diesels
  Twin Perkins T6 354M 160-hp diesels

Performance (Based on 317 gallons of fuel.)

With twin 107-hp Aifo diesels

Top speed	16 kn (18.2 mph)
Cruising speed	14 kn (16.0 mph)
Cruising endurance	50 hr
Cruising range (14 kn)	700 nm (800 mi)

With twin 140-hp Aifo diesels

Top speed	19 kn (21.7 mph)
Cruising speed	16 kn (18.2 mph)
Cruising endurance	42 hr
Cruising range (16 kn)	672 nm (766 mi)

The broad, tumbling wake of the catamaran should be a natural for raising school tuna. Cruising at 14 knots, Harrauer's cat has an endurance of 50 hours and range of 700 nautical miles. (Photo courtesy of Mondo Sommerso)

With twin 160-hp Perkins diesels

Top speed	20 kn (22.8 mph)
Cruising speed	18 kn (20.5 mph)
Cruising endurance	35 hr
Cruising range (18 kn)	630 nm (718 mi)

Description

Imagine a 38½-foot fishing cruiser with a beam of more than 18 feet, capable of 20 knots top speed with a total of only 320 hp in two small diesels, and able to cruise 700 nautical (800 statute) miles on one modest load of 317 gallons of fuel, while cranking out a respectable 14 knots! This is the remarkable performance record of Italian designer Franco Harrauer's unconventional 11.75-meter fishing catamaran.

View from the catamaran's bridge, looking forward. (Photo courtesy of Mondo Sommerso)

Actually, the extreme overall beam of this boat is deceptive, because instead of one short, fat hull she has two long, slim hulls decked over with a comfortable cabin-bridge. The twin hulls are asymmetrical mirror images with straight inboard hull sides. This is claimed to reduce inter-hull wave interference, especially at speed. Speed is helped by the high coefficient of fineness of the hulls, which have the bearing center situated 35 percent of the waterline length forward of the stern.

Construction is by a single mold for the two hulls and the platform. Incorporated into the cockpit molding is a fishwell with pumped water circulation for live bait. The between-hull portion of the transom can be dropped as a loading ramp to take aboard large fish.

The main cabin includes an L-shaped dinette and complete galley with sink, stove, refrigerator, and lockers. Two control stations are provided, one in the main cabin and one on the bridge. The short tower could easily be made much

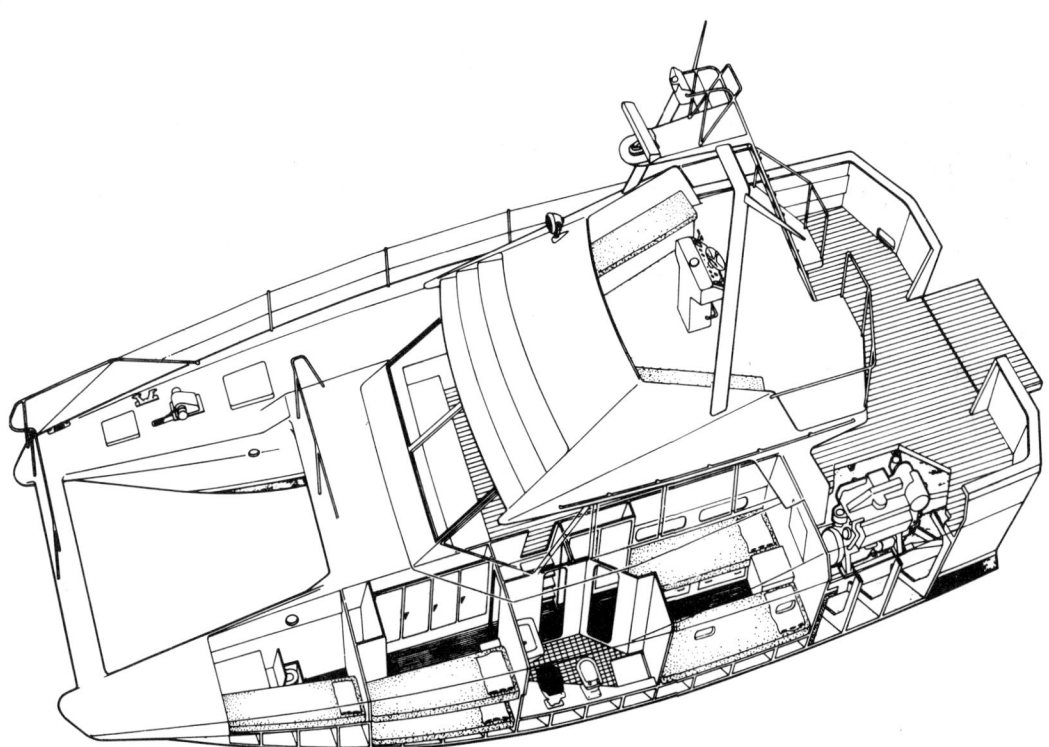

taller in view of the catamaran's great stability, with a complete remote-control operating station.

The interiors of the twin hulls are totally utilized for living and working space. They are reached from the main cabin, and the engine compartments in the sterns are reached from the cockpit through hatchways. Engines drive through V-drives to lower the shaft angle. Each hull has a double stateroom under the wings of the main cabin, with private entrance to a head, which is next forward. Forward of the head, under the break of the main cabin windshield, are double-berth staterooms. A corridor runs fore and aft. In the bow of the port hull is a crewman's separate bunkroom with W.C. A matching room to starboard can be used as a general storeroom or another single-berth sleeping room.

Thus, we count up to 10 berths in six sleeping compartments, plus two lavatories with W.C., shower, and sink, and two other W.C.s with sinks, in a boat that is less than 40 feet long. Truly a remarkable achievement in the use of space.

The advantages of the catamaran hull for offshore fishing are easily spelled out.

1. High degree of stability, no rolling, little pounding.
2. Good maneuvering qualities due to the distance between the two propellers and rudders.
3. Consistent economy of fuel, cruising or trolling.
4. Very generous living space considering the length of the vessel.

On the other side of the coin, there are a few caveats learned from American experience with commercial, fishing-party, and private power catamarans.

1. Inter-hull structure must be super-strong to withstand the great stresses of rough water at high speed.
2. Catamarans are quite weight-sensitive and soon lose their edge of hull efficiency when heavily loaded.
3. Their great beam in proportion to length can cause berthing problems at some marinas and piers.
4. Ton for ton, catamarans are more expensive to design and build.
5. Having had little experience with the craft, insurance brokers are sometimes loath to give them coverage.

But these are quibbles that apply in some degree to all specialized powerboats, among which sportfishing boats are well out in front. Properly designed and built, a 50-foot or 60-foot, twin-hull, fast powerboat carrying, say, a pair of 17-foot center-console fishing skiffs and a one-man minisub could be a perfect long-range fishing base for exploring distant waters where fish have never seen a trolled ballyhoo nor tried to catch up with a silver spoon towed 10 fathoms deep behind a downrigger.

Franco Harrauer's Italian fishing catamaran bids fair to break new ground in the constant struggle to reach perfection in boats that carry fishermen to sea.

VIKING 40-FOOT CONVERTIBLE

Designer	Viking Yacht Co.
Builder	Viking Yacht Co. Route 9 New Gretna, NJ 08224
Construction	Hand-layup fiberglass hull, deck, and superstructure. Balsa-core hull sides, decks, cabin top. Solid keel, strakes, and chines.

Specifications

Length overall	40 ft 4 in	12.29 m
Length, waterline	NA	
Beam, maximum	14 ft 6 in	4.42 m
Draft	3 ft 6 in	1.06 m

Continued

Specifications *continued*

Cockpit area	100 sq ft	9.30 m²
Freeboard forward	5 ft 8 in	1.73 m
Freeboard aft	3 ft 4 in	1.02 m
Height above waterline	11 ft 9 in	3.58 m
Weight, normal	30,000 lb	13,608 kg
Fuel capacity	350 gal	1,325 l
Water capacity	90 gal	341 l
Interior headroom	6 ft 6 in	1.98 m
Sleeping accommodations	6	

Power options
   Twin 350-hp Crusader gasoline
   Twin 3208 Caterpillar diesels
   Twin Detroit 671N or 671TI diesels
   Other engines by arrangement

Performance

Builder's test-boat performance: Three persons, full fuel tanks; twin 225-hp Caterpillar diesels, 1.97:1 reduction gear; propellers 23-inch diameter by 21-inch pitch; trim tabs not used.

RPM	MPH	GPH*	MPG	Endurance	Range	Angle
1000	7.19	2.5	2.88	140.0 hr	1,006 mi	1.0°
1500	9.94	4.6	2.16	76.0 hr	755 mi	2.5°
2000	12.20	9.5	1.28	36.8 hr	450 mi	5.0°
2500	17.90	22.2	0.81	15.8 hr	282 mi	7.0°
2600	19.58	25.0	0.78	14.0 hr	274 mi	8.0°

*Fuel rate is interpolated from engine manufacturer's test data. Endurance and range are calculated for comparison only.

With Viking Boat Leveler trim tabs in operation

RPM	MPH	Angle
2500	19.99	4.00°
2750	22.92	4.25°

Use of trim tabs improved engine top speed by 150 rpm and boat top speed by 3.34 mph, or 17 percent. At a normal fast cruising engine speed of 2500 rpm, with tabs, the effective cruising range would be extended to well over 300 miles.

Description

The very low trunk molded into the forward deck of the Viking 40-foot Convertible is not apparent at first glance and contributes to the generous interior headroom of 6½ feet. The gentle reverse sheer terminates at the forward end of the cockpit and gives the hull a forward-thrusting look at full speed.

   The commodious cockpit can accommodate a fixed fighting chair and two fixed or portable fishing chairs. A step-up from cockpit deck level to deckhouse floor provides good engineroom space and keeps cockpit slop and gurry from invading the living quarters. There is space for a lower steering and control station to port on the deckhouse after bulkhead, and for a tackle and freezer setup to starboard under the bridge ladder.

The convertible concept in cruising-fishing powerboats has proved popular, and this model from Viking has comfortable accommodations for six while offering speeds of over 20 mph with twin 225-hp 4-cycle diesels. (Photo by Viking Yacht Co.)

Bridge controls are located well aft, and there is plenty of room for seating volunteer lookouts and bridge riders. The console has locker space for essential electronic gear. A Venturi windshield of tinted safety glass or heavy plastic deflects the wind of high-speed travel from the operator. A Bimini top or full-sized tower can be added as desired.

Three different interior plans affect only the lower living spaces. In each the arrangement of the salon is unaltered. A combination settee-bed is placed to port with occasional chairs arranged as desired. In Plan A, the master stateroom to port, below, has a double bed with its own head forward of that. In Plan B, the master stateroom has upper and lower single berths arranged in the "crossover" position, one fore-and-aft, the other athwartships. In Plan C, the master stateroom is replaced by an L-shaped lounge in the stateroom space, and the bulkhead between deckhouse and lower cabin area is left out. The L-lounge has a table and can be converted into sleeping quarters.

In each plan the galley is to starboard, below, with lockers forward of the galley. A bow stateroom has V-berths. Three deck hatches provide ventilation and emergency exits. An interesting feature is the provision of lockers in the lower deckhouse sides for stowing rods and tackle. This obviates the need to hang the rigged rods from overhead hangers, from which they can occasionally bounce free in rough water to the detriment of the tackle and the heads of passengers.

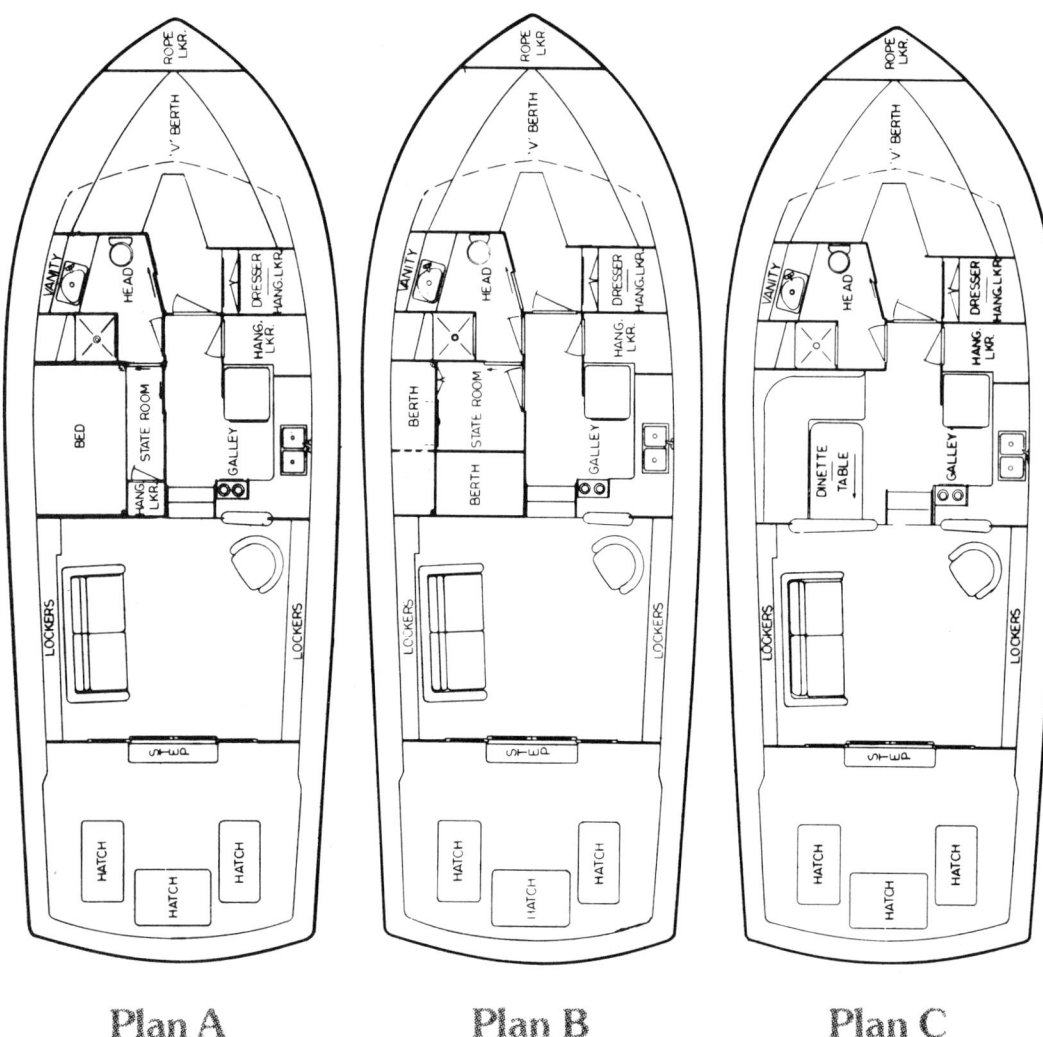

Plan A   Plan B   Plan C

Owner's Evaluation

Ron Essner of Pitman, New Jersey, reports on his 1978 Viking 40-foot Convertible. He fishes the southern New Jersey ocean areas and also in South Florida, averaging 375 operating hours per year. His boat is powered with twin GM J&T 671TI diesels rated at 375 hp each. He estimates top speed at 29 mph and cruising range at 270 miles at 24 mph, carrying 360 gallons of fuel. He uses the boat 80 percent for cruising and 20 percent for game-fish trolling. Here is his evaluation score.

Fuel economy	Good
Handling qualities	Super
Seaworthiness	Super
Overall design	Super
Cruising comfort	Good
Fishing efficiency	Good
Ease of maintenance	Good
Investment value	Super

Essner is definite in his priorities when it comes to the qualities that make up a good sportfishing boat. Following are the qualities in his order of priority.

Seaworthiness
Handling ability
Investment value
Ease of maintenance
Fishing efficiency
Fuel economy
Cruising range
Personal comfort

The boat, according to Essner, is dry-running, with excellent directional stability, especially in following or quartering seas. The hull is a modification of the familiar deep-V and apparently requires trim tabs to achieve maximum efficiency at cruising speeds. Motion and handling qualities at trolling speeds, where tabs have little effect, are excellent.

Like the majority of owners contacted, Essner declares that in the future he will continue to fish at his present rate of effort, fuel being available.

Standard Equipment

Propulsion

Engines, twin 350-hp Crusader gasoline (diesels optional)
Engine alarm system, audible
Engine stringers, structural-steel channel
Mufflers, fiberglass
Propellers, 3-blade
Rudders, struts, manganese bronze
Shafts, 1½-in dia. SS

Fuel and Water

Fuel lines, flexible aircraft-type
Fuel manifolds, filters, crossover valves
Fuel tanks, welded aluminum
Hot-water heater, 12-gal capacity
Water connection, dockside, with relief valve
Water lines, high-pressure nylon reinforced, FDA-approved
Water system, pressurized, welded aluminum tanks

Electrical

Batteries, 6 v. DC in series (4), fiberglass box
Battery charger
Battery paralleling switch, vaporproof
Battery systems, individual, port and starboard
Bilge blowers
Bilge pumps, automatic, with indicator lights (2)
Bonded electrical system, color-coded wiring
Dockside 115 v. AC system with 50-ft cable
Duplex electrical outlets, 115 v. AC
Engineroom light, vaporproof, with indicator light
Generator, 6.5-kw, gasoline, with muffler
Horn, dual electric
Instrument panel lights
Lights, interior, combination 12 v. DC/115 v. AC throughout

Master control panel, 12 v. DC and
115 v. AC circuit breakers, control
switch, voltmeter, polarity light
Navigation lights

Flying Bridge

Compass
Covers, Dacron, instruments and helm
seat
Full instrumentation
Handrails, SS
Lockers, windshield, Venturi-type
Seat, pedestal, helm
Seats, companion, upholstered

Salon (Deckhouse)

Carpeting throughout
Cabinets, storage
Chair, upholstered
Convertible sofa
Lighting, indirect
Table (stateroom interior only)
Windows, sliding, with screens

Galley

Countertops, Formica
Electric range, 3-burner, with oven
Exhaust fan
Pressure water system, hot and cold
Refrigerator-freezer, 10 cu ft
Cutlery and utensil drawers
Sink, double, SS

Dinette Interior

L-shaped upholstered lounge with sliding
table and locker below, converts into
bed (dinette booth optional)

Master Stateroom Interior (optional)

Carpeting throughout
Double bed or crossover bunks with
mattresses
Drapes with glide track
Hanging locker
Storage lockers

Forward Stateroom

Carpeting
Hanging locker
Storage lockers and shelves
V-berths with mattresses

Head

Formica vanity with sink, SS
Monomatic toilet
Medicine cabinet
Stall shower

Cockpit

Recessed cleats and hawsepipes
Recessed storage boxes
Side lockers
Teak cockpit boarding ladder

Miscellaneous

Anchor, 25-lb, with chain and rode
Bow chocks and cleats
Docklines
Bow rail, SS
Drapes throughout
Fire extinguishers (3)
Flagstaff and ensign, fog bell
Life jackets (6 adult)
Nonskid decks, fore and aft
Safety glass, all windows
Screens on all opening windows and
portlights
Springline cleats (4)

OCEAN YACHT 40-FOOT AND 42-FOOT SUPER SPORT*

Designer	John E. Leek Associates
Builder	Ocean Yachts P.O. Box 312 Egg Harbor, NJ 08215
Construction	Fiberglass hull, decks, and super-structure. Teak and mahogany trim.

Specifications

*At the time of this writing, Ocean Yachts was phasing in a new 42-footer based on their original 40-foot hull. Specifications below are for the 40-footer. Illustrations and data for the 42-footer are so marked.

Length overall	40 ft 2 in	12.26 m
Length, waterline	35 ft 10 in	10.95 m
Beam, maximum	14 ft 4 in	4.37 m
Draft	3 ft 6 in	1.07 m
Cockpit area	100 sq ft	9.3 m²
Freeboard forward	5 ft 5 in	1.68 m
Freeboard aft	3 ft	0.92 m
Height, waterline to bridge	12 ft	3.66 m
Weight, normal	30,000 lb	13,636 kg
Fuel capacity	450 gal	1,700 l
Water capacity	100 gal	378 l
Sleeping accommodations	6	

Power options
  Twin 671N Detroit diesels
  Twin 671TI Detroit diesels
  Twin VT 555 Cummins diesels
  Twin 653N Detroit diesels

Performance

The following table is from data on the 40-footer prepared by David P. Martin, N.A.

Power	Twin GM J&T 671TI diesels with M95 injectors
BHP	410 each engine
SHP	390 each engine
Reduction gear	1.5: 1
Propellers	24-in dia. × 26-in pitch, Michigan Ni-Bral, cupped
Fuel data	Johnson & Towers propeller load curve

Viewed from aft, the Ocean Yacht 40-footer is all fishing machine. (Photo by DeJon Photography Studio Inc.)

RPM	Speed	Total GPH	NMPG
1400	8.8 kn	11	.810
1600	13.4 kn	13	1.020
1800	18.5 kn	16	1.130
2000	22.5 kn	22	1.050
2200	25.6 kn	28	0.910
2400	28.7 kn	37	0.780
2500	31.0 kn	45	0.688

The same data indicate that at a cruising speed of 2300 rpm, the boat moves at 27 knots with a fuel consumption of 34 gph. This suggests a cruising endurance of 13.24 hours and a range of 357 nautical miles at that speed. By contrast, the

1400-rpm, 8.8-knot speed with fuel consumption of 11 gph suggests an endurance of almost 41 hours at that speed and a range of about 360 miles. The boat's most economical speed appears to be 17 knots at about 1740 rpm, with a fuel rate of 1.17 mpg, or about 14½ gph. Endurance at this speed would be 31 hours and extreme range would be 528 nautical miles.

Description

The Ocean Yacht 40- and 42-foot Super Sports are very modern, yet completely nautical fishermen. The sweeping reverse sheer is understated, yet it provides generous headroom in the cabins forward. The deckhouse is not large in proportion to the rest of the vessel, placing the center of daytime living and the bridge control station only a jump away from the cockpit. The cockpit, with more than 100 square feet of space, is large enough for a full-sized fighting chair plus two portable fishing chairs. A hardtop bridge cover with radar antenna (illustrated) gives the impression of a low enclosed tower.

The boat's length-beam ratio of 2.93:1 suggests a hull that is a trifle slimmer than others of the 40- to 42-foot length class. This may, in part, account for the excellent speed and range provided by two 390-hp TI diesels.

The layout calls for a cockpit control station on the port side at the forward end of the fishing area. To starboard is space for a large bait freezer and tackle station. A live-bait well is underdeck well aft on the centerline. Plan A provides for a complete galley setup on the port side of the deckhouse with cabinet, sink, range, refrigerator, and freezer. To starboard is a large L-shaped lounge with dropleaf table and an icemaker and bar forward. The master stateroom to port, below, features a double berth fore and aft, vanity, and locker. Forward of this is the head, with doors to the master stateroom and forward stateroom.

The forward stateroom has V-berths, a seat, vanity, and locker. There is a separate Pullman-type berth to starboard of the main companionway and deckhouse steps. A generous rope locker is located in the forepeak.

Plan B moves the galley below in the place of the single Pullman berth. The remainder of the below-decks layout is essentially the same as in Plan A. The Plan B deckhouse layout is the same as Plan A to starboard but substitutes an entertainment center to port, forward, and open space for deckhouse furniture where the galley is in Plan A. The layouts are conventional, but the workmanship and attention to detail are excellent.

Jack Leek, the head of John C. Leek Associates, is one of the Leek brothers who for years built the well-known Pacemaker boats. A hard-fishing angling competitor, he puts into his vessels a wealth of experience gained in tournaments and in everyday fishing from Florida to New England.

Owner's Evaluation

J.W. Blackwell of Pennington, New Jersey, reported on his 40-foot Super Sport just as he was trading in the older model for one of the new 42-footers. His report gives his personal opinion of the two very similar models.

(continued on page 249)

*Above: Thoroughbred styling marks this tournament-quality 40-footer with the Jack Leek stamp strong on its design. Accommodating six, the 40-foot design is credited with a top speed of 31 knots (35.3 mph) with twin J&T 671TI diesels. Calculated maximum range is over 500 miles at cruising speed of 17 knots. **Right:** Running fast and dry at 25 knots in rough water. (Photos by DeJon Photography Studio Inc.)*

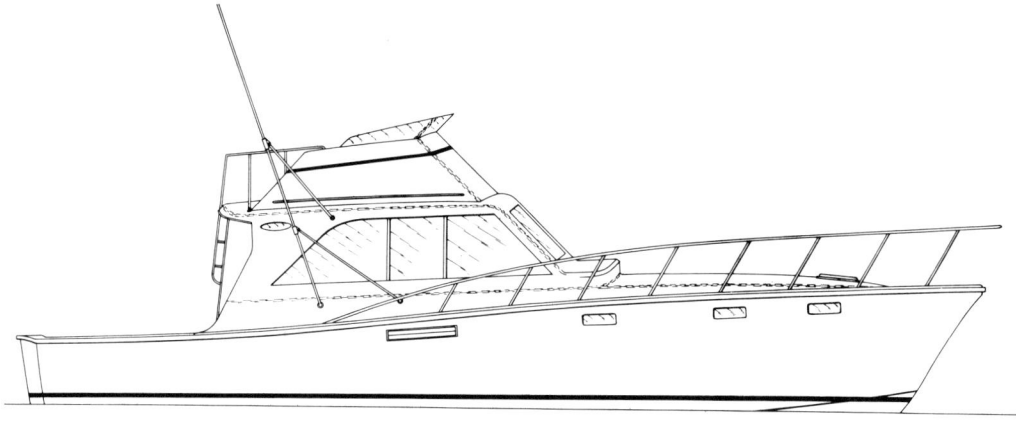

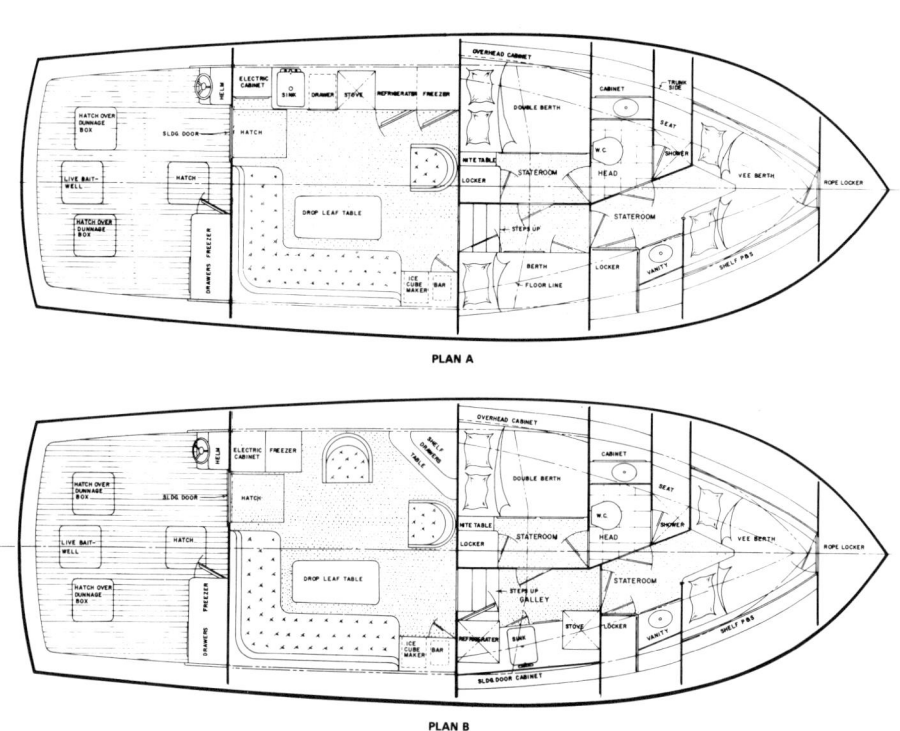

Two plans for the newer 42-footer differ mainly in the location of the galley. The cockpit is slightly larger than in the 40-footer. (Courtesy of Ocean Yachts)

	40-Footer	42-Footer
Fuel economy	Good	Good
Handling qualities	Good	Super
Seaworthiness	Super	Super
Overall design	Good	Good
Cruising comfort	Good	Good
Fishing efficiency	Super	Super
Ease of maintenance	Good	Good
Investment value	Good	Good

Blackwell averages up to 550 hours of use per year, fishing off Cape Hatteras and southern New Jersey to Baltimore and Wilmington Canyons. He claims a 31-knot top speed with two 380-hp 671TI Detroit J&T diesels. His 40-footer, the *Rammer*, cruised at 27 knots at 2300 rpm or 23 knots at 2150 rpm. He claims a 325-nautical-mile cruising range at 25 knots, and he finds the usable fuel capacity to be 420 gallons.

The 42-footer is his ultimate fishing machine "until something better comes along." He evaluates the 42-footer as "super" when considered against other boats he has owned. He rates fishing ability, handling ability, and cruising range as the most important qualities he looks for in a fishing boat, closely followed by seaworthiness, fuel economy, ease of maintenance, and, finally, investment value. Answering the question about whether he will fish in the future if fuel is available, he gave a simple, "Yes!"

Standard Equipment, 40-foot Super Sport

Power and Propulsion

2 engines, as per arrangement
Propellers, 3- or 4-blade, Dyna Jet
 Ni-Bral
Shafts, 3½-in Aquamet 22
Struts, 2 main, 2 intermediate,
 manganese bronze
Rudders, manganese bronze
Mufflers, fiberglass
Fuel strainers (4)
Full engineroom insulation
External strainers
Freshwater spigot in engineroom
Trim tabs

Electrical

Cigarette lighter, 12 v. DC
Converter, 60-amp
Radio ground tubes
50-ft shore cable, 50-amp, 220 v. AC,
 shoreline switch
Voltmeter
Duplex outlets with covers, 115 v. AC
Electrical control center, 12 v. DC and
 115 v. AC, with breakers
Internal bonding system
Batteries, 205-amp (2)

Battery power relay, aircraft-type
Generator, 7.5-kw, diesel
SSB antenna counterpoise
Fire and smoke detectors
Zinc anodes, shafts and rudders

Lighting

International navigation lights
Cockpit courtesy lighting
Portable searchlight
Overhead, bunk, engineroom, docking
 lights

Water System

Hot-water heater, 17-gal
Pressure water system
Lovett 12 v. DC automatic shower sump
 pump
Single-lever faucets
Central main drain aft eliminates all side
 through-hull fittings

Deck and Outfitting

SS handrails
SS bow anchor-line deck hawse, anchor
 chocks
8-in to 10-in SS mooring cleats (6)

Docklines, 25-ft, nylon (5)
Stern quarter dockline fairleads, SS (2)
Cabin door hooks
Deck hatch forward, ½-in Plexiglas
Fenders, 6 in × 26 in (2)
Forward lounge cushion and cover
Deck flanges, SS

Safety and Navigation

22-lb Danforth anchor, 5-ft vinyl-coated
    chain
200-ft nylon anchor line
Fog bell, deluxe electric horn
2½-lb fire extinguishers (4)
Halon 5-lb system (engineroom)
First-aid kit
Type 1 life jackets (6), Type IV
    cushion (1)
Bow rail, bridge rail, ladder, SS
Sumlog, quartz ship's clock
Constellation 4-in flush-mounted compass
Quick-action ball-type fuel shutoff valves
Fuel shutoff valves, seacocks on all
    fittings below waterline
Bilge blowers, 4-in, with thermostats (2)
Lovett automatic bilge pumps (2)
Hydraulic steering, 2-station
Engine alarm system, hour meters, fuel
    gauges
VHF/FM radio, 55-channel, 8-db antenna

Salon (Deckhouse)

Teak sliding door with security lock
Carpeting, decor selection
Chairs, as per layout plan
L-lounge, sleeps 2, seats 6
High-low table
Freezer, Plan B
AM/FM 8-track tape and radio
Built-in vacuum system
3-zone air conditioning, heating
Roman drapes with teak trim and cornice
Windshield covers or solid fiberglass
Tinted safety glass
Tinted portlights below

Galley

Water-tank level gauge
Garbage disposal
Instant hot-water faucet
Range, Princess Model 33, 3-burner,
    oven, rotisserie
Refrigerator, 6.6-cu-ft, freezer, 6.6-cu-ft,
    Plan A

Refrigerator, 6.6-cu-ft, Plan B
Deluxe icemaker, SS front
Corningware dishes, 8-place setting
Spacious drawers and storage
    compartments
Hanging locker
Exhaust blower

Forward Stateroom

Carpeting, drapes
Mattresses, 5-in foam, pillows (2),
    mattress covers
Full-length mirror, decor selection
Drawers for storage of clothing
Sink and vanity
Hanging locker

After Stateroom

Carpeting, drapes
Mattresses, 5-in foam, with covers,
    pillows (2)
Full-length mirror, decor selection
Drawers and hanging locker

Head

Holding tank, 45-gal
Vanity with Corian sink and top
Shower with tempered-glass door
Towel bars, toothbrush and tumbler
    holders
Soap dish, gold faucet
Exhaust blower

Cockpit

Rodholders, flush-type (4)
Cockpit side lockers
Tackle locker
Cockpit steering station
Transom door
Boarding step
Bait freezer
Seawater washdown hose and valve
Teak cockpit deck, covering boards,
    toe rails
Padded cockpit coaming
Live-bait well
Dockside freshwater connection
    and spigot

Flying Bridge

Molded fiberglass, complete
    instrumentation
Helmsman and companion seats
Windshield, safety rail, ladder, lockers
Lounge seat front

Ocean Yachts does not supply a list of optional equipment. Their standard list is so complete that an optional list is not necessary. The Super Sport models come as complete living and fishing packages. Owner's choice is exercised in selection of outriggers, tower, chairs for cockpit, fishing tackle, and electronic aids to fish location, navigation, and communication.

UNIFLITE 42-FOOT CONVERTIBLE

Designer	Uniflite Inc.
Builder	Uniflite Inc. P.O. Box 1095 Bellingham, WA 98225 P.O. Box 68 Swansboro, NC 28584
Construction	Fiberglass hull, decks, and super-structure. Fire-resistant resin used throughout.

Specifications

Length overall	42 ft	12.10 m
Length, waterline	37 ft 9 in	11.51 m
Beam, maximum	14 ft 9 in	4.50 m
Draft	3 ft 9 in	1.14 m
Cockpit area	110 sq ft	10.23 m²
Freeboard forward	5 ft 2 in	1.59 m
Freeboard aft	3 ft 6 in	1.07 m
Headroom, interior	6 ft 6 in	1.98 m
Height, waterline to bridge	15 ft	4.58 m
Weight, normal	35,000 lb	15,455 kg
Fuel capacity	500 gal	1,890 l
Water capacity	160 gal	605 l
Sleeping accommodations	4-6	

Power options

Twin 350-hp Crusader gasoline, 2.57:1 reduction gear
Twin 210-hp Cummins diesels, 3:1 reduction gear
Twin 240-hp Cummins diesels, 3:1 reduction gear
Twin 310-hp J&T Detroit diesels, 2:1 reduction gear
Twin 320-hp Cummins diesels, 2:1 reduction gear
Twin 210-hp Caterpillar diesels, 2.5:1 reduction gear

Designed and built originally in Washington state, the Uniflite 42-foot Convertible shows many East Coast fishing features. Sleeping from four to six people, she is capable of up to 29 mph with a wide selection of gasoline and diesel power available. Maximum cruising range is about 400 miles at 15 or 16 knots. (Photo by Uniflite Inc.)

Performance

With twin 350-hp Crusader gasoline engines
4-blade N/C propeller, 24-in dia. × 24-in pitch
2.57:1 reduction gear

Top speed	26 kn (29.6 mph) @ 4200 rpm
Top fuel rate	52 gph
Top fuel economy	0.50 nmpg (0.57 mpg)
Top fuel endurance	9.6 hr
Top-speed range	250 nm (285 mi)
Cruising speed	18 kn (20.5 mph) @ 3000 rpm
Cruising fuel rate	32 gph
Cruising fuel economy	0.56 nmpg (0.64 mpg)
Cruising fuel endurance	15.6 hr
Cruising-speed range	281 nm (320 mi)

With twin 210-hp Cummins diesels
4-blade N/C propellers, 26-in dia. × 24-in pitch
3:1 reduction gear

Top speed	18 kn (20.5 mph) @ 3300 rpm
Top fuel rate	26 gph
Top fuel economy	0.69 nmpg (0.79 mpg)
Top fuel endurance	19.2 hr
Top-speed range	346 nm (395 mi)
Cruising speed	15 kn (17.1 mph) @ 3000 rpm
Cruising fuel rate	18 gph
Cruising fuel economy	0.83 nmpg (0.95 mpg)
Cruising fuel endurance	27.8 hr
Cruising-speed range	417 nm (475 mi)

With twin 240-hp Cummins diesels
4-blade N/C propellers, 26-in dia. × 26-in pitch
3:1 reduction gear

Top speed	19 kn (21.7 mph) @ 3300 rpm
Top fuel rate	28 gph
Top fuel economy	0.68 nmpg (0.77 mpg)
Top fuel endurance	17.9 hr
Top-speed range	339 nm (387 mi)
Cruising speed	16 kn (18.2 mph) @ 3000 rpm
Cruising fuel rate	20 gph
Cruising fuel economy	0.80 nmpg (0.91 mpg)
Cruising fuel endurance	25 hr
Cruising-speed range	400 nm (456 mi)

With twin 310-hp J&T Detroit diesels
4-blade N/C propellers, 26-in dia. × 25-in pitch
2:1 reduction gear

Top speed	23 kn (26.2 mph) @ 2500 rpm
Top fuel rate	34 gph
Top fuel economy	0.68 nmpg (0.77 mpg)
Top fuel endurance	14.7 hr
Top-speed range	338 nm (386 mi)
Cruising speed	20 kn (22.8 mph) @ 2300 rpm
Cruising fuel rate	30 gph
Cruising fuel economy	0.67 nmpg (0.76 mpg)
Cruising fuel endurance	16.7 hr
Cruising-speed range	333 nm (380 mi)

With twin 320-hp Cummins diesels
4-blade N/C propellers, 26-in dia. × 25-in pitch
2:1 reduction gear

Top speed	23 kn (26.2 mph) @ 2600 rpm
Top fuel rate	34 gph
Top fuel economy	0.68 nmpg (0.77 mpg)
Top fuel endurance	14.7 hr
Top-speed range	338 nm (386 mi)
Cruising speed	20 kn (22.8 mph) @ 2300 rpm

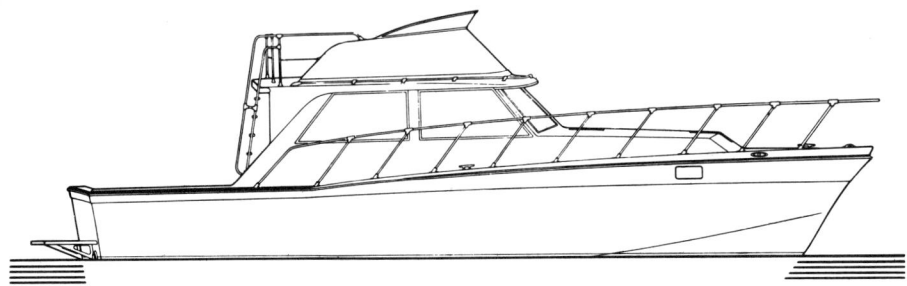

Cruising fuel rate*	20 gph
Cruising fuel economy	1.00 nmpg (1.14 mpg)
Cruising fuel endurance	25 hr
Cruising-speed range*	500 nm (570 mi)

In view of the extremely consistent speed/fuel data of the other five engine combinations, it seems possible that this fuel rate and cruising-speed range may be the result of calculating or typographical error.

With twin 210-hp Caterpillar diesels
4-blade N/C propellers, 24-in × 24-in pitch
2.5:1 reduction gear

Top speed	17 kn (19.4 mph) @ 2800 rpm
Top fuel rate	26 gph
Top fuel economy	0.65 nmpg (0.75 mpg)
Top fuel endurance	19.2 hr
Top-speed range	327 nm (373 mi)
Cruising speed	14 kn (16.0 mph) @ 2400 rpm
Cruising fuel rate	18 gph
Cruising fuel economy	0.78 nmpg (0.89 mpg)
Cruising fuel endurance	27.8 hr
Cruising-speed range	389 nm (443 mi)

Description

The Uniflite 42-foot Convertible is in every respect a high-quality cruising fisherman with tournament capability. Built originally in this company's Bellingham, Washington, yard, the 42-footer is now also produced in the newer Swansboro, North Carolina, facility. The flying bridge is slightly unusual from the West Coast point of view, in that it incorporates the after position for the helmsman, typical of East Coast style. This after position gives the operator complete visibility of the cockpit, essential when working large, active game fish. The large cockpit can easily take a full-sized fighting chair and a pair of fixed or portable fishing chairs.

West Coast owners are partial to the transom platform, and the Uniflite 42-footer offers a transom door and platform (they call it a "boarding platform") as standard equipment. This is one western convention that is starting to become popular in eastern and southern waters. The hull is a modified deep-V, and the use of fire-retardant fiberglass resin throughout is a welcome safety note. Uniflite has built many hulls for the U.S. government, and government specifications are followed in much of their civilian production.

The commodious deckhouse is unusual in its arrangement. A lower control station is provided forward on the port side. Most similar stations are positioned to starboard. The semi-open companionway to the lower cabin area creates a feeling of space and light. A convertible settee is placed to starboard in the deckhouse, and there is space for several arrangements of furniture. Craftsmanship is of a high order.

Plan C is the standard for below-decks arrangement and has the galley to starboard, below, flanked by the owner's stateroom to port. The owner's stateroom may have either twin beds or one double berth. Forward, to port, is a large toilet room with head, sink, vanity, and shower. It has doors opening to the master stateroom and also to the companionway. Forward, to starboard, are upper and lower single berths. Locker and drawer space is generous.

Hull construction is one-piece with glassed-in foam-core stringers. The superstructure is fastened to the hull with stainless-steel rivets, then bonded with fiberglass to form a solid unit. Plan E is a slight variation on Plan C and incorporates a second head to starboard in the space borrowed from the galley and a hanging locker. This makes the port head completely private to the master stateroom.

The Uniflite 42-foot Convertible illustrates the growing tendency of manufacturers to borrow good fishing practice and apply it to create powerboats that are truly "convertible" from fishing to cruising, and vice versa. It also shows the influence of competent game-fishing professionals in layout, choice of equipment, and basic design. The result is a boat that will acquit itself well in any fishing or cruising territory or in any nautical company.

Standard Equipment

Hull and Deck

Gunwale guard, heavy-duty
Hull drain plug
Ventilation portholes
Anchor combination
    Danforth anchor, 20-ft chain
    Deck pipe and chocks
    200-ft, ½-in nylon rode
Boarding platform and transom door
Cleats (4) and chocks (2), SS
Cleats (2), springline, SS
Cockpit bulkhead, white Formica
Emergency escape hatch forward
Ventilation hatches over master stateroom, galley
Fishbox, cockpit-type
Flagstaff with socket
Fuel deckplates with chains
One-piece nonskid deck surfaces
Railing, SS

Superstructure

Command bridge, rails, ladder, single swivel seat, cover

Door, sliding-glass, after bulkhead
Door hardware chrome-plated
One-piece, nonskid bridge deck surface
Tip-out electronics bins in bridge console
Windows, tinted safety glass
Windows, sliding, salon with screens

Interior Furnishings (Plan C standard)

Carpeting, all floors, with padding
Drapes, lined
Paneling and joinerwork, teak
Vinyl headlining

Master Stateroom

Beds, owner's choice, twin or double
Dresser/vanity, Formica top
Hanging lockers
Linen cabinets

Forward Stateroom

Deluxe hull liner
Full-length clothing locker
Hanging locker
Large berths with foam-filled cushions
Privacy door

Galley-Dinette

Countertops, heat- and stain-resistant
Dish and food lockers
Garbage bin
Large galley counter
Refrigerator, upright, 14-cu-ft, 115 v. AC
Spice rack, utensil and cutlery drawers
Sink, double, SS
Stove, 3-burner, electric, oven, cover,
    cutting board

Head(s)

Carpeted floor covering with pad
Marine toilet, holding tank, sea/dockside
    discharge
Mirror, forward head
Roll-away clothesline in shower
Shower, enclosed, fiberglass
Towel ring and paper holder
Vanity cabinet with sink and Formica top

Propulsion and Controls

DC alternators
Approved all-copper-line fuel system with
    selector valves and filters
Bronze propellers, 4-blade
Compass, 5-in
Controls, Morse
Engine mounts, vibration-eliminating
Engines (standard), twin Crusaders,
    350-hp gasoline
Fuel filters and gauges
Heat exchanger, freshwater cooling
Engine hour meter
Insulation, engineroom
Instrument spray covers on bridge
Full instrumentation, bridge and deck-
    house

Mufflers, watercooled exhaust pipes
Seawater strainers for cooling system
Self-aligning stuffing boxes
Shafts, 1¾-in SS
Synchronizer, engines, single-station

Electrical-Mechanical

Battery boxes with hold-downs
Battery paralleling switch, isolator system
Battery charger
Circuit breakers on AC and DC circuits
Color-coded and marked wiring
    throughout
Dockside power, 115 v. AC inlet with
    50-ft, 30-amp cable
Electrical control panel in salon
Generator, Onan, 7.5-kw, all accessories,
    115 v. AC
Generator, Onan, 6.5-kw, all accessories,
    115 v. AC
Lighting, 12 v. DC throughout,
    fluorescent in salon
Outlets, 115 v. AC, receptacle
160-gal freshwater system, pressurized
12-gal electric hot-water heater
Single-lever swing faucets

Safety Equipment

Alarm system, fumes, water temperature,
    oil pressure, gear oil (for gasoline or
    diesel)
Bilge pumps, automatic (3)
Bilge blowers (gasoline only)
Fire extinguishers (4)
International navigation lights
Ship's bell, trumpet horn
Shutoff valves on all underwater
    through-hull fittings

Optional Equipment

Hull, Deck, Superstructure

Paint, bottom, antifouling
Shipping cradle
Cockpit coaming, padded
Rodholders, flush-type
Outriggers, Lee's Sr., with 22-ft poles,
    6-ft bases
Pulpit, bow, teak, with anchor roller
Rail, bow, teak
Rail, toe, teak

Solid after bulkhead with one opening
    door
Transom door
Washdown pump, seawater
Anchor bow roller, Plath, 19-in, rope
Anchor chain, 200-ft galvanized, with
    shackles
Anchor bow roller-chock combination, SS
Anchor winch, heavy-duty, 12 v. DC,
    rope only

Anchor winch, heavy-duty, 12 v. DC, chain and rope
Bridge seat, additional, with cover
Bridge seat, back-to-back reclining lounge
Sliding door, bridge, portside
Tournament-fishing bridge console and controls with seat forward

Deckhouse (Salon)

Chairs, occasional
Lounge, L-shaped
Sofa, convertible to 58-in double bed
Sofa, convertible to 66-in double bed
Table, high-low
Wet bar with automatic icemaker

Master Stateroom

Wall mirror, full-sized, Plan C

Galley and Head

Refrigerator, 8-cu-ft, 12 v. DC/ 115 v. AC, Norcold
Refrigerator, 14-cu-ft, with automatic icemaker
Stove, 3-burner, electric, cook top with radar range under
Marine toilet, Microphor waste-treatment system with Raritan electric toilet
Marine toilet, Mansfield Vacu-Flush (1) with 20-gal holding tank
Marine toilet, Mansfield discharge kit

Electrical-Mechanical-Freshwater

Air conditioning, includes split AC circuits
Cigar lighters
Electric circuit, split AC (standard with air conditioning)
Extra 115 v. AC dockside inlet with single buss
Extra 115 v. AC dockside inlet with split buss
Fans, defrost
Water hookup, dockside, port and starboard
Heaters, electric, thermostat-controlled
Lights, docking, Morse
Searchlight, dual-station, electric operation
Searchlight, single-station, electric operation

Propulsion and Controls

Engines, as per Power Options in Specifications
Fuel water separators
Helm, lower station, with chair, windshield wipers
Shaft, spare, stowed
Steering, cockpit controls
Synchronizer, engine, dual-station, gas or diesel
Trim tabs

Safety Equipment

Air horn, twin Buell, with compressor
Ship's bell
Bilge pumps, automatic, extra
Fire extinguisher system, Halon Automatic 1301
Windshield washers

Boat Canvas

Bimini top
Bimini top with weather enclosure
Command-bridge dash cover
Tournament flying-bridge console cover

Navigation and Communication

Autopilot, Benmar 21R, single- or dual-station
Chart storage, overhead, salon
Fathometer, Raytheon DE 738
Fathometer, extension bracket for bridge with switch
Hailer, Ray 250 with intercom horn
Intercom, 2-station
Radar, Ray 2700, flying-bridge front mount
Radio, VHF/FM Ray 50A, 25-watt, with antenna
Radio, VHF/FM Ray 48A, with antenna
Radio, SSB, Ray 1209, with antenna
Radio, VHF/FM remote station
Stereo, AM/FM tape, 8-track, with 6 speakers and selector switch

Water Delivery Kit

Mooring lines, 30-ft (4)
Life jackets, adult (6)
Life ring (1)
Emergency flares and projector
Fender (4)
First-aid kit

BERTRAM 46-FOOT CONVERTIBLE

Designer	Bertram Yacht Division, Whittaker Corp.
Builder	Bertram Yacht 3663 N.W. 21st Street Miami, FL 33142
Construction	Fiberglass hull, subdecks, and super-structure. Teak cockpit, deck, and trim.

Specifications

Length overall	46 ft 6 in	14.18 m
Length, waterline	40 ft	12.20 m
Beam, maximum	16 ft	4.88 m
Draft	4 ft 6 in	1.37 m
Cockpit area	130 sq ft	12.09 m²
Freeboard forward	6 ft 3 in	1.91 m
Freeboard aft	3 ft 7 in	1.10 m
Height to flying-bridge windshield	13 ft 9 in	4.24 m
Weight, normal	44,000 lb	20,000 kg
Fuel capacity	642 gal	2,430 l
Water capacity	200 gal	756 l
Sleeping accommodations	6	

Power options
  Twin 435-hp 8V-71TI GM diesels
  Twin 420-hp VTA-903 Cummins diesels

Performance

With twin 435-hp 8V-71TI GM diesels
(642 gallons — 2,430 liters)

Top speed	29.6 mph (44.1 kph) @ 2300 rpm
Cruising speed	19.3 mph (28.8 kph) @ 1500 rpm
Cruising range	475 mi (700 km) @ 1500 rpm

With twin 420-hp VTA-903 Cummins diesels
(same tankage)

Top speed	31.3 mph (46.6 kph) @ 2600 rpm
Cruising speed	24.1 mph (35.9 kph) @ 2000 rpm
Cruising range	512 mi (763 km) @ 2000 rpm

Speeds and cruising ranges are test averages and may vary among similar boats depending on weight, engine condition, and bottom condition.

"Unstoppable in any fishable weather" is the phrase for this big Bertram. Six can cruise and fish the tournament circuit in air-conditioned comfort. Top speed with twin 420-hp Cummins diesels is over 31 mph and range is over 500 miles at 24 mph cruising speed. (Photo by Bertram Yacht)

Description

With a length of 46 feet 6 inches and a beam of 16 feet, this Bertram model is not a small boat. Yet serious competitive offshore fishermen do not hesitate to include it in the rather exclusive class of "tournament" boats. The word *tournament* can be misleading. Actually, almost any old boat can participate in a fishing tournament, but the term *tournament boat* is usually applied only to sportfishing boats that meet or exceed very high standards of performance, handling qualities, equipment, and imaginative design. Tournament-class boats may be as small as 25 feet, in which case they are frequently used by light-tackle specialists, or they may exceed 50 feet in length. Generally speaking, true tournament sportfishing boats are between 35 feet and 50 feet in length. Smaller than 35 feet, they may lack the weight and body to fish in really rough water. Larger, they may lack some of the cutting-horse maneuverability that tournament fishing frequently requires.

The distinctive Bertram sheerline is broken by a slanted step-down at the after deckhouse bulkhead. This effectively reduces cockpit freeboard, a necessity in the larger sportfishing vessels. Otherwise, the Bertram profile is so perfectly preserved that, at a distance, it is sometimes difficult to distinguish the 46-foot Convertible from smaller Bertrams in the 38-foot and 42-foot classes. Close aboard, however, the boat's size and generous space are quite evident.

The cockpit area of about 130 square feet may appear small when compared to the boat's overall size, but it is completely adequate for all serious offshore fishing. A larger cockpit would not increase fishing efficiency and would merely detract from interior living space. Standard practice calls for mounting the fish-lifting gin pole on the starboard side, fastened to the deckhouse overhang. This is also the logical location for a cockpit control station if this option is desired.

To port is the flying-bridge access ladder, with space forward of the ladder for a deck bait freezer and tackle locker. The fighting chair, when fitted, is mounted on the centerline with space for a portable, deck fishbox or gearbox between the extended footrest and the stern. Some owners prefer a built-in stern door for boating large fish. This option can be installed at the time of building.

As in many boats of this class, the bridge control station is considered the normal station for handling the boat, even in very bad weather. The controls and instrument group are located in a fiberglass console to port of the bridge centerline, just forward of the access ladder. There is adequate angle of view of the cockpit for the operator, always an important factor in big-game fishing. Seating is provided for up to six other persons, since the bridge of any sportfishing boat is a popular place for nonfishing guests, and for lookouts when cruising fast for sight of finning game fish.

The deckhouse after bulkhead has sliding doors. There is a bar to port on entering and a convertible lounge that can sleep two when made up for the night. A high-low table serves the lounge during the daytime. A full-length rod and tackle locker can be built into the starboard deckhouse side. There is ample room for two or three large easy chairs.

The galley is to starboard at the step-down level of the lower staterooms. Normal equipment includes a 6-cubic-foot refrigerator, 6-cubic-foot freezer with icemaker, stove, oven, stainless-steel sink, hot- and cold-water outlets, and freshwater supply indicator. Interior ventilation is complete and air conditioning is a popular option.

The owner's stateroom is to port, forward of the deckhouse, and features twin 36-inch by 77-inch beds. There is an owner's toilet forward of the stateroom, entered from the stateroom. A second, guest toilet room is to starboard. Both facilities have built-in showers. The forward stateroom is equipped with twin V-berths and access to the guest toilet. Locker and stowage space is lavish throughout.

According to the builders, special features include:

- A "floating" electrical system, isolated from everything except the generator to minimize currents that cause electrolysis, together with a 32-volt DC boat's system.
- "Constant trim" design for fuel and water tanks.
- Both positive and negative sides of electric circuits protected by circuit breakers.
- Air horns operated by bottled CO_2, not a power-driven compressor.
- Structural parts built into the hull while the hull is still in the mold, assuring a "true" hull.
- Separate 30-gallon drinking-water system with stainless-steel tank.
- Heavy-duty vinyl paneling throughout.
- All wiring harnessed and color-coded for safety and convenient service.
- Special "trouble-shooter" alarm system that spots problems without tedious personal inspection.

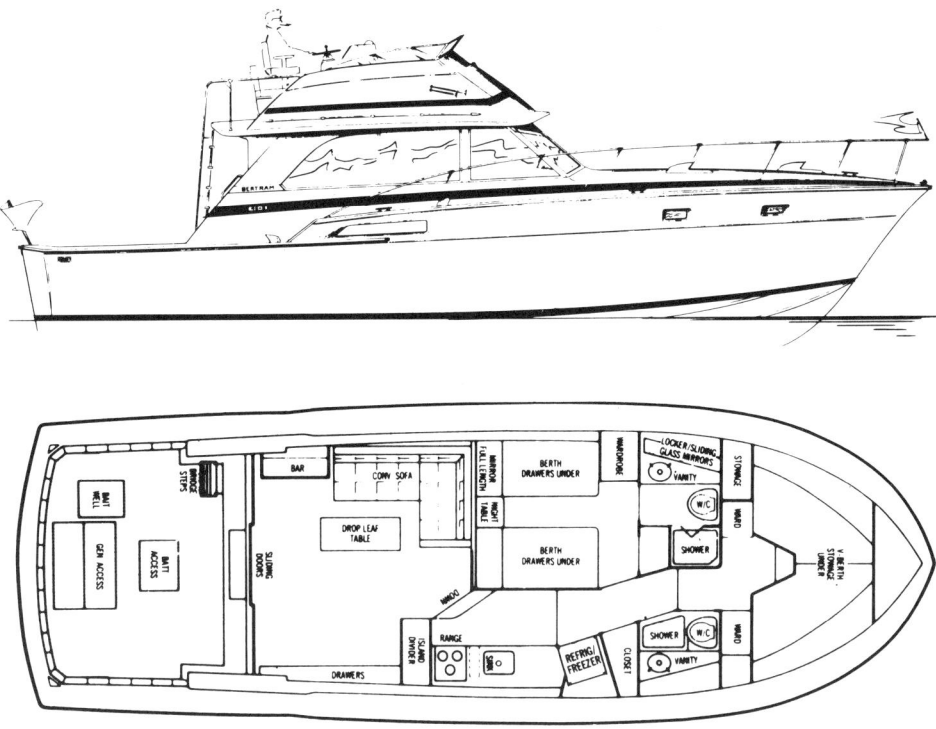

The dynamic stability of the Bertram 46 is dramatic. The author rode a 46-foot Convertible from Miami to Bimini with a stiff northwest wind raising a short, steep, confused chop on the Gulf Stream. Beneath the heavy chop was a massive groundswell from the south, remnant of an earlier storm. The Bertram never slowed from her 20-knot cruising speed and tracked as straight as a ruled line through that broken water. Later, sailfishing off Cat Cay was a delight, with the big hull holding trolling speed with, across, or against the prevailing wind and chop.

Owner's Evaluation

Bertram 46 owner Johnnie Baker of Wrightsville Beach, North Carolina, uses his boat at least 300 hours a year, averaging 30 percent cruising time and 70 percent fishing-trolling. He calculates a top speed of 28 mph and cruising range of 400 miles at 24 mph with twin Detroit diesel 8-71 TI engines of 435 hp rating each. He rates the Bertram 46 "the best one yet — it has proved to be a super fish-raiser, including blue and white marlin. Better sea boat than the Bertram 38."

Johnnie Baker's performance evaluation of the Bertram 46-footer gives the boat excellent marks.

Fuel economy	Good
Handling qualities	Super

Seaworthiness	Super
Overall design	Super
Cruising comfort	Super
Fishing efficiency	Super
Ease of maintenance	Good
Investment value	Super

When asked about the satisfaction he gets from sportfishing, Baker replied, "With the exception of tournaments, we are past the fish-kill type of billfishing. It is gratifying to see my family and young people fail or succeed at fishing. And we make many new friends."

Baker's remark about the superiority of the Bertram 46-footer over the same builder's 38-foot boat is typical of the reaction that many owners have to the experience with a boat larger than the one they operated before. It has been proved many times that, all else being equal, nothing replaces size and weight for comfort in rough water.

Standard Equipment

General

Complete drapes throughout
32 v. DC, 115 v. AC lighting
115 v. AC outlets
Separate drinking-water system
Water-pressure system
2½-ton air-conditioning system
Carpeting throughout

Forward Stateroom

V-berths with Polyfoam mattresses
Drawers under berths (6)
Hanging lockers, port and starboard
Private access to guest bath
60-in mirror
Ventilating hatch and skylight
Portlights in hull sides

Owner's Stateroom

Twin beds, 35 in × 77 in,
  with Polyfoam mattresses
Storage drawers under each bed
3-drawer nightstand between berths
Hanging lockers (2)
Mirror, full-width, after bulkhead

Owner's Bath

Clothes hamper
Stall shower
Vanity with locker and drawer storage
Electric toilet
Ventilating hatch and skylight

Guest Bath

Access door from companionway or
  forward stateroom
Fiberglass vanity
Stowage lockers
Mirror
Telephone-type shower with curtain
Electric toilet
Ventilating hatch

Galley

6-cu-ft refrigerator
6-cu-ft freezer with icemaker
3-burner range with oven
Exhaust fan
Dish locker
SS sink with chopping-block cover
Single-lever hot and cold faucet
Freshwater tank-supply indicators

Deckhouse

Bulkhead with sliding doors
Bar unit portside
Cold cathode lighting
Curved convertible lounge with high-low
  table
Screens on side windows
Color television
Stereo tape player with 4 sets of speakers

Cockpit

White vinyl deck

Live-bait well below deck
Access hatch to generator, rudders, tanks,
 battery compartment
Stowage lockers, port and starboard
Washdown outlet, seawater

Flying Bridge

Seating for 8, including adjustable
 helmsman's seat
Complete controls, instrumentation
Safety monitor system (fire, bilge,
 engines, oil and water)
Compass, 5-in
Padded coaming

Mechanical Equipment

Hynautic hydraulic steering
Dual-lever engine controls
Seacocks
SS propeller shafts
Freshwater cooling, main engines,
 generator
CO_2 fire-extinguisher system
Dockside water-supply inlet, port and
 starboard
Vibration mounts on all engines

Machinery Space

DC lighting
Thermal insulation

Sea strainers
Bilge blowers (2)
Bilge pumps, automatic (3)
Hot-water tank, freshwater pump system

Electrical

Automatic 30-amp converter
115 v. AC air conditioning
32 v. DC ship's system
200-Ah batteries, 2 banks with parallel
 switch
Bonding system with large ground plates
20-gal, 115 v. AC water heater
Electro-hydraulic trim tabs
Twin-trumpet air horn
International navigation lights
32 v. DC fuel-system priming pump
2½-ton air conditioning with port and
 starboard 50-amp service
Generator, 7.5-kw, diesel

Deck Hardware

Heavy-duty foredeck cleats, 12-in (2)
Heavy-duty springline cleats, 10-in (4)
Flush stern-deck chocks
Heavy-duty stern cleats in cockpit (2)
SS bow rail
40-lb Danforth anchor with 300-ft, ¾-in
 nylon line

Optional Equipment

Additional 30-amp automatic converter
Automatic pilot
Bimini bridge top, Dacron
Bridge cover, Dacron
Cabin heater with fan
Cockpit controls
  Steering
  Engine controls
  Engine start-stop switches
  Vinyl cover
Cockpit cover, Dacron
Deckhouse controls
  Steering and engine controls
  5-in compass
  Instruments, switches, safety panel
Deckhouse windshield cover, Dacron
Fishbox, curved to fit transom
Forward docking lights

Garbage-disposal unit
Generator, 12-kw, diesel
Gin pole
Mansfield toilets
Marlin Blue Fin fighting chair
  with cover
Outrigger mounts, 8-ft
Propellers, extra pair
Searchlight with electric control
Freshwater maker
Rodholders, cockpit (4)
SS shaft, spare
Teak cockpit deck
Teak bow pulpit
Transom docking lights, remote control
Transom steps
Windscreen for Bimini top, Dacron
Windshield washers (3)

POST 46-FOOT SPORT FISHERMAN

Designer	Post Marine Company
Builder	Post Marine Company River Road Mays Landing, NJ 08330
Construction	Fiberglass hull, decks, and super-structure. Teak trim.

Specifications

Length overall	46 ft	14.03 m
Length, waterline	NA	
Beam, maximum	15 ft 9 in	4.80 m
Draft	NA	
Cockpit area	110 sq ft	10.23 m²
Freeboard forward	6 ft 4 in	1.93 m
Freeboard aft	3 ft 3 in	1.00 m
Height, waterline to bridge	12 ft 6 in	3.81 m
Weight	NA	
Fuel capacity	656 gal	2,480 l
Water capacity	120 gal	454 l
Sleeping accommodations	6-8	

Power options
    Twin Detroit 671N 310-hp diesels
    Twin J&T Detroit 671TI 410-hp diesels

Performance

Literature announcing the Post 46-footer describes the top speed as "almost 35 mph" with twin 410-hp J&T Detroit 671TI diesels. A statement from the builder's office gives the following speeds with the same power:

2300 rpm	25 kn	(28.5 mph)
2500 rpm	28 kn	(31.9 mph)

Using J&T propeller-load curves for fuel consumption, the following fuel rate, endurance, and range have been calculated:

RPM	GPH	Endurance	Range
2300	32.6	20 hr	570 mi
2500	48.24	13.5 hr	430 mi

These figures, of course, are estimates and should not be considered builder's claims. They are given for the sake of comparison only. Boat loading, sea and weather conditions, and condition of bottom and propellers will affect speed and range and may produce figures different from these.

The Post 46-footer's proportions are so good that she could be mistaken for a larger vessel. The curtain-protected bridge becomes almost an elevated pilothouse, but there is adequate voice and eyeball contact with the cockpit. Speeds to 32 mph with twin J&T 671TI diesels and range to over 550 miles at 25 knots. (Photo by Post Marine Company)

Description

The Post 46-footer, which updated their earlier 42-foot sportfisherman in 1979, is described as a sedan cruiser laid out for serious game fishing, with emphasis on speed, performance, and fuel economy. The fiberglass has four S-section longitudinal stringers running the full length of the bottom and is hand-built with layers of fab-matt and polyester resin. A honeycomb of cross members, plus bulkheads and floors, gives great structural strength. The word *floor* in this context does not signify a surface to be walked on, but rather the older nautical definition of a transverse-strength member built into the hull, running across the keel from bilge to bilge.

Solid teak is used externally for trim and cockpit coaming covering boards. Interior woodwork and trim are of cabinetmaker quality. The deckhouse salon is finished in stained and varnished natural wood and can be equipped with a wet bar, special cabinets, and the owner's selection of salon furniture. The latter can include an L-lounge that converts into sleeping space for two.

Moving below, there is a dinette to port that can be converted into a double berth. Immediately forward is the galley. Dinette and galley look out onto the salon, preserving the feeling of open space between the two levels. To starboard of the dinette is the master stateroom, which may be equipped with twin berths or a large double berth. The master stateroom has its own private head, and there is a second head forward, to starboard, for the forward stateroom and the guest accommodations. The forward stateroom features upper and lower berths to port and an optional child's berth to starboard. This allows for considerable flexibility of sleeping arrangements.

Access to the bridge is by conventional ladder, and the operator's station is placed well aft, providing an unobstructed view of the entire cockpit. A Bimini top and clear plastic side curtains fastening to the raised bridge wings give excellent protection to the main control station while preserving excellent vision around the full circle. Locker and console space is provided for a full complement of electronic fish-finding and navigating aids.

While the decor is very modern, the treatment is nautical, minimizing the boudoir effect found in some heavily styled powerboats. Pleated and lined draw drapes give privacy to the salon. Six-inch foam mattresses are used on all berths. Bedspreads, pillow covers, wall coverings, etc., are selected by the owner. Ceilings are off-white perforated leatherette for heat and sound reduction, except in the shower and over the galley stove, where smooth laminate is used.

The overall result is a distinctive boat with conservative, modern good looks and an excellent record in the rough-and-tumble of competitive tournament fishing.

Standard Equipment

Bridge

Windshield, compartments
Constellation compass
Front and side seats
Adjustable helm chair
Electronics cabinet
Console cover
SS railings
Bimini top, curtains

Mechanical

Twin GM 671N diesels, standard
Twin GM 671TI diesels, optional
Full instrumentation, safety and alarm
  systems
Shafts, 1¾-in SS
Struts, V-type with Cutless bearings
Strainers, nonfouling, engine and
  generator
Generator, 7.5-kw, diesel, 115 v. AC
Trim tabs, electro-hydraulic, bridge
  controls
Fuel tanks, heavy welded aluminum

Water tanks, polyethylene
Full copper-wire bonding system
Insulation from solar and engine sources
Hydraulic steering accepts additional
  stations

Electrical

All systems conform with AB&YC and
  USCG standards
40-amp battery charger
Independent 12 v. DC and 115 v. AC
  systems
Giant Dynaplate radio ground system
17-gal electric water heater
Auto/manual bilge pumps (2)
12 v. DC automatic bilge sump pump
Exhaust blowers, engineroom, shower,
  galley
215-amp, 12 v. DC starting batteries (2)
50-ft shore current cable, 30-amp
Duplex (12 v. DC/115 v. AC) lighting
  fixtures and outlets
Central control panel with circuit
  breakers

Interior and Hardware

Glazing, all windows and ports tinted safety glass

Screening, for all windows and hatches

Port windows, 7 in × 14 in, with screens and drapes

Deck hatches, 3 forward for light, ventilation

Toilet rooms

  Approved heads, white or matching colors

  Matching lavatories, towel bars, etc.

  Mirrors, glass and brush holders, coat hooks

  Shower, access from either toilet room

Galley

  14-cu-ft refrigerator, top freezer, icemaker

  3-burner electric range, oven, rotisserie

  Exhaust hood and blower, duplex outlets

  Trash receptacle, cupboards, dish cabinet, drawers

Salon, tinted glass, center opening, screened

Full draperies and carpeting

SS handrails, guards, chafing strips

L-lounge/sleeper, cabinet each end

Cockpit step stool

Safety steps and grabrail on transom

Cockpit hatches (2), over struts and rudders

Halon fire-extinguisher system, auto-manual

Personal flotation vests (8)

Portable fire extinguishers

Fog bell, dual trumpet air horn

International navigation lights

Anchor with chain and 300-ft, ⅝-in nylon rope

⅝ in × 25 ft nylon docklines (6)

No charge for launch and make-ready with 200 gal fuel

The builder does not list optional equipment for the 46-foot Sport Fisherman but will discuss such equipment as outriggers, tower, fishing and fighting chairs, bait freezer, and tackle station with each owner to provide complete personal satisfaction.

HATTERAS 46-FOOT CONVERTIBLE

Designer	J.B. Hargrave, N.A., Inc. 205½ Sixth Street West Palm Beach, FL 33401
Builder	AMF — Hatteras Yachts 2100 Kivett Drive P.O. Box 2690 High Point, NC 27261
Construction	Fiberglass hull, deck, and superstructure, with teak and hardwood trim and decor.

Forty-six feet of length seems to be almost a magic number among larger sportfishing boats. This Hatteras 46-footer is large enough for a professional crew of two and owner's party of four, yet not so large as to be unwieldy in fast competitive fishing. Top speed with twin 425-hp 8V-71TI diesels is 30 mph. Range at 27 mph cruising speed is calculated at well over 400 miles. (Photo by AMF — Hatteras Yachts)

Specifications

Length overall	46 ft 2 in	14.07 m
Length, waterline	41 ft 3 in	12.58 m
Beam	14 ft 9 in	4.50 m
Draft	4 ft 2 in	1.27 m
Cockpit area	120 + sq ft	11 + m²
Freeboard forward	6 ft 8 in	2.03 m
Freeboard aft	3 ft 7 in	1.09 m
Headroom, interior	6 ft 5 in	1.96 m
Height, waterline to windshield	13 ft 8 in	4.17 m
Weight, normal load	41,000 lb	18,595 kg
Fuel capacity	650 gal	2,460 l
Water capacity	180 gal	680 l
Sleeping accommodations	4-6	
Power, standard	Twin 425-hp GM 8V-71TI diesels	

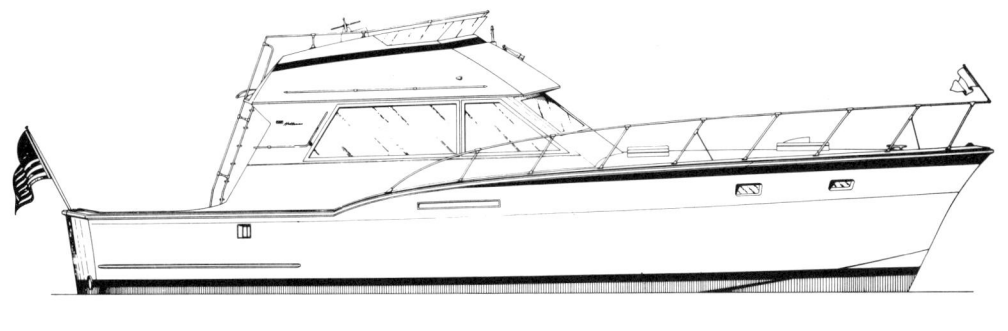

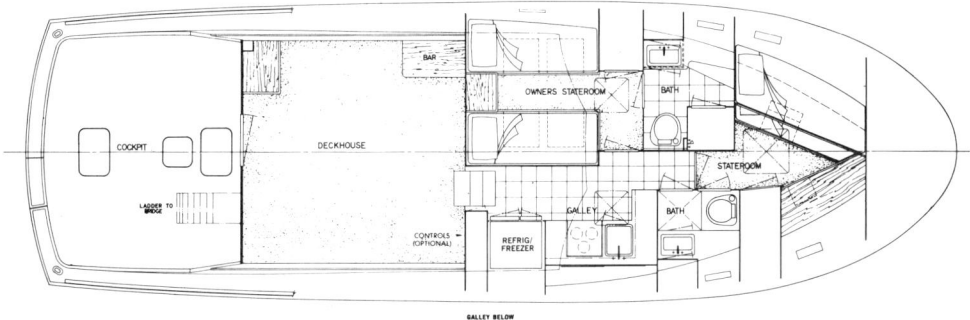

GALLEY BELOW

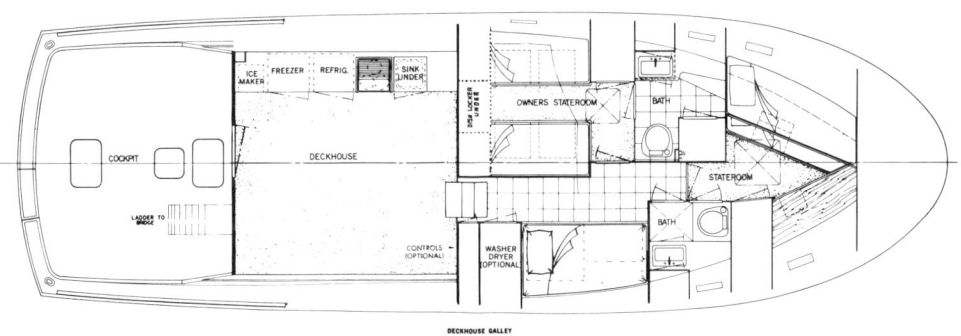

DECKHOUSE GALLEY

Performance (normal full loads of fuel and water)

With twin GM 8V-71TI diesels
(425 hp × 2 = 850 total hp)

Top speed	30 mph @ 2300 rpm
Top fuel rate	50 gph, or 0.60 mpg
Cruising speed	27 mph @ 2100 rpm
Cruising fuel rate	40 gph, or 0.68 mpg

Calculated endurance and range
(from builder's data, 650 gallons)

Top-speed endurance	13 hr
Cruising endurance	16¼ hr
Top-speed range	390 mi
Cruising range	440 mi

The builder notes that "speed and consumption figures are attained by measuring under ideal weather and sea conditions with substantially full fuel and water tanks. Performance above can be expected under similar conditions, but is not guaranteed." Performance data with alternate power were not available.

Description

Two optional interior plans distinguish the handsome Hatteras 46-foot Convertible. One features the galley below in the space that otherwise would be devoted to a guest stateroom. This version has twin berths in the large master stateroom and upper and lower berths in the forward stateroom. Placing the galley below to starboard leaves the deckhouse uncluttered for entertaining. At least two can sleep in the deckhouse on a convertible lounge.

The second arrangement has the galley in the deckhouse on the port side and a double-bed guest stateroom below to starboard. This arrangement sleeps six below and at least two more in the deckhouse on a convertible lounge. Both versions provide a private toilet and shower for the master stateroom and a second head with shower for the rest of the vessel. An optional washer-dryer is available with the guest-stateroom arrangement.

The flying bridge is in the typical Hatteras style, with the control station located well aft for a complete view of the large cockpit. With a width of more than 14 feet, the cockpit has plenty of room for a full-sized tournament fighting chair and a pair of flanking fixed or portable fishing chairs. A transom door is standard equipment.

With 41,000 pounds normal displacement — 12,000, or 41 percent, more than the 37-foot Convertible — the 46-footer shows from builder's data a respectable cruising range of 440 miles at 27 mph. The length-beam ratio of 3.13:1 is about average for boats of this length class. Air conditioning and heating are both standard, and the boat, from the factory, is ready to handle any climate from the chilly fogs of Nova Scotia to the baking summer heat of the Gulf of Mexico.

The Hatteras bridge station is worthy of special mention. The broad, low bridge wings enclose a commodious bench seat placed forward of the control station. The control station features complete integrated instrumentation immediately in front of the wheel, with a weather-tight electronics compartment and panel extending to the port bridge wing. Everything from radiotelephone to sounder, RDF, Loran, and radar scope is within easy reach and in view of the operator. The entire structure is fiberglass and forms part of the deckhouse top.

Some observers of the nautical scene are inclined to minimize the importance of electronic equipment for fishing. "Fishing is mainly a matter of luck, of being in the right place at the right time," is the pronouncement offered. The second half of this statement is true enough — but being in the right place at the right time requires much more than luck.

Modern electronics take much of the guesswork out of fish location and offshore navigation. Installing the equipment where it will do the operator some good when he needs it is the job of design engineers who understand the problems of modern offshore game fishing. Hatteras engineers have resolved this problem to a high degree.

Styling and interior decor is very modern and entirely nautical. Special attention is paid to ventilation and insulation. The long lists of standard and optional equipment are essentially the same as those for the 37-foot Convertible. Among additional options are:

      Maxim water-maker
      Hailer-intercom, Raytheon, Model 350
      Baitwell with circulating pump
      Washer-dryer
      Hanging bar bunk cover

The overall effect of the Hatteras 46-foot Convertible is that of a big, powerful, seagoing fishing cruiser combining the best attributes of a quality power cruiser with those of a well-thought-out, modern, deep-sea fishing machine.

PACIFICA 48-FOOT SPORTFISHERMAN

Designer	Kipper Yachts
Builder	Pacifica by Kipper Yachts 928 West 17th Street Costa Mesa, CA 92627
Construction	One-piece fiberglass hull. One-piece fiberglass deck and hardtop.

Specifications

Length overall	48 ft	14.64 m
Length, waterline	42 ft 8 in	13.01 m
Beam, maximum	15 ft 2 in	4.64 m
Draft	4 ft	1.22 m
Cockpit area	130 sq ft	12.09 m²
Freeboard forward	7 ft	2.14 m
Freeboard aft	3 ft 9 in	1.14 m
Height, flying-bridge windshield	13 ft 5 in	4.09 m
Weight, light	40,000 lb	18,181 kg
Fuel capacity	1,000 gal	3,780 l
Water capacity	160 gal	605 l
Sleeping accommodations	6	

Power options
    Twin 570-hp 8V 92TI GM diesels, 2:1 reduction gear
    Twin 8V 92N GM diesels, 2:1 reduction gear

Pacifica sportfishermen have earned a name for performance and fishability in West Coast and Hawaiian waters. This handsome 48-footer accommodates up to six and has unusual high-speed, long-range capability. (Photo by Kipper Yachts)

Performance

With twin 570-hp 8V 92TI GM diesels

Top speed	36.0 mph (53.6 kph)	@ 2500 rpm
Fast cruise	32.0 mph (47.7 kph)	@ 2200 rpm
Range	550 mi (820 km)	@ 2200 rpm
Fuel rate	0.55 mpg (0.22 km/l)	@ 2200 rpm

Description

The tendency among West Coast powerboat designers is to give their vessels a very healthy fuel capacity. The Pacifica's capacity of 1,000 gallons is up to twice what could be expected in some similar East Coast hulls. The reason, of course, is the relatively greater distances between ports along Pacific shores. With a cruising range of over 500 miles at better than 30 mph, the Pacifica can be expected to do considerably better than this distance at its most efficient planing hull speed. This would be a considerable asset in long hauls — for example, from San Diego to the lower tip of Baja California.

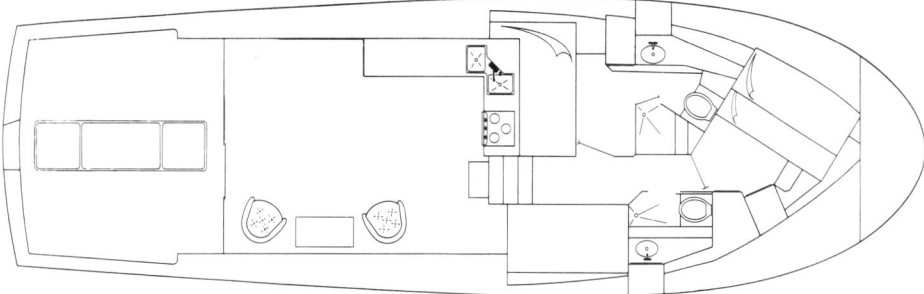

The reverse sheer forward, blending into a straight sheerline well aft, is pleasing. The slope of the deckhouse and flying-bridge front adds to the relatively low profile, which is also pleasing. Scrutiny of the flying-bridge plan reveals a characteristic of many West Coast boats that is not regarded as truly efficient for serious game fishing. This is that the control station is placed so far forward as to obscure a large portion of the cockpit from the operator's backward view.

This tendency of western designers and builders has been explained as a preoccupation with providing maximum visibility forward to sight floating driftwood, of which western coastal waters have a plentiful supply. Experience with many different types of bridges has shown, however, that placing the bridge control station a few feet farther aft does not detract from visibility of the water surface to the detriment of safety, and it vastly increases the ability of the bridge operator to coordinate boat movements with the requirements of an angler fighting a large, active fish.

Another nonfishing feature is the fore-and-aft lineup of deck hatches in the cockpit sole, extending almost from the transom to within a foot of the forward bulkhead. This would make it difficult to mount a full-sized fighting chair in the cockpit without either bridging over or bolting down the long central hatch. One explanation of the present hatch arrangement is that the use of a fighting chair was not contemplated when the boat was designed, and much West Coast game fishing does not require such a chair. This is probably true, but the ability to mount a permanent fighting chair in the cockpit, plus bridge-cockpit eyeball contact, are two points that the knowledgeable fishing-boat buyer uses to judge the "fishability" of any powercraft.

As a large, fast, family fishing cruiser with exceptional cruising range, the Pacifica 48-footer is hard to beat. The deckhouse galley to port leaves plenty of room for chairs and a convertible lounge that can sleep two. Down below, the master stateroom to port has a double berth placed athwartships with its own private connecting head and shower. To starboard are upper and lower bunks in a small guest stateroom and a second head serving the guest and forward staterooms. The forward stateroom has upper and lower bunks to port with ample lockers to starboard. Decor and finish are superior.

In the final analysis, the Pacifica 48-footer is an excellent example of the modern western cruising fisherman. Most of these boats are owner-operated without professional crews, and the layout and design have been created to satisfy this specialized market.

Standard Equipment

Hull and Superstructure

One-piece fiberglass hull, deckhouse, hardtop
Flying bridge, molded fiberglass
Adjustable bridge helm seat
Custom back-to-back seat for 6, convertible to double bed
Windshield, tinted reverse
SS bridge rails and ladder with teak steps
Outboard grabrails
110 v. AC bridge outlet
Control station fully instrumented on bridge
Lighted compass, dual-lever controls
Hydraulic steering

Engineroom and Propulsion

Twin diesels as per option
Electric light in engineroom
7.5-kw diesel generator
Freshwater pressure system, electric hot-water heater
Automatic electric bilge pump
Engineroom blower
Seacocks on all underwater through-hull fittings
Engine-temperature and oil-pressure alarms
Electrically bonded throughout
Stuffing boxes with self-aligning shaft logs
Manganese bronze struts, rudders (rubber bearings)
8-D, 12 v. DC, heavy-duty batteries (3), boxes, etc.
Watertight bulkheads (2)
Full insulation for sound, fire protection
Custom fiberglass, louvered air vents

Electrical Systems

40-amp, 12 v. DC battery charger
Custom panel with AC and DC breakers, ammeter, 3 engine meters, voltmeters, distribution switches
110 v. AC ship's service with shoreline connection
Light fixtures: 110-v. duplex fixtures, outlets (12)
Navigation lights

Salon (Deckhouse)

Tinted safety glass windshield, sliding side windows
Engine access hatches
Stereo/tape player, wet bar with storage
3-burner, 110 v. AC range, oven, rotisserie
6.5-cu-ft refrigerator, door to match decor
SS sinks
Dish and storage lockers, glass rack
High-pressure laminate countertops

Master Stateroom

Double berth
Hanging locker
Storage drawers
Berth lights, 110 v. AC duplex outlet
Portlight, opening overhead hatch

Master Head

Vitreous china lavatory
Medicine cabinet with mirror
Light, 110 v. AC duplex outlet
Linen storage, built-in laundry hamper
Stall shower, built-in bench and door

Guest Accommodations (amidships)

Deep lounge, converts to upper and lower berths

Guest Head

SS lavatory
Medicine cabinet with mirror
Portlight
Light, 110 v. AC duplex outlet
Linen storage
Shower, electric toilet

Guest Accommodations (forward)

Private stateroom, upper and lower bunks
Hanging locker, storage drawers
Berth lights, 110 v. AC duplex outlets
Portlights and opening overhead hatch

Cockpit

Molded fiberglass, 3 large scuppers
Underdeck access hatches with overboard drains
Teak strips under gunwale for accessory hangers
12-in mooring cleats

Hardware

All hardware, chrome on brass, SS, anodized aluminum
Anchor, anchor bitt and hawsepipe

Stern cleats (2), spring cleats (2), 12-in
All safety rails SS
Horn
Zincs on transom

Miscellaneous

Custom draperies throughout
Carpeting throughout
Nylon anchor and mooring lines
Anchor chain
Fire extinguishers (4)
Life preservers (8)

Factory-Installed Options

Anchor winch, chrome heads and foot
  switch
Upper berth in master stateroom
Padded cockpit coaming
Cockpit control station, deckhouse control
  station
Bow pulpit, roller, safety rail
Transom door, swim step (teak)
Molded tower, furniture package

HARGRAVE 50-FOOT SPORTFISHERMAN

Designer	J.B. Hargrave, N.A., Inc. 205½ Sixth Street West Palm Beach, FL 33401
Builder	Hull: Halmatic Ltd., Havant, Hants., England. Finished to custom order by selected domestic yards.
Construction	Hull, deck, and superstructure — one- piece fiberglass layups to Lloyd's specifications. Marine plywood bulkheads.

Specifications

Length overall	50 ft	15.25 m
Length, waterline	45 ft	13.73 m
Beam, maximum	16 ft	4.88 m
Draft	4 ft 6 in	1.35 m
Cockpit area	100 + sq ft	9.3 + m²
Freeboard forward	6 ft 7 in	2.01 m
Freeboard aft	4 ft	1.22 m
Heights above waterline		
Bridge windshield top	15 ft 4 in	4.68 m
Bimini top	17 ft 4 in	5.29 m
Weight (see text)		
Fuel (one option)	800 gal	3,000 l
Water (one option)	300 gal	1,134 l
Sleeping accommodations	6-8	
Power options (see Performance and Description)		

Performance

This is essentially a custom-built vessel. Power, weight, and other performance-altering factors will vary from boat to boat. The designer, however, has provided a comprehensive speed-power-weight chart that graphically depicts speed versus displacement, power-for-power ratings of 400 to 1,200 hp, and displacements between 30,000 pounds and 50,000 pounds. Three different sets of performance data are available, two from the designer and one from an owner who kindly cooperated with the research for this book.

Example 1   *(Data from the designer)*

Power	Twin 12V71N GM 2-cycle diesels
Fuel capacity	800 gal
Water capacity	300 gal
Top speed	25 kn (28.5 mph)
Cruising speed	22 kn (25.1 mph)
Endurance	NA
Range	NA

Example 2   *(Data from the designer)*

Power	Twin 425-SHP Detroit 2-cycle diesels with 2:1 reduction gear
Fuel capacity	490 gal
Water capacity	250 gal
Top speed	22 kn (25.1 mph)
Cruising speed	19 kn (21.7 mph)
Endurance	NA
Range	NA

Example 3   *(Data from an owner)*

Power	Twin 8V71TI GM diesels, each 425 hp
Fuel capacity	958 gal
Water capacity	380 gal
Top speed	23 mph (20.2 kn)
Cruising speed	20 mph (17.5 kn)
Endurance	30 hr @ 20 mph (estimated)
Range	600 mi @ 20 mph
Fuel rate	.63 mpg @ 20 mph (estimated)

Description

While not exactly one-of-a-kind, this big Hargrave-designed sportfisherman is highly customized within the limits of a standardized fiberglass hull. The result is a series of very individual boats bearing a strong family resemblance. All materials used in the manufacture of hull, decks, bulkheads, and superstructure conform to Lloyd's specifications.

The hull is a one-piece molding with overlaminated foam-core longitudinals. Foam density is 1.8-pounds-per-cubic-foot Coolag, except between bulkheads C and D, where it is 4 pounds per cubic foot. A Douglas-fir packet is inserted on top of the longitudinals between bulkheads C and D. Four bulkheads are of marine plywood. Bulkhead A is ⅝-inch thick; bulkheads B, C, and D are ¾-inch thick and

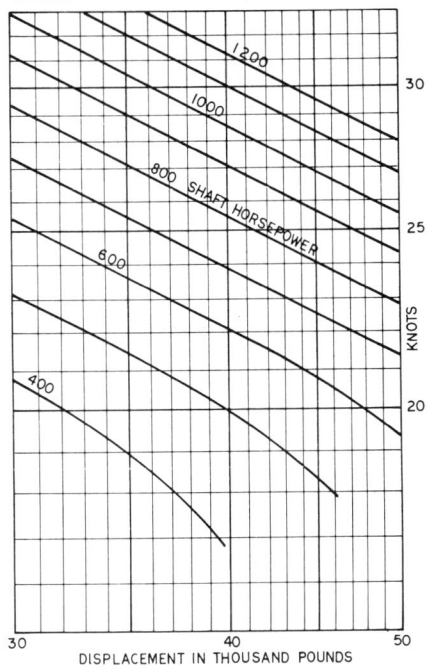

Left: Knowing displacement of the Hargrave 50, speed can be calculated for any reasonable planned power installation.

Below: There is nothing heavy-footed about the way the Hargrave 50-footer walks on the water. Accommodations for six to eight, according to plan, and custom appointments throughout. Top speed is quoted at 25 knots with cruising at 22, propelled by twin 12V71N GM diesels. (Photo courtesy of J.B. Hargrave, N.A., Inc.)

laminated to the hull. Forward stringers are triangular-section foam, overlaminated, and positioned port and starboard, running aft from bulkhead A to the forward face of bulkhead B.

Wheelhouse and cockpit soles are similar in construction to forward stringers, running between engine-compartment bulkheads C and D and around topsides and transom in the cockpit area aft of bulkhead D.

Deck and superstructure are a one-piece molding of sandwich construction. The superstructure top is reinforced in way of the flying bridge by including hardwood pads instead of the usual balsa-core material. The result is an excellent blend of strength with light weight. Deck and hull are bolted together before overlamination.

The flying bridge is a one-piece double molding, consisting of front and side panels stiffened with foam and overlaminated. Aluminum-alloy securing plates are laminated into the bridge structure.

Normal tank plan is as follows: 1 forward water tank, 1 reserve fuel tank, 2 wing fuel tanks (port and starboard), and 1 center after fuel tank.

Other standard items from the designer's list include: 8 portlight spigots, 2 engine louver spigots, 2 water traps, 2 water inlets, 2 shaft tubes and tail pipes, 2

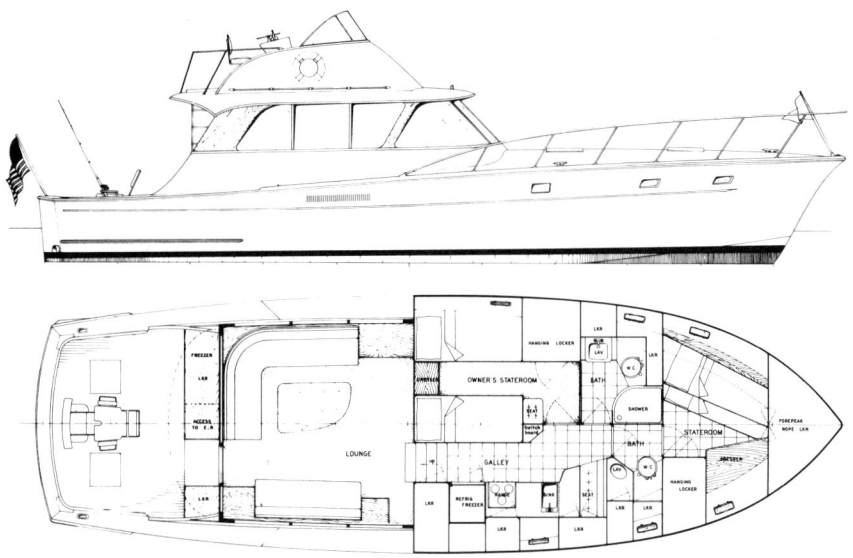

This customized version of the Hargrave 50 has the galley located down below.

molded rubbers (port and starboard), and arrow emblem and cavita line molded into hull.

Two different interior plans are illustrated in the two sets of sketches from the designer. One features a deckhouse galley with three staterooms sleeping six persons below. The large deckhouse lounge can be converted into sleeping quarters for two more. The other features a galley below with two staterooms sleeping four persons. In both cases, the forward stateroom would normally be for the crew of captain and mate or steward. Separate heads are provided for each stateroom.

The commodious cockpit can easily accommodate a full-sized fighting chair and two auxiliary fishing chairs. There is freezer space for bait and a large tackle locker planned into the bulkhead of the deckhouse at the forward end of the cockpit. The bridge controls are located so as to give the operator a clear view of the working portion of the cockpit. Neither boat shown in the designer's sketches has deckhouse controls. Flying-bridge controls and instrumentation make that location the logical command center.

The question arises: Is this a luxury cruiser or a fishing machine? The answer is: It is both.

A boat this large and complex demands a professional crew, experts in boat handling, housekeeping, and competitive sportfishing. In such capable hands, with experienced anglers on the tackle, the overall length of 50 feet does not exceed the limits for top-quality, tournament-class fishermen.

The hull is large enough to carry fuel for upwards of 600 miles cruising range at the respectable cruising speed of 20 mph. This, for example, translates into an easy noon-to-noon run for the 410 miles from Key West to the island of Cozumel, off the Yucatan Coast, allowing an average speed-over-the-bottom reduction of 3 mph to account for the adverse Gulf Stream and Yucatan Channel currents.

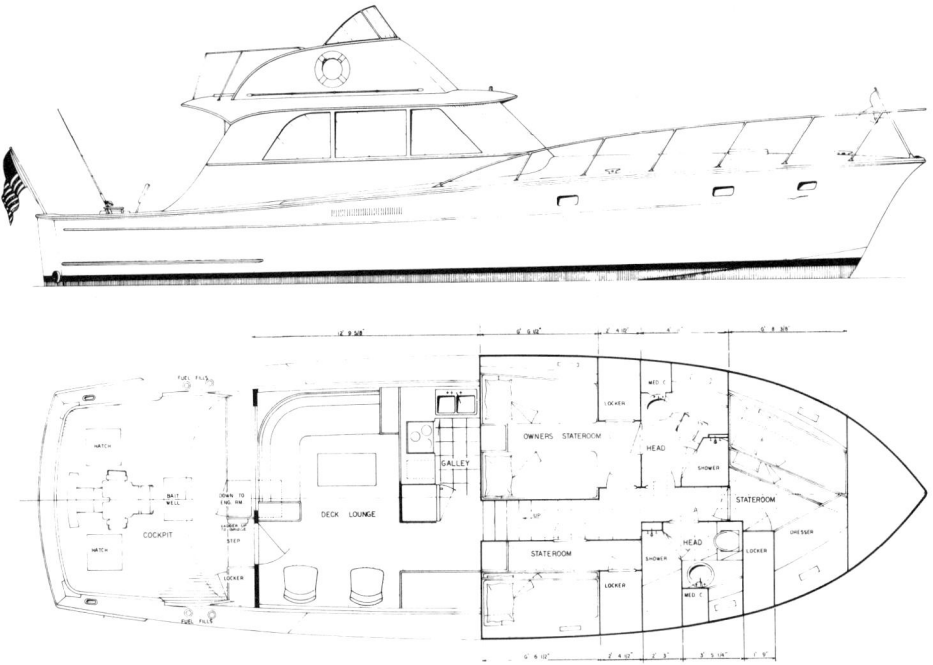

Galley is in the deckhouse in this model.

Owner's Evaluation

Fuel economy	Poor*
Handling qualities	Super
Seaworthiness	Super
Overall design	Super
Cruising comfort	Super
Fishing efficiency	Super
Ease of maintenance	Poor**
Investment value	Super

Owner professes to be concerned with excessive fuel consumption of any type and calls for a switch to slower, more fuel-efficient fishing boats.

**Owner's qualifying remark: "Too much teak."*

This owner does not consider the Hargrave 50-footer to be his ultimate fishing machine. He claims the Gulf of Mexico and the Out Islands of the Bahamas as his fishing ground, averaging 3,400 miles and 200 hours of annual use, of which 80 percent is spent cruising and 20 percent trolling. He says that when it comes time to sell, he will buy a more fuel-efficient (slower) boat in the same size/price range. His closing remark was, "Best boat I have had, except for fuel economy and maintenance."

The Hargrave 50-footer is not a light boat. According to the designer's speed-power-weight chart, a top speed of 25 knots with 50,000 pounds of displacement would require just under 1,000 SHP. This is a lot of boat to push at that speed. But "a lot of boat" adds up to seakindliness and comfort in less than popcorn weather. In offshore fishing, that is the bottom line.

Franco Harrauer 55-foot Tiger Shark. *(Foto Zampa, Genoa, Italy)*

SECTION THREE
Boats 53 to 85 feet

HATTERAS 53-FOOT CONVERTIBLE

Designer	J.B. Hargrave, N.A., Inc. 205½ Sixth Street West Palm Beach, FL 33401
Builder	AMF — Hatteras Yachts 2100 Kivett Drive P.O. Box 2690 High Point, NC 27261

Specifications

Length overall	53 ft 7 in	16.33 m
Length, waterline	48 ft 3 in	14.71 m
Beam, maximum	16 ft	4.88 m
Draft	4 ft	1.22 m
Cockpit area	150 + sq ft	14 + m²
Freeboard forward	7 ft 6 in	2.29 m
Freeboard aft	3 ft 9 in	1.14 m
Headroom, interior	6 ft 7 in	2.01 m
Weight, normal load	61,000 lb	27,670 kg
Fuel capacity	1,100 gal	4,160 l
Water capacity	250 gal	945 l
Sleeping accommodations	6-8	

Power options
 Twin GM 550-hp 8V-92TI diesels
 Twin GM 650-hp 12V-71TI diesels

Performance (Normal full loads of fuel and water)

With twin GM 8V-92TI diesels
(550 hp × 2 = 1,100 total hp)

Top speed	27.5 mph @ 2300 rpm
Top-speed fuel rate	54 gph, or 0.51 mpg
Cruising speed	25.0 mph @ 2100 rpm
Cruising fuel rate	40 gph, or 0.63 mpg

With twin GM 12V-71TI diesels
(650 hp × 2 = 1,300 total hp)

Top speed	29.0 mph @ 2300 rpm
Top-speed fuel rate	67 gph, or 0.43 mpg
Cruising speed	26.5 mph @ 2100 rpm
Cruising fuel rate	52 gph, or 0.51 mpg

Twenty-five-mph cruising speed is deceptive in a boat the size of the Hatteras 53-foot Convertible. Accommodations are for six in the owner's party and a paid crew of two. Cruising range of over 680 miles is calculated for power of twin 550-hp 8V92TI diesels. (Photo by AMF — Hatteras Yachts)

Calculated Endurance and Range   *(from builder's data, 1,100 gallons)*

	Twin 8V-92TI Diesels	Twin 12V-71TI Diesels
Top-speed endurance	20.37 hr	16.42 hr
Cruising endurance	27.50 hr	21.15 hr
Top-speed range	560 mi	476 mi
Cruising range	688 mi	560 mi

The builder notes that "speed and consumption figures are attained by measuring under ideal weather and sea conditions with substantially full fuel and water tanks. Performance above can be expected under similar conditions, but is not guaranteed." Calculated endurance and range were figured by the author from builder's information.

Description

Here is another example of a boat so well proportioned that it must be viewed at a distance together with smaller craft of similar design to appreciate its larger size. Emphasis is on spaciousness in the cockpit and below decks, rather than on trying to crowd in accommodations to make the vessel a floating dormitory. Two standard layouts are offered, one with galley in the deckhouse and the other with galley below. Both offer below-decks sleeping for six, the galley-below design having two heads and the galley-in-deckhouse having three.

Above: The divan in the well-appointed deckhouse of the galley-below model converts to a double bed. Rods are stowed in overhead racks. Below: The galley is compact and fully equipped. (Photos by AMF — Hatteras Yachts)

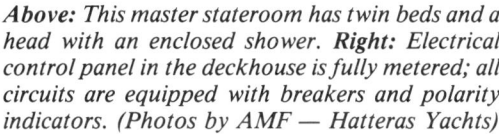

Above: This master stateroom has twin beds and a head with an enclosed shower. Right: Electrical control panel in the deckhouse is fully metered; all circuits are equipped with breakers and polarity indicators. (Photos by AMF — Hatteras Yachts)

The huge cockpit is small only in proportion to the entire vessel. Cockpit area of more than 150 square feet is sufficient for a large fighting chair and two deck-mounted flanking fishing chairs, plus movable guest chairs. The ingenious Hatteras tackle center occupies only a portion of the forward end of the cockpit. This center, available in all Hatteras models, incorporates a bait freezer, tackle drawers, sink, and working surface. It is placed behind and is part of the lower portion of the bridge ladder. A set of cockpit controls in a separate pedestal complements the tackle center as an available option.

Interior styling and decor follow the nautical-modern Hatteras pattern. The large deckhouse is very light and airy, but it can be completely shielded for dockside privacy by curtains and window drapes. A deckhouse lounge can be made over into a double bed at night for extra guests. With this arrangement, the boat can sleep eight — six in the owner's party and a crew of two in separate quarters forward.

As in other Hatteras vessels, the standard system of rod stowage is to use overhead hangers in the deckhouse. Presumably, a full-length tackle locker could be built into the deckhouse side if arranged for at the time of contract.

A four-step stairway leads from the deckhouse level to the forward space sole, and there is no enclosing bulkhead. This creates the illusion of vast space in this

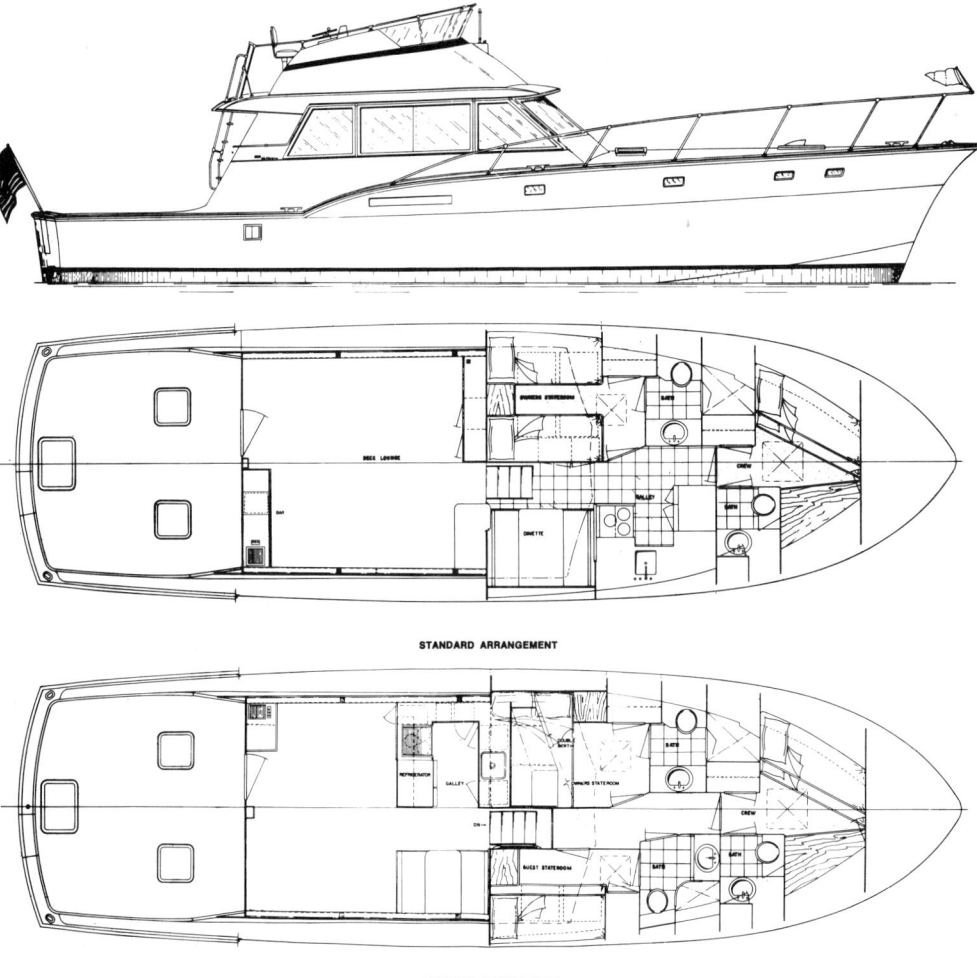

STANDARD ARRANGEMENT

OPTIONAL ARRANGEMENT

split-level arrangement. A dinette seating four is located to starboard beside the stairway and can be converted to a double berth. Locker space is adequate and the interior finish of matched-grain mahogany is superior.

The twin-berth master stateroom is opulent, but not to a degree that would degrade the rest of the interior. Fine-quality appointments and finish are consistent throughout. The inclusion of air conditioning and heating as standard equipment ensures that installation will be done to builder's standards without having to tear up finish work.

The lists of standard and optional equipment follow those already stated earlier for Hatteras craft. The 53-footer's DC electrical system is 32-volt, with two banks of heavy-duty batteries. The 15-kw diesel generator supplies 120 to 240 volts AC. A single-sideband radio ground screen is molded into the hardtop.

The tradition of Hatteras fishability was originated by the late Willis Slane, who competed vigorously in earlier Hatteras models in major tournaments from Florida to Long Island. Nothing stimulates designers, engineers, and building technicians to view fishing problems with a careful eye as much as actually participating in competitive fishing in the boats they create.

Hatteras boats are not the only ones developed in the tournament school, but they combine the elements of modern style and comfort with the necessities of fishing to an unusual degree.

FRANCO HARRAUER 55-FOOT "TIGER SHARK"

Designer	Franco Harrauer, N.A. Via Aurelia or. 286-a 16035 Rapallo, Italy
Builder	Soc. Aereonautica Italiana ing. Ambrosini Genoa, Italy
Construction	Welded aluminum Peraluman 35.

Specifications

Length overall	55 ft	16.80 m
Length, waterline	42 ft 7 in	13.00 m
Beam, maximum	15 ft	4.60 m
Draft, hull only	2 ft	0.70 m
Freeboard forward	6 ft 8 in	2.04 m
Freeboard aft	4 ft 10 in	1.48 m
Height above waterline	23 ft 5 in	7.14 m
Displacement	37,000 lb	17,000 kg
Fuel capacity	704 gal	2,660 l
Water capacity	265 gal	1,000 l
Sleeping accommodations	8	
Power	Twin 455-hp D336A-TA Caterpillar diesels	

Performance

The only performance information available for the *Tiger Shark* was the designer's statement of a top speed of "over 25 knots." If we were to interpret this to mean, for example, 26.32 knots (30 mph), we would have a reasonable top speed from which to work out a calculated performance table, using known parameters. These are:

Accepted top speed	26.32 kn (30 mph)
Stated total power	910 hp (diesel)
Fuel capacity	704 gal
Normal diesel fuel rate	20 hp/gal/hr
Cruising speed	24 kn (approx. 90% of top speed)
Cruising power	820 hp (approx. 75% of top power)

The first four parameters are known or assumed. The last two, cruising speed at 90 percent of top speed and cruising power at 75 percent of top power, are substantiated by performance of U.S. boats of generally similar type, size, and power rating.

Table of Calculated Performance

Top speed	26.32 kn (30.0 mph)
Top fuel rate	45 gph
Top fuel mileage	0.58 nmpg (0.67 mpg)

At speed the hull shows strong dynamic lift and level trim. Hydraulic trim tabs at the transom control running angle. On trials, the boat lacks fishing equipment. (Photo by Foto Zampa, Genoa, Italy)

Top endurance	15.6 hr
Top range	411 nm (469 mi)
Cruising speed	24.0 kn (27.36 mph)
Cruising fuel rate	33.75 gph
Cruising fuel mileage	0.71 nmpg (0.81 mpg)
Cruising endurance	20.9 hr
Cruising range	502 nm (572 mi)

Description

Like something out of *Star Wars*, Franco Harrauer's big *Tiger Shark* cleaves the Mediterranean, displaying her distinctive Italian approach to powerboat design. Superficially, she is a very classy, radical, high-performance cruiser with luxurious accommodations for eight, but actually she is 100 percent long-range, high-speed fishing cruiser, built and equipped for Mediterranean competitive fishing.

Welded-aluminum construction by the Italian Aeronautical Society matches aircraft excellence. The unusual, self-supporting, spoonbill bow pulpit is great for handling ground tackle or harpooning swordfish. In the Mediterranean, harpooning by noncommercial fishermen is not yet a mortal sin. The huge cockpit can accommodate many fishing chairs, ice and fish boxes, scuba gear, and the like. A fold-down platform drops out of the stern for swimming, diving, gaffing fish, or boarding from a small tender.

Left: Access to crew's quarters in the bow is by the ventilator-hatch built into the capstan housing. The wooden grating forward of the deckhouse is for stowing dock lines, etc. Below: Scale model of Tiger Shark shows imaginative design. Waterline side exhaust tubes double as docking fenders. Deadrise at stern is moderate. (Photos by Foto Zampa, Genoa, Italy)

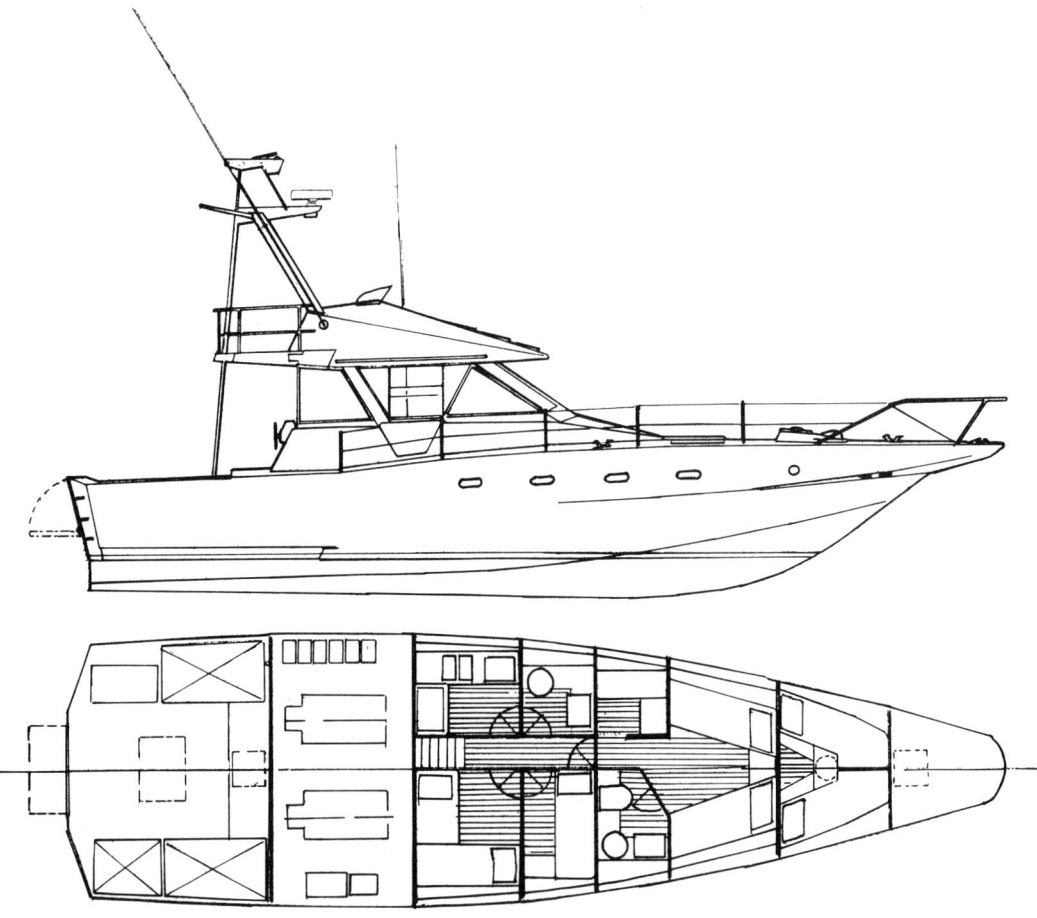

The accommodation layout is unusual. Starting in the long, sharp bow, the crew's quarters come first, with access by means of a ventilating forward deck hatch. Next aft is the master stateroom, with twin beds, toilet room to starboard, and dressing room to port. This head shows the Continental influence, boasting that instrument of elegance, a bidet. The bulkhead between crew's quarters and master stateroom is watertight.

Next aft on the starboard side is another stateroom with conventional upper and lower bunks placed athwartships. Opposite is another head. Amidships is another stateroom to starboard, with upper and lower berths set at a 90-degree angle to each other. The commodious galley, freezer, and storage lockers are to port.

The two big Caterpillar diesels occupy a large engineroom under the deckhouse. Ratio of reduction gears and type and size of propellers were not available. The diesels exhaust through unique exhaust tunnels welded to the outside of the hull at the waterline, extending back to the transom. Muffling is accomplished by water injection and internal baffles. The exhaust tubes, looking somewhat like the exhausts of a rocketship, only smaller, act as effective waterline hull bumpers.

Three control stations are provided: deckhouse, tower, and forward end of cockpit. Insulated fish and ice wells are underdeck. Watertight integrity is unusually complete. Four watertight bulkheads divide the hull into five compartments, each with its own bilge-pumping system. Hull stiffening is by means of longitudinal frames and four massive metal girders extending forward from the engine beds. Hydraulic trim tabs position the hull for the most effective fore-and-aft trim.

Interior decor is very modern, relieved by teak trim. Hardly what one would call a production model, *Tiger Shark* demonstrates forcefully what can be accomplished when a gifted architect and highly competent shipbuilding crew get together to create a vessel that, once seen, is not easily forgotten.

BERTRAM 58-FOOT CONVERTIBLE

Designer	Bertram Yacht Division, Whittaker Corp.
Builder	Bertram Yacht 3663 N.W. 21st Street Miami, FL 33142
Construction	Fiberglass hull, decks, and super-structure. Teak cockpit deck and trim.

Specifications

Length overall	58 ft 3 in	17.70 m
Length, waterline	51 ft 6 in	15.71 m
Beam, maximum	17 ft 10½ in	5.45 m
Draft	5 ft	1.52 m
Cockpit area	168 sq ft	15.62 m²
Freeboard forward	7 ft 6 in	2.29 m
Freeboard aft	4 ft 2 in	1.27 m
Heights above waterline		
Flying-bridge windshield	17 ft 4 in	5.28 m
Flying-bridge hardtop	17 ft 10 in	5.44 m
Add for light	2 ft 1 in	0.64 m
Weight, dry (approx)	70,000 lb	31,751 kg
Weight, cruise (approx)	80,000 lb	36,287 kg
Fuel capacity, standard	1,300 gal	4,921 l
Fuel capacity, optional	2,000 gal	7,560 l
Water capacity	300 gal	1,136 l
Sleeping accommodations	6-10	
Standard power		

Twin 650-hp 12V-71TI GM diesels
Power options available by arrangement with builder

"Majestic" is the word for this 58-foot Bertram Convertible sliding at 26 mph top speed with twin 650-hp 12V71TI diesels spinning the props. Up to 10 persons can sleep in various accommodation plans. Cruising range is 750 miles at 22.5-mph cruising speed. The huge cockpit has three chairs abreast plus tackle and bait station and lower control station. (Photo by Bertram Yacht)

Performance

With twin 650-hp 12V-71TI GM diesels

Top speed	26.0 mph (38.7 kph) @ 2300 rpm	
Cruising speed	22.5 mph (33.5 kph) @ 2000 rpm	
Cruising range	500 mi (745 km)	@ 2000 rpm (1,300 gal)
Cruising range	750 mi (1,146 km)	@ 2000 rpm (2,000 gal)

Speeds and cruising range are test averages and may vary among similar boats depending on weight, engine condition, and bottom condition.

Description

A question frequently asked is, "Can a boat this big actually fish efficiently?"

It's a good question, one voiced most frequently by the owner of a smaller sportfishing boat who is thinking of trading up to a vessel with longer range and more personal comfort. The answer is a slightly qualified "yes," the qualification consisting of two parts.

1. A sportfishing boat this size almost automatically requires a professional crew. A good professional fishing captain can fish almost any size of boat with a high degree of efficiency.

2. Surprisingly, large sportfishing boats do quite well in light-tackle competition, where one of the rules is that the contestants must fish from a dead boat. The term *dead boat* refers to an almost complete restriction on maneuvering to help the angler. Some tournaments permit the captain to turn the boat so the stern faces the fish but do not permit running or backing to save line. With this rule in effect, much of the maneuvering advantage of smaller boats is lost. The larger boats offer a steadier platform for stand-up fishing in rough weather.

The author saw this demonstrated at Cozumel off the Yucatan Coast of Mexico during a tie-breaking fishoff between two high-scoring tournament contestants. The fish were sailfish and the tackle was 12-pound test. Both contestants fished dead-boat from 57-foot vessels of another manufacturer. The sea was quite choppy, with a fresh wind from the east. The contestants fished standing up and were permitted up to four lines in the water at one time. The winner was credited with four releases in as many hours of sudden-death fishing. There was no question that the size, weight, and inherent stability of the 57-foot boats contributed materially to the success of the fishoff.

The builder is not exaggerating in describing this boat as "impressive." At a distance, the Bertram look is so perfectly preserved as to diminish the apparent size of the vessel, but up close, with human figures to provide scale, the effect is that of a large, fast power yacht quite successfully adapted to sportfishing. The cockpit, for example, is wide enough to accommodate two full-sized fishing chairs with footrests, although this is seldom done.

The fact that the boat is primarily a fishing cruiser and not a tournament machine is revealed in the layout of the flying bridge, in which the operator's control station is placed rather well forward, immediately behind the windscreen. This might cause some inconvenience in fish-fighting, especially if guests were to occupy the seats behind the skipper's perch, blocking the view into the cockpit. The illustration of *Aquarius* shows this and also shows a popular way of enclosing the bridge with a sun cover and plastic curtains supported by the tower structure.

The deckhouse is very commodious, with a convertible double lounge to port on entering from the cockpit and movable seats and a table to starboard. Farther forward on the starboard side are a convertible dinette-berth and wet bar, flanked on the port side by a U-shaped galley with double sink, freezer-refrigerator, range and oven, and plenty of locker space and countertop space. An electrical panel and color TV and stereo system are built into the port deckhouse side.

Three staterooms occupy the space forward and below. The owner's stateroom, to port, features a large double bed flanked by lockers and drawers. Forward are the owner's private bath and hanging lockers. A guest stateroom to starboard contains upper and lower berths against the boat's side, with lockers

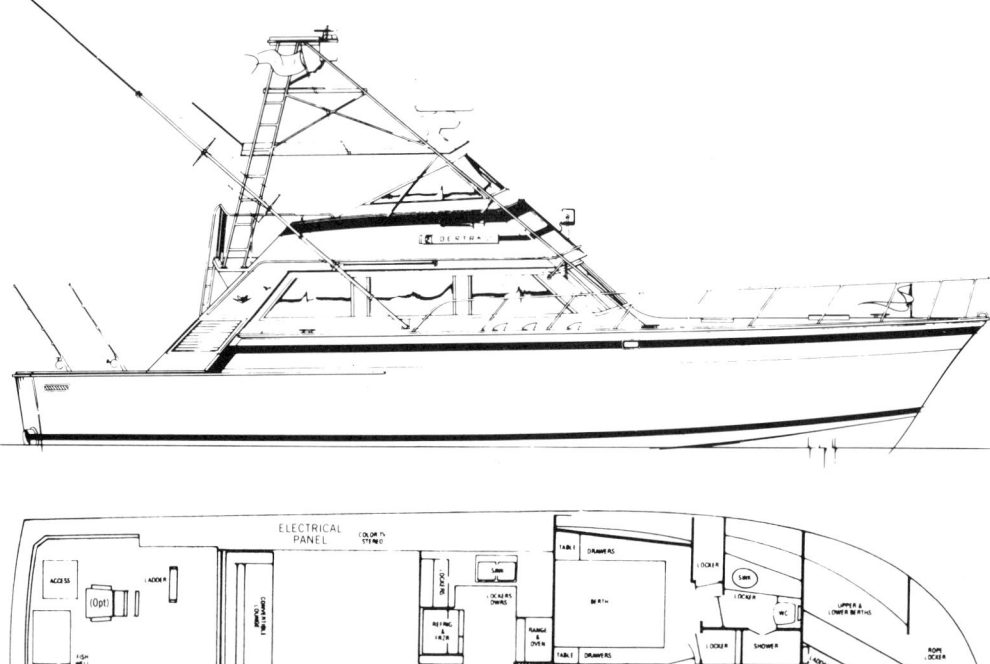

and drawers and access to a guest's bath, which can also be entered from the main companionway. The forward stateroom has upper and lower berths to port and drawers and lockers to starboard. A door closes off this stateroom from the other two, and there is a third bath with shower stall, etc., on the starboard side immediately forward of the guest bath. Six can sleep in the staterooms, plus four more in the two deckhouse double berths.

Owner's Evaluation

An owner from Mississippi, who wishes to remain anonymous, gives the following performance evaluation.

Fuel economy	Good
Handling qualities	Super
Seaworthiness	Super
Overall design	Good
Cruising comfort	Super

Fishing efficiency	Good
Ease of maintenance	Good
Investment value	Super

This owner admits to using the boat about 500 hours a year, part of which is tied up with business entertainment. Cruising takes about 70 percent of the time and fishing about 30 percent. "But the boat is very good at raising blue and white marlin, and tuna," the owner explains. He likes the low cockpit for fishing and the large deckhouse for entertaining.

He names his primary satisfactions from sportfishing as "a change of pace, plus getting important thinking done and decisions made in a relaxed and friendly atmosphere. And with the care my crew gives the boat, it is actually increasing in value faster than the present rate of inflation."

Standard Equipment

General

Air compressor with tank, filter, regulator
Air conditioning throughout
AM/FM 8-track stereo throughout
Anchor-line locker
Anchors, chocked (2)
Battery-condition meter, universal
Bilge blowers
Bilge pumps, automatic (3), engine-driven (1)
Boathooks, chocked (2)
Bottom paint, antifouling, with boot stripe
Bow rail, heavy-duty
Burgee staff and burgee
Chocks, stern (2), custom (1), forward
Cleats, foredeck (2), aft (2), springline (4)
Deck and cabin: marine aluminum with thermal insulation
Docklines: ⅝ in × 50 ft (3), ⅝ in × 30 ft (3), nylon
Drip pans, fiberglass, under engines
Dual-lever Panish engine controls
Electric flying-bridge windshield wipers with washers
Electro-hydraulic trim tabs
Emergency engine-stop system
Ensign pole and socket
Fog bell, 6-in
Freshwater cooling, main engines and generator
Freshwater supply for engine cooling
Fuel filters, water-separator type
Hydraulic steering
Life jackets, adult (8)

Manual/automatic CO_2 fire-extinguisher system
Mufflers, custom design
Navigation lights
Radio ground plates, dual
Raw-seawater strainers
Safety center, engine oil and water ·
Safety rails and ladder, bright anodized aluminum
Saltwater foredeck and cockpit wash-down outlets
Seacocks on all through-hull fittings
Soundproof generator compartment
SS propeller shafts, 2½-in dia.
Teak toe rail on raised deck
Telephone service, port and starboard outlets, jacks in salon and owner's stateroom
Thermal and acoustic insulation
Twin air horns
Water heater, 30-gal, 220 v. AC
Water inlet, dockside supply, with regulator, port and starboard
Water-pressure system, electric
Windows, smoked safety glass

Electrical

32 v. DC boat's electrical system
115/220 v. AC system
180-Ah storage batteries, 2 banks with parallel device
Bonding system with 2 large ground plates
Converters, automatic (3)
Generator, 20-kw, 115/230 v. AC

Shore service, port and starboard, in
cockpit

Interior

Carpeting throughout
Drapes throughout

Main Salon

Cold cathode lighting
Color television
Natural-teak window frames and panels
Rod locker, starboard side
Stowage, outboard
Windshield cover, Dacron

Galley

Dishwasher
Double SS sink
Freshwater-supply indicator
Lockers and drawers for provisions
Oven, range
Refrigerator/freezer, upright, with
automatic icemaker
Single-lever faucet with rinsing hose
Teak cabinets with butcher-block
countertop
Vent hood over range
Vinyl floor covering

Master Stateroom

Bedspread and pillow shams
Cold cathode lighting
Drawers under bed
Nightstand with drawers
Portlights with Soji screens
Queen-size walkaround bed
Telephone jack
Wardrobes (2)

Master Bath

Exhaust blower
Lockers with sliding mirror panels
Marbleized vanity with molded sink
Mirror on door
Shower, extra-large
Toilet, Raritan Crown with Lectra San
Ventilating deck hatch

Guest Stateroom

Drawers under berths
Private access to guest bath
Upper and lower bunks, 6-in foam
mattresses
Ventilating deck hatch
Ventilating portlights

Guest Bath

China sink with Formica cabinet
Exhaust blower
Locker
Mirror, with vanity
Shower, molded fiberglass pan
Toilet, Raritan Crown with Lectra San

Forward Stateroom

Access ladder to deck hatch
Access to private head
Foam mattresses with coverlets
Hanging lockers and stowage
Mirror, 48-in, on companionway door
Portlight to port side
Upper and lower berths, 30 in × 80 in
Ventilating deck hatch

Forward Stateroom Bath

Exhaust blower
Locker with sliding mirrors
Molded fiberglass vanity with sink
Shower, telephone-type
Toilet, Raritan Crown with Lectra San

Cockpit

Access to all enginerooms
Boarding lights (2)
Coaming padding
Cockpit steps, port and starboard mounted
Extra-large transom scuppers
Overboard scuppers for hatch drains
Rodholders (4)
Shore freshwater service, port and
starboard
Stereo speakers (2)
Stowage lockers, port and starboard
Teak covering boards
Saltwater washdown outlets, port and
starboard
Vinyl-covered sole

Flying Bridge

Chart stowage
Compass, 6-in
Curved lounge
Drawer stowage
Electronics distribution panel, 12 v. DC
Electronics lockers, port and starboard
Forward control with helm seat
Safety monitor system
Stereo speakers, with controls (2)
Windshield, 3-piece, outboard ventilating,
tinted safety glass, wipers, washers

Optional Equipment

Deck Hardware

Anchors, additional, as required
Anchor line, additional, as required
Chain, anchor, 300 ft
Pulpit, bow
Windlass, vertical capstan
Windlass with wildcat, horizontal
  capstan

Electrical

European shore power with Cable-
  master
European shore power without Cable-
  master
Generator, 15-kw, additional
Generator, 30-kw, in place of standard
  20-kw unit
Shoreline reels, electric cable, automatic
Cockpit floodlights (2)
Docking lights, bow
Docking lights, transom
Searchlight, 10-in, 32 v. DC, with cover

Interior

Garbage disposal
Trash compactor
Twin berths, owner's stateroom
Chairs, deckhouse
Convertible sofa, deckhouse
Dinette
Salon wet bar
Stowage locker, extra

Canvas Coverings

Flying-bridge controls, forward, Dacron
Flying-bridge lounge, Dacron
Helm seat, bridge, Dacron

Flying Bridge

After control station with cover
Aluminum hardtop with sliding side
  windows and clear vinyl enclosure
Companion seats forward, 2 each, with
  covers
Galley with refrigerator, icemaker, sink,
  stowage, cover
Weatherboard, smoked Plexiglas

Fishing Equipment

Cockpit windlass for hoisting fish
Fighting chair with cover (Tournament)
Fishbox in cockpit sole (icebox)
Outriggers, 25-ft, with 3 spreaders
  (Tournament)
Preparation center with cover:
  3.3-cu-ft freezer
  Live-bait well
  Sink with fresh and salt running water
  Cutting board
  Stowage drawers
Rodholders, transom-mounted
Transom door (2 pieces: covering board
  gate and transom door)
Transom door, with swim ladder

General

Chocks and davits, for 13-ft Boston
  Whaler only
Cockpit sole, teak
Shipping and storage cradle
Extra fuel capacity, 2,000 gal total
Freshwater maker
Life raft, 10-person capacity, inflatable
Propellers, extra pair, stowed
Propeller shaft(s), stowed
Swim platform, fiberglass
Synchronizer, Glendenning, dual
Synchronizer, Glendenning, single

RYBOVICH 58-FOOT CUSTOM SPORT FISHERMAN "LITTLE PETE"

Designer	John Rybovich & Sons
Builder	John Rybovich & Sons West Palm Beach, FL
Construction	Triple-planked wood, Honduras mahogany diagonal-laid, epoxy-bonded. No frames, monocoque construction. Interior teak veneer over marine plywood. Teak cockpit sole and covering boards. Mahogany deckhouse with laminated pine beams and strength members.

Specifications

Length overall	58 ft	17.69 m
Length, waterline	55 ft 6 in	16.93 m
Beam, maximum	17 ft 6 in	5.34 m
Draft	4 ft 6 in	1.37 m
Freeboard forward	NA	
Freeboard aft	NA	
Height above waterline	NA	
Displacement	59.44 t gr.	54,036 kg gr.
	47.00 t net	42,727 kg net
Fuel capacity	1,500 gal	5,670 l
Water capacity	400 gal	1,512 l
Sleeping accommodations	7 +	

Power
  Twin GM 12V-71TI diesels, 675-hp each
  1.5:1 reduction gears
  Propellers: 28½-in dia. × 26½-in pitch, 4-blade

Performance

From data provided by Florida yacht broker Bill Dunne, the following performance has been calculated.

Low cruise	20 kn @ 1850 rpm
Low-cruise fuel rate	44.0 gph, or 0.45 mpg
High cruise	23 kn @ 2000 rpm
High-cruise fuel rate	52.0 gph, or 0.44 mpg
Top speed	26.2 kn @ 2300 rpm
Top-speed fuel rate	60.4 gph, or 0.43 mpg
Low-cruise range	675 nm
Low-cruise endurance	34 hr

High-cruise range	660 nm
High-cruise endurance	28.8 hr
Top-speed range	645 nm
Top-speed endurance	24.8 hr

Efficiency of the hull in the 20- to 26-knot speed range is demonstrated by the almost flat miles-per-gallon fuel rate. Despite the boat's gross displacement of almost 60 tons, the hull is a true planing type that could make the 400-mile run from Key West to Cozumel off Mexico's Yucatan Coast against an average 3-knot head current in a comfortable 24-hour period, and still arrive with 10 hours' reserve of fuel if speed were held to a "modest" 20 knots. The length-beam ratio of 3.3:1 is quite low for a boat of this length and contributes to great stability and comfort in rough water.

Description

The 58-foot custom-built *Little Pete* was described in its year of building, 1975, as the "Queen of the Rybovich fleet." The unusual stressed-skin construction consists of three separate layers of selected mahogany planking laid at diagonal angles to each other, held together with epoxy bonding material. The hull was built over a master frame, but it has no interior framing of the conventional kind. Laminated

The long, forward-reaching reverse sheer is distinctive in Florida-built custom sportfishing boats. Little Pete *runs low, fast, and level at more than 20 knots.*

wooden longitudinal keel and engine bearer members and stringers are bonded to the skin internally. The result is an extremely strong, light, rigid, one-off type of molded self-frame hull that is very expensive to build but of great fidelity to designed shape and almost indestructible.

Starting forward, the forward stateroom is laid out with two V-berths and a third lower berth. This area is considered crew's quarters and provides comfortable accommodations for professional captain, mate, and cook-steward. It has its own head with shower and generous drawer and locker space.

The master head is located forward of the master stateroom, with access from the master stateroom only. It features a black marble sink and counter, decorator fixtures in gold and marble, a storage locker, drawers, medicine chest, stall shower with seat, and a hamper.

The master stateroom features large crossover berths and is trimmed with imbuya wood. The lower berth is a full-sized double. The forward hanging locker is done in the style of a Queen Anne armoire, with four storage drawers below. The controls for the air conditioner and communications-entertainment speaker system are hidden in the closet. There is a parqueted vanity with a chair, side mirror, and storage drawers. A land telephone jack and single-sideband radio remote control are located under the upper berth.

The guest head is located forward of the guest stateroom and features a black marble countertop and bronze hardware. There is a large stall shower and ample locker and drawer space. Access is from the companionway or the guest stateroom.

The guest stateroom is trimmed with imbuya wood and has fore-and-aft twin-size upper and lower bunks with a reading light over each bunk. There is a storage locker outboard of the upper berth and a separate eight-drawer upright chest. Air conditioner and speaker controls are located in the hanging locker. Two large drawers are under each berth.

The galley is complete, with refrigerator and freezer built into the forward part of the port bulkhead. Opposite to starboard is the main cooking area, with all units hidden in teak cabinetry. Units include a Whirlpool trash compactor, Kitchen-Aid disposer, Jenn-Air four-burner electric stove with separate grill and oven, and Nutone home center unit. The stainless-steel sink has hot and cold water with dishwasher head. There is generous storage space for dishes, utensils, and canned and dry-packaged foods.

The large deckhouse main salon has a Sony color TV forward, wet bar aft on the port side with a large Whirlpool icemaker, stainless-steel sink, Bar Boy unit, and glass and bottle storage, all enclosed in teak cabinetry. There is a large, custom-built, queen-size convertible settee aft on the starboard side, with a custom teak-and-tile high-low table and two custom occasional chairs with matching footstools. There are three vacuum-cleaner outlets for housekeeping. Interior drapes provide privacy alongside the pier.

The large cockpit has three boarding locations for cockpit steps. The Rybovich fighting chair is electrically operated and there are two large underdeck baitwells. Flush hatches give access to the lazarette space and separate generator compartment. There are rod and gaff storage compartments below the gunwales and a starboard location for custom cockpit steering and throttle controls. To port, forward, is a custom locker with two chill boxes that convert to freezers and two

Bows-on at full speed, Little Pete *has the purposeful, military look of high-quality sport-fishing craft.*

separate bait freezers. Salon access doors and engine-space access are located center, forward.

The large bridge area has the control station located well aft for complete cockpit visibility. Guest seats are forward of the console. The console contains radio, sounder, Loran, and radar units. The radar antenna sits atop the bridge sun-canvas frame halfway up the tower. Roll-up front and side curtains of transparent plastic can be dropped and buttoned down to enclose the bridge against inclement weather. The tower has complete engine, steering, and radio remote controls and an intercom connection to the bridge and salon.

To recapitulate, *Little Pete* is a complete sportfisherman with tournament capability but also a complete, long-range, cruising power yacht capable of operating far from home base.

Equipment

Since *Little Pete* is a one-of-a-kind custom boat, the equipment list reflects the taste and requirements of the owner and the judgment of the designer and builder. Components may vary from owner to owner and between sister vessels of the same builder.

Decca Model 914 48-mi radar

Northstar 2000A automatic-acquisition tracking Loran-A with tower remote control and readout

Northern Model N550 150-watt SSB radiotelephone

Konel KR160 150-watt AM radio

Mariner Intech Model V108 25-watt VHF/FM radio

Johnson Messenger 5-watt CB radio on tower

Johnson Messenger 5-watt CB radio on bridge

Benmar 14B Autopilot with tower remote control

Simrad EX recording depth sounder

Datamarine Pacifica digital sounder with alarm, bridge

Datamarine Pacifica digital sounder with alarm, tower

Unimetrics Model Seacall-1 hailer, intercom, and foghorn

Sea-Temp sea-temperature gauges (2), bridge and tower

Englehard 90W12D Capac System

Automatic 15# Halon fire-extinguisher system

General 2¾-lb fire extinguishers (2)

Bell engine-oil and temperature alarm system

Thermostatically controlled engineroom exhaust blowers (5)

Lovett 12 v. DC automatic electric bilge pumps (2)

Par 12 v. DC emergency bilge pumps (2)

Rule sump pump

30-gal waste holding tank

Automatic fuel transfer system

Automatic lubricating-oil filler system

Automatic, main-engine, fresh cooling-water filler system

Racor Series 1000 fuel fillers (4)

Rybovich fuel coolers (2)

Air compressor

Ritchie 6-in master compass

Rybovich helm seat

Rybovich tower, completely anodized, including welds

Tower station includes:
  2 seats
  Wheel
  Single-lever controls
  Tachometers
  Compass
  Digital sounder
  Sea Temp gauge
  Autopilot clutch switch
  CB radio
  Cockpit and foredeck lighting
  Safety padding, sun top
  Fiberglass platform

Rybovich outriggers, triple spreaders, 41-ft poles

Bridge outrigger release system

Transom door
Rybovich electrically operated fighting
   chair
Custom rod and gaff cockpit lockers (2)
Cockpit freshwater washdown
Coaming rodholders (2)
Bridge-rail rodholders (3)
Flush-deck baitwells (2)
Cruisaire 4-zone reverse-cycle air
   conditioner
VacuMaid central vacuum system
SenDur 10-gal hot-water heater
Sony 12-in color TV
Winegard rotating TV antenna
Panasonic AM/FM, 8-track, 4-channel
   stereo system

National Instant Hot Water tap (galley)
Whirlpool trash compactor
KitchenAid disposer
Dishwashing tap
Whirlpool icemaker
Jenn-Air electric stove, grill, oven
   (galley)
Jenn-Air electric grill (cockpit)
Moen combination shower heads
Jet electric toilets with holding tank
Full galley equipment
Complete glassware set
Ideal electric anchor windlass
300-ft, 1-in anchor rode
60-lb Danforth high-tensile anchor

HARGRAVE 64-FOOT SPORTFISHERMAN

Designer	J.B. Hargrave, N.A., Inc. 205½ Sixth Street West Palm Beach, FL 33401
Builder	Hull: Halmatic Ltd., Havant, Hants., England. Finished to custom order by selected domestic yards.
Construction	Hull, deck, and superstructure — one-piece fiberglass layups to Lloyd's specifications. Marine plywood bulkheads.

Specifications

Length overall	64 ft	19.52 m
Length, waterline	58 ft 9 in	17.92 m
Beam, maximum	16 ft 4 in	4.98 m
Draft	4 ft 6 in	1.37 m
Cockpit area	120 + sq ft	11.2 + m²
Freeboard forward	9 ft	2.75 m
Freeboard aft	5 ft	1.53 m
Heights above waterline		
Bridge windshield top	16 ft	4.88 m
Top of tower	24 ft 6 in	7.47 m

Continued

Specifications *continued*

Weight, hull only	11,000 lb	5,000 kg
Weight, half-load	62,000 lb	28,182 kg
Fuel capacity (variable option)	1,890 gal	7,144 l
Water capacity (variable option)	460 gal	1,739 l
Sleeping accommodations	6-10	
Power options (see Performance and Description)		

Performance

Like the 50-footer by the same designer, this 64-foot boat is custom-finished from a standardized fiberglass hull. The designer's speed-power-weight chart for the 64-foot version indicates that, at the half-load displacement of 62,000 pounds, approximately 875 SHP is required to produce a speed of 20 knots. Designer's specifications also list the displacement at 20 to 30 tons (20,100 to 30,150 kg).

Performance data for two examples are provided by the designer.

Example 1

Power	Twin 550-hp Caterpillar diesels
Displacement	62,000 lb (half-load)
Fuel capacity	1,890 gal

Sea Ranger *is a fisherman of super-cruiser proportions with a cruising range of over 500 miles. Six to 10 persons can be accommodated, depending on interior arrangements. The unique tower gives the vessel a naval air as she cruises at 20 knots. While the hull is stock, built of fiberglass by Halmatic of Great Britain, each Hargrave 64-foot fisherman is custom-finished in a U.S. yard selected by the designer and the prospective owner. (Photo by J.B. Hargrave, N.A., Inc.)*

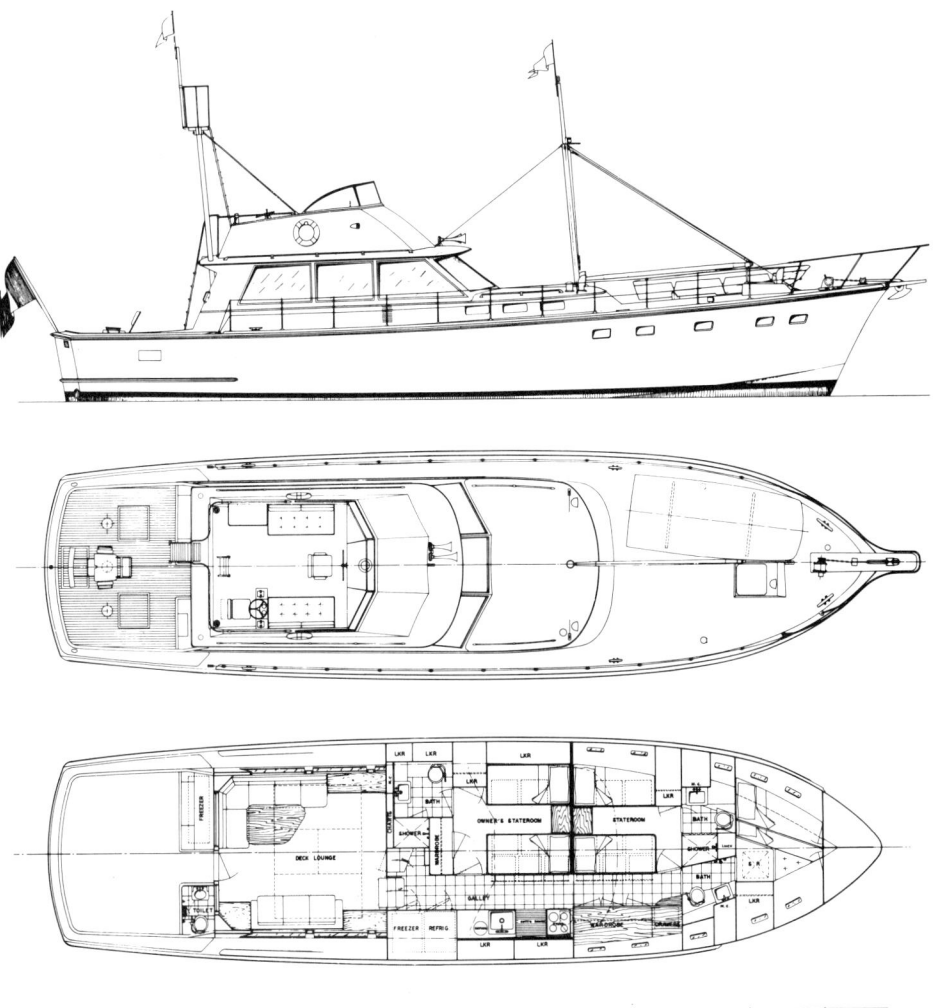

Another version of the Hargrave 64 with open bridge and military mast-lookout station.

Water capacity	460 gal
Top speed	22 kn (25.1 mph)
Cruising speed	20 kn (22.8 mph)
Endurance	NA
Range	NA

Example 2

Power	Twin 478-hp GM diesels
Displacement	62,000 lb (half-load)
Fuel capacity	1,880 gal
Water capacity	580 gal
Top speed	22 kn (25.1 mph)
Cruising speed	18 kn (20.5 mph)
Endurance	NA
Range	NA

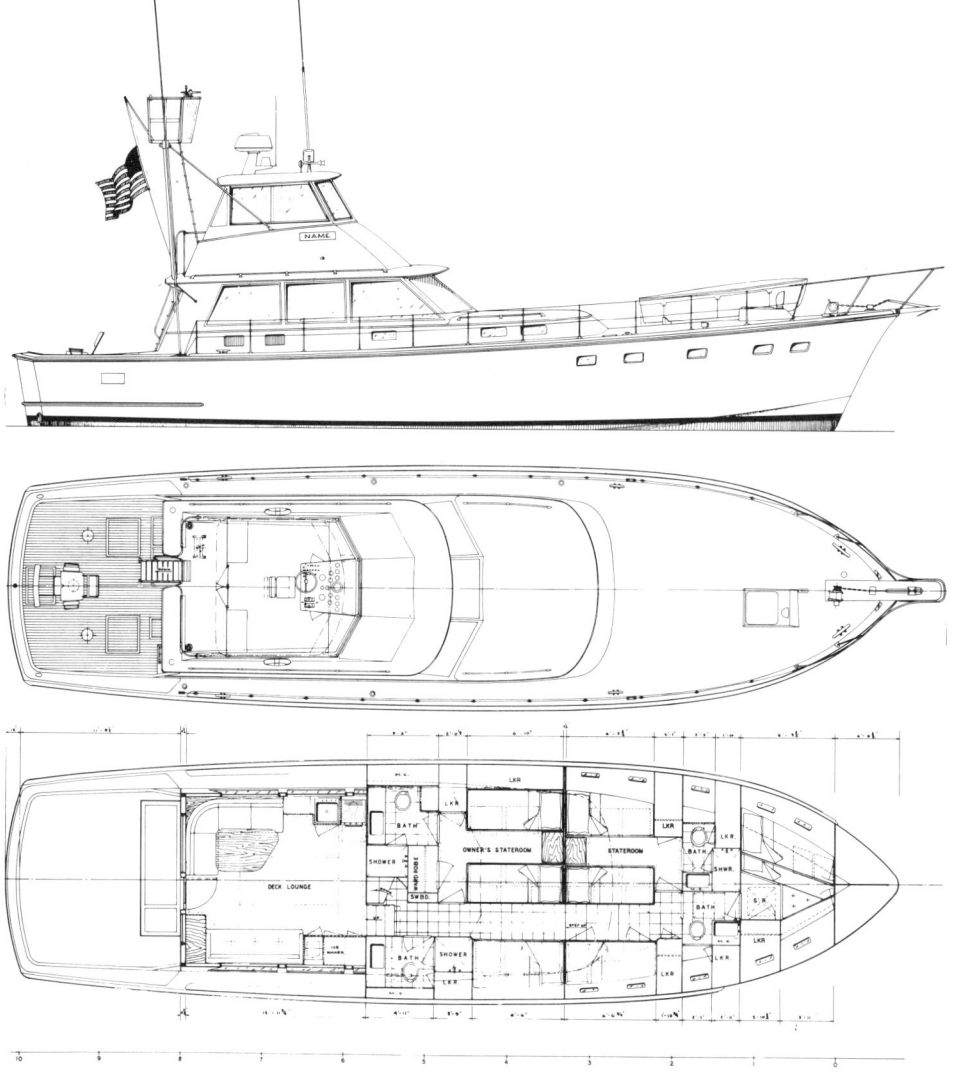

This version of the Hargrave 64 has an enclosed wheelhouse atop the deckhouse.

Comparison of power, displacement, and speed data for the Hargrave 50-foot and 64-foot sportfishing models suggests that the 64-footer is probably more fuel-efficient at 20 knots than the 50-foot version. Hull length of the larger boat is 14 feet (28 percent) greater than its smaller sister, while beam is only 4 inches greater, a negligible increase. This suggests that the longer hull with greater displacement but equal beam is inherently less wasteful of fuel. This is not to disparage the 50-footer's design and concept, but rather to point out the well-established fact that in many cases the longer hull of a proven type is more efficient.

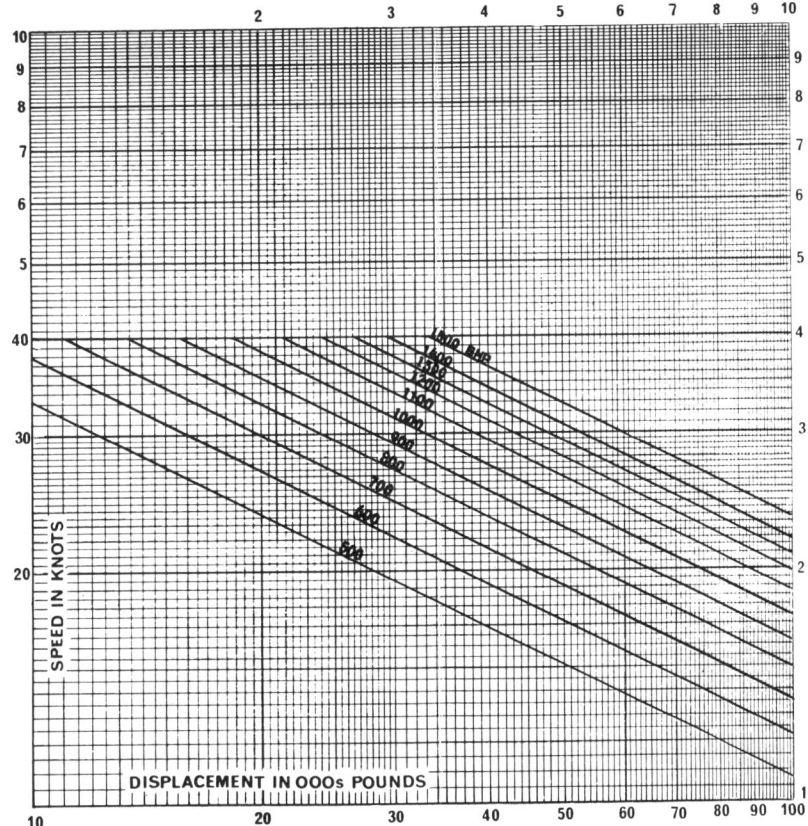

Speed/displacement/horsepower curves. (Courtesy of Halmatic Ltd.)

Interpolating these conjectures into the realm of range and endurance, we can guess that at the same expenditure of fuel per hour, the 64-footer may run 15 percent slower for a basic cruising speed of 17 knots or mph against the 50-footer's theoretical basic cruising speed of 20 knots or mph. This would reduce the 50-footer's estimated cruising range of 600 miles to about 510 miles.

But the 64-footer's larger fuel capacity, averaging at least twice that of the 50-footer, would increase the ultimate 17-knot cruising range to about 1,000 miles for the larger vessel. Readers are cautioned that these estimates are the author's alone and are not to be regarded as designer information. They are set forth to show what can be done by careful interpolation of related sets of data.

Description

The Hargrave 64-foot Sportfisherman is a truly handsome little ship, so well proportioned that one has to view it in relation to other boats of known size to appreciate its generally larger dimensions. *Sea Ranger* (see photo) runs fast and level with a minimum of spray and bow wave. The effect is that of a miniature light naval cruiser questing in advance of a fleet.

Construction follows the plan and quality of the 50-footer previously described. The interior plans illustrated merit careful study. Despite their similarity, there are major differences that reflect owners' individual requirements. No attempt is made for this model, or the 50-footer, to list standard or optional equipment. In vessels of this type, every item of equipment is a matter of agreement between the designer and builder on the one hand, and the owner or his agent on the other.

The designer's recommended power range of 800 to 2,000 SHP and speed range of 10 to 35 knots imply a hull that is equally efficient at displacement and fast planing speeds. This is rather unusual in sportfishing craft and suggests that at the most efficient displacement speed, which may fall within the 8- to 10-knot range, the 64-footer could have transoceanic cruising ability on a standard load of fuel. Data on slow-speed operations should be available from the designer.

Once again the question arises: Is this a fast, long-range cruising boat, or is it a fisherman? And once again, this time with qualifications, the answer is: It is both.

The qualifications, naturally, have to do with the boat's size. Much has been made in popular writing of the need for quick and sudden maneuverability to fight game fish. Most of these claims are made by people wishing to sell small, fast, highly maneuverable boats, and by writers who have had limited big-boat fishing experience. In this writer's opinion, the 64-foot Hargrave hull approaches, but does not exceed, the upper limit for boats well suited to competitive tournament-style fishing.

The modern trend is toward light tackle and the dead-boat restriction on maneuvering. (Dead-boat means that the captain may turn the vessel to keep it pointed toward the fish but may not back up or run ahead to help the angler regain lost line.) Skillful big-game skippers do a minimum of boat maneuvering under these circumstances, and the so-called maneuvering advantage of the small, fast boat diminishes to the vanishing point. Where backing and running are allowed under fishing rules, however, the small, fast boat definitely has a strong advantage.

The Hargrave 64-foot Sportfisherman looks like a natural for the adventurous angler who craves action in distant places, or who has a strong interest in the science of fishing. The vessel is an excellent base for a group of trained scientist-anglers, carrying one or two smaller boats like Boston Whalers for light-tackle work in sheltered waters or even at sea under good weather conditions.

Modification of stateroom space could provide a small but versatile oceanographic laboratory, and the boat's size and load capability make it self-sufficient for considerable periods of time. Its relatively shoal draft opens many shallow areas to exploration. Navigation and communication capabilities are limited only by the owner's imagination and pocketbook.

You may not find a Hargrave 64-footer tied up to every marina or fuel pier, but when you do see one of these outstanding vessels, you recognize it instantly for what it is — a magnificent example of functional, nautical design, built to the highest standards of the marine trade.

FEADSHIP 85-FOOT YACHT/FISHERMAN "IMPETUOUS"

Designer	Ir F. De Voogt Haarlem, Holland
Builder	C. Van Lent & Zonen Kaag, Holland
Decorator	Pierre Tanter Cannes, France
Construction	Aluminum hull and superstructure. Teak and holly decks, mahogany interior trim.

Distinctly European is the look of Impetuous, *designed and built in Holland for a U.S. owner. Accommodations are for six in the owner's party and a crew of three. Twin 1220-hp MTU 12V-331TC-71 diesels give a top speed of 21.3 knots (24.3 mph) and cruising range of more than 700 nautical miles at 17 knots. (Photo by Marty's Photographic Service, Fort Lauderdale, FL)*

Specifications

Length overall	85 ft	25.91 m
Length, waterline	71 ft 6 in	22.80 m
Beam, maximum	20 ft 6 in	6.25 m
Draft, normal	5 ft 7½ in	1.72 m
Cockpit area	112 sq ft	10.42 m²
Freeboard forward	10 ft	3.04 m
Freeboard aft	6 ft 2 in	1.88 m
Heights above waterline		
Top of deckhouse	14 ft 2 in	4.32 m
Top of wheelhouse	21 ft 2 in	6.45 m
Top of tower	34 ft 4 in	10.46 m
Displacement	140,000 lb	63.6 mt
Fuel capacity	4,100 gal	15,500 l
Water capacity	1,000 gal	3,780 l
Sleeping accommodations, guests and crew	9	

Performance

With twin 1,220-hp MTU 12V-331TC 71 diesels

Top speed	21.30 kn*	36.18 kph
Cruising speed	17.0 kn*	28.88 kph
Fuel rate at cruise	95 gph	359 l/hr
Endurance at cruise	42 hr	
Fuel mileage at cruise	0.18 nmpg	0.08 km/l
Fuel range at cruise	714 nm	1,164 km

Since speed is described in knots, distance is quoted in nautical miles (nm).

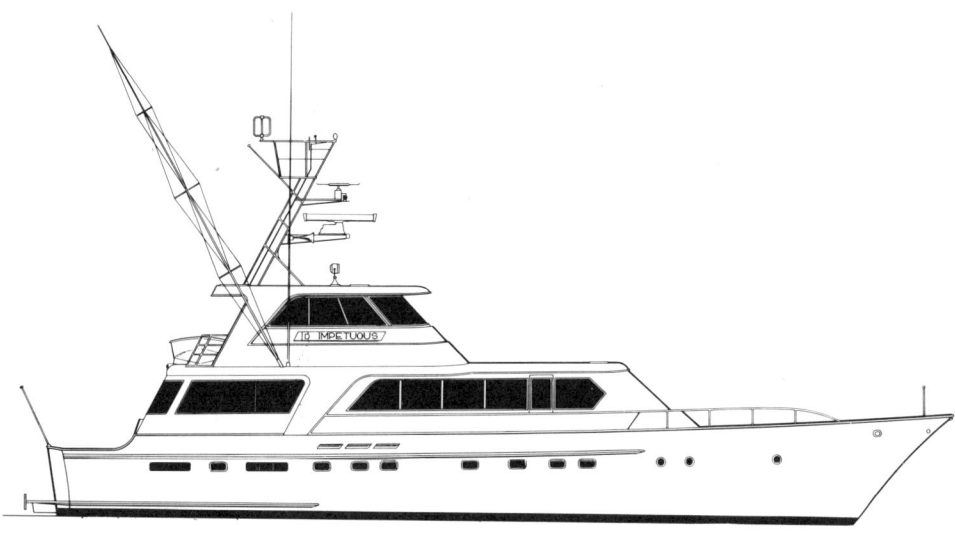

Description

Impetuous is a one-of-a-kind vessel that stops nautical and shoreside traffic wherever it goes. The deeply raked bow is European in style, while the wheelhouse and fishing cockpit combination is strictly American. The tremendous cockpit is wide enough to take three fighting chairs abreast if need be, although one centerline fighting chair is all that is needed for competitive fishing. The big transom door exits onto a low stern platform for gaffing and tail-roping large fish, or for the use of scuba- and skin-divers.

The cockpit is equipped with Rybovich 36-foot outriggers and a Rybovich teak fighting chair, a live-bait well, and a hot-and-cold shower. Diving equipment includes four sets of tanks and a Mako compressor. A 60-gallon gas tank is located under the swim platform to fuel the 55-hp outboard motor of the 14½-foot Seasquirt tender.

The interior includes a very modern galley, salon, and dining area. The after deck includes a wet bar, Bar Boy, icemaker, and chilled wine locker, and it is air-conditioned, as is the rest of the boat's interior. The master stateroom has a king-size bed, stereo, TV, and an attached master bath with sauna. The two guest staterooms are located just aft of the master stateroom, each having its own head with sink, W.C., and stall shower. Twin beds are installed. The crew's quarters forward contain large bunks for three, with lockers and a separate head.

The twin 1,220-hp MTU diesels are located well aft in an engineroom of big-ship proportions and hospital-white atmosphere. They are capable of driving the boat 700 to 800 miles at 15 to 17 knots, and much greater range if speed is held down to displacement value of 8 to 10 knots. *Impetuous* has a pair of 6-square-foot Naiad stabilizers, a 20-kw Westerbeke diesel generator, and a GM 371 30-kw generator with a heat-recovery muffler that makes 20 gallons of fresh water per hour with a Triton freshwater maker. There is an Aqua Air chilled-water system and a Bradford bow thruster for close maneuvering beside the pier.

Electronic equipment is complete, probably the working equivalent of a World War II destroyer-escort. Included are a Decca 1626A radar, Decca 550-GM autopilot with a Plath gyro, two Decca STR-25 VHF-FM radios, and a CAI 35 MkII all-channel SSB marine radio with 1,000-watt linear amplifier for around-the-world communication. Also included are a Decca LAZ 43 sounder with port and starboard transducers, a Datamarine Model 2700 digital sounder, Plath Navigon ADF, 40-channel CB transceiver, Northstar 6000 Loran C with microprocessor, Danforth Sea Slave hailer, complete instrumentation, Bogen phone system, and Kahlenberg D-4 horns.

The vessel's clean lines are almost severe. The teak-planked forward and side decks are protected by a bulwark topped with a stout handrail that gives big-ship security to sun-lounging or bad-weather deck work. The after freeboard of six feet is a lot for game fishing, but the full-width after swim ladder makes gaffing and fish-handling a simple matter.

While the designer and builder's agents do not class this as a tournament fisherman, the boat should be able to give good account of herself in competitive fishing in the hands of an experienced big-boat fishing captain. *Impetuous* is a long-range power cruiser with strong fishing capability, one that would be com-

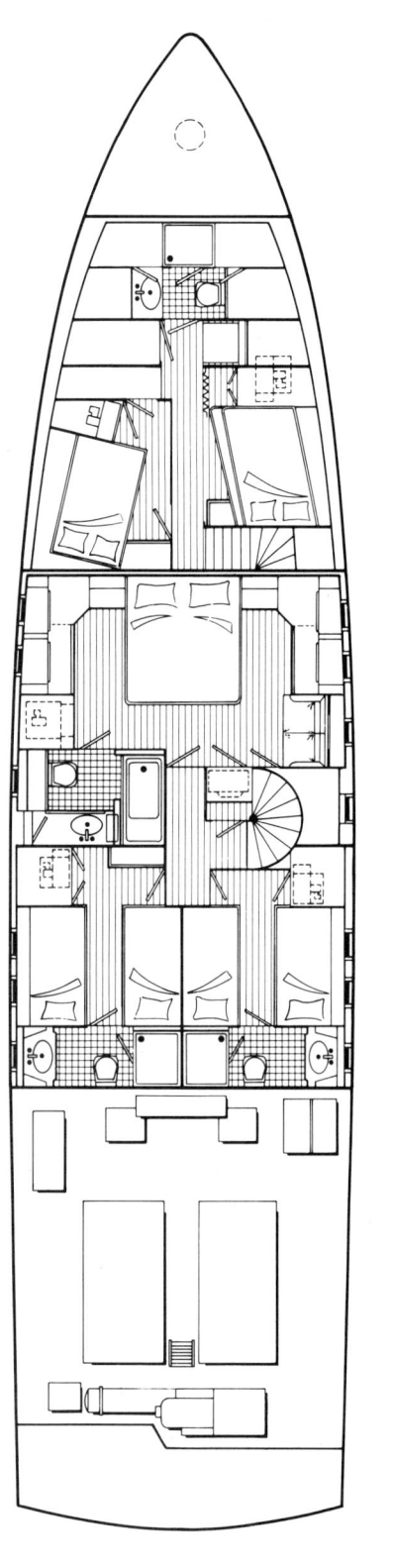
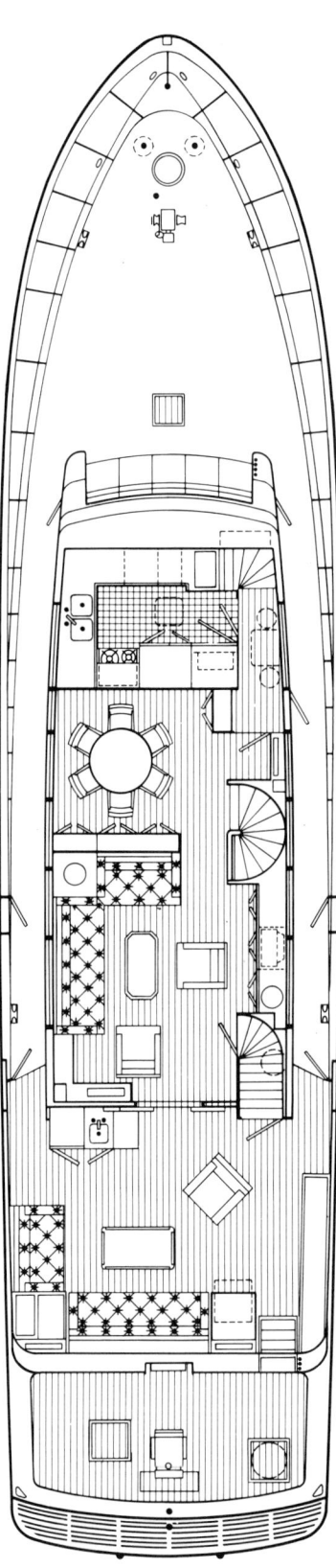
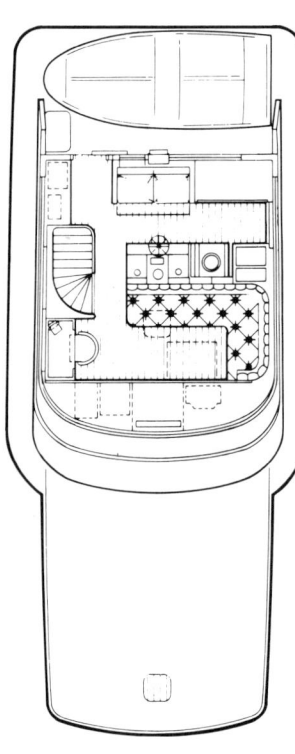

pletely at home exploring virgin waters in the South Atlantic or Central and South Pacific, where self-contained operational capability and comfort for the participants are more important than the last possible percentage point of fishing maneuverability.

Boats like *Impetuous* may not be everyone's dish, but they give everyone who sees them something to think about.

Left: Lower deck plan shows master stateroom forward of amidships, spanning the hull's width. Abaft this are two double-occupancy guest staterooms with private heads. Crew's quarters are forward. Main deck plan shows galley forward followed by dining area, main saloon, and after cabin with bar. Master control station is in the center of the wheelhouse, with a large, L-shaped lounge forward and a chart table and navigating desk aft. (Courtesy of Nautical Quarterly*)*

Index